Economic Theory
and the Underdeveloped Countries

H. MYINT

The London School of Economics
and Political Science

New York

OXFORD UNIVERSITY PRESS

London   1971   Toronto

Second printing, 1973

Copyright © 1971 by Oxford University Press, Inc.
Library of Congress Catalogue Card Number: 79–135973
Printed in the United States of America

Economic Theory and
the Underdeveloped Countries

Preface

Although this volume is not a complete collection it does contain most of my papers on the economics of the underdeveloped countries written since the early days of the subject in the 1950s.

I am very grateful to Gerald M. Meier for editing my papers and improving the coherence of the collection as a whole by judicious cuts and minor revisions. He has also done me the honour of publishing this volume as the first in the Series on World Poverty. I hope that it may, as he believes, have some value in providing a general background to the more specialised volumes which are to follow in the series.

I should like also to thank the editors and publishers of the following journals and conference volumes for permission to reprint the papers in this collection: *The Journal of Political Economy; The Teaching of Development Economics,* eds. K. Martin and J. Knapp (Frank Cass & Co. Ltd., 1967); *Economica; Oxford Economic Papers; The Review of Economic Studies; The Economic Journal; International Trade Theory in a Developing World,* eds. R. Harrod and D. C. Hague (Macmillan & Co. Ltd., 1963); *International Economic Relations,* ed. P. Samuelson (Macmillan & Co. Ltd., 1969); *Social and Economic Studies; Pacific Affairs; The Brain Drain,* ed. W. Adams (Macmillan & Co. Ltd., New York, 1968); *Economic Development and Structural Change,* ed. I. G. Stewart (Edinburgh University Press, 1969); *The Malayan Economic Review;* Japan Economic Research Centre (1968); Banca Nazionale del Lavoro *Quarterly Review.*

September 1970   H. M.
London, England

Contents

Introduction

The papers collected in this volume are concerned with the middle level of analysis between "pure" formal economic theory and detailed empirical studies of particular underdeveloped countries. Their aim is to examine the realism and the relevance of theoretical concepts and doctrines, both orthodox and modern, in relation to the broadly observable patterns of economic change, the salient features of the economic situation, and the general aims of development policy in the underdeveloped countries.

I have always been a firm believer in the fruitfulness of the older, classical economic theory in the study of the underdeveloped countries. But, like many others who sought a broader dynamic approach to economic development, I started out with considerable reservations concerning the relevance of the static neo-classical theory, particularly the international trade theory, for the underdeveloped countries. This skepticism is apparent in the three earliest papers reprinted here as chapters 3, 4, and 5. But subsequently, in the light of accumulating factual information about the post-war economic experiences in the underdeveloped countries, I became increasingly aware of the dangers of misapplying sophisticated "dynamic" theories to justify what in commonsense terms appear to be glaring cases of inefficient use of available economic resources. This led me to revise my views about the static optimum theory. This change in outlook is reflected in the rest of the volume, particularly in chapters 1, 2, 7, 13, and 14. In these chapters, I was mainly concerned with defending the static optimum theory against the advocates of the "dynamic" approach; but it is also possible to raise objections against the optimum theory from the side of welfare economic theory, in terms of the Second Best Theorem and the distribution of income. Here I am content to leave it to the reader to judge for himself how far these objections are likely to be serious in the actual contexts in which I have tried to use the optimum theory.

The general plan of this collection is as follows. Part I contains two introductory chapters setting out my present views on the relation between economic theory and the underdeveloped countries. Part II contains five chapters mainly concerned with the application of international trade theory to the underdeveloped countries. Part III contains four chapters on education and economic development; and Part IV contains three chapters exploring the relationship between the internal aspects, including economic planning, and the external aspects of development policy.

There are two unifying threads which link the different parts of the book. (1) In the international trade chapters, I have been concerned not only with the direct effects of trade, but also with the indirect "educative" effects of alternative trade policies. In the education chapters, I have been concerned not only with formal training and education in the narrower sense but with the broader educative effect of the whole economic environment as it is shaped by economic policies. (2) I have always been interested in the intimate relationships which exist between the external and the internal aspects of economic development. This was what prompted me to write the earliest paper in this volume (chapter 3). These relationships as I see them now are summed up in the last chapter in this volume, which examines the concept of economic dualism in the underdeveloped countries.

I | The Relevance of Theory

1 | Economic Theory and the Underdeveloped Countries

How far is the economic theory of the industrially advanced countries applicable to the underdeveloped countries? This question has been raised, at one time or other, by a variety of people. Some of the sociological writers have questioned the applicability of the concept of the "economic man" to the underdeveloped countries where traditional values and attitudes still prevail. The historical and institutional economists have argued that the generalizations of economic theory are based on the particular circumstances of the advanced countries and are, therefore, not "universally valid." Finally, there has been a long line of critics from the underdeveloped countries. In the nineteenth century, Hamilton, Carey, and List questioned the applicability of the English classical free-trade theory to the underdeveloped countries of that period, namely, the United States and Germany. They have been followed, among others, by Manoilesco from southeast Europe and by Prebisch from Latin America. With the emergence of the underdeveloped countries of Asia and Africa, the questioning of the usefulness of the "Western" economic theory to these countries has become widespread. Now,

Reprinted from *The Journal of Political Economy,* Vol. LXXIII, No. 5, October 1965, pp. 477–91. Copyright 1965 by the University of Chicago.

many Western economists, not normally regarded as historical or institutional economists, have joined the ranks of the critics.

There are two main lines of criticism currently adopted against economic theory. The first is to elaborate the older line of criticism, stressing the differences in the social and institutional settings and stages of development between the advanced and the underdeveloped countries. This may be described as attacking the "realism" of economic theory. The second and newer line of attack is to question the "relevance" of economic theory to the underdeveloped countries. It is argued that "Western" economic theory is geared to the pre-occupations of the advanced countries which, having already achieved sustained economic growth, are concerned with other problems, such as the optimum allocation of resources, the maintenance of full employment, and perhaps the prevention of "secular stagnation." Thus the conventional economic theory is likely to be out of focus, if not largely irrelevant, for the central problem of the underdeveloped countries which is to initiate and accelerate the "take-off" into sustained growth.

Critics vary considerably in the emphasis they attach to these two different lines of attack.[1] But they share a common viewpoint on other issues. First, their attack on the applicability of economic theory to the underdeveloped countries is closely linked up with their attack on the applicability of free trade and laissez faire policies to these countries. Thus, their sharpest attack on "Western" economic theory is reserved for the "orthodox" classical and neoclassical theory associated with the laissez faire approach. The "modern" Keynesian and post-Keynesian economics is accepted less critically and is frequently used in support of deficit financing for economic development, or as a basis for over-all economic planning in terms of aggregate capital requirements to achieve a target rate of increase in national income, assuming a fixed capital-output ratio. Other

1. D. Seers, in "The Limitations of the Special Case," *Bulletin of Oxford Institute of Economics and Statistics,* May, 1963, stresses the "realism" aspect, while G. Myrdal, in *Economic Theory and Underdeveloped Regions* (London, 1957), stresses the "relevance" aspect.

modern developments of the neoclassical general equilibrium theory, such as welfare economics, input-output analysis, linear programming, etc., are also acceptable provided they are used not as techniques for studying the performance of the market economy but as techniques of planning.

Further, all the critics share a common suspicion of the dispassionate "positivist" approach advocated by some of the orthodox economists.[2] The critics feel strongly that something should be done very urgently to relieve the poverty in the underdeveloped countries. They are also sceptical of the possibility of maintaining strict ethical neutrality in economics and regard "positivism" merely as a cloak for inertia and an underdeveloped social conscience. Thus, they feel that economists should give up the pretence of traditional academic detachment and become the champions and spokesmen for the underdeveloped countries. Some of them have come to look upon the economics of the underdeveloped countries not as a subject of impartial study but as an exercise in making out a persuasive case for increasing international economic aid to these countries.

The aim of this paper is to clarify and appraise some of the issues that have arisen at the present stage of the discussion on the question of the applicability, particularly the "relevance," of economic theory to the underdeveloped countries. Since this is closely bound up with the further question of the applicability of the laissez faire policy to these countries, we shall make use of the arguments directed against the market mechanism to illustrate the arguments directed against economic theory. To clear the air, the underlying standpoint adopted in this paper toward planning and private enterprise in the underdeveloped countries may be stated as follows: There is no reason to suppose that economic policies considered appropriate for the advanced countries will prove to be equally appropriate to the underdeveloped countries. But this "realistic" objection to generalizations should apply not only to the laissez faire but also to the planning policies in the underdeveloped countries. Further, given

2. For example, G. Myrdal, *op. cit.*, chap. xii; D. Seers, *op. cit.*, p. 83.

the wide differences that exist among the underdeveloped countries themselves with respect, say, to the degree of population pressure, the over-all size of the economy, the general level of administrative efficiency, and the coherence of the institutional framework, etc., it is highly unlikely that any single standard model of development planning will be appropriate for all of them.[3]

The plan of this paper is as follows: In Section I we shall examine the various arguments directed against the market mechanism in the underdeveloped countries and use them to illustrate and clarify the various arguments directed against the applicability of economic theory to these countries. In Section II we shall argue that while the need for a greater "realism" is fully conceded, the arguments directed against the "relevance" of the "Western" economic theory to the underdeveloped countries are more debatable. In particular, we shall argue that the orthodox static theory of the optimum allocation of resources is as relevant as any other part of the existing economic theory. In Section III we shall argue (1) that a realistic approach to the underdeveloped countries has been hindered not only by the tendency to generalize from the "special case" of the advanced countries (as some critics have maintained) but also from the tendency to generalize from the "special case" of a particular underdeveloped country, such as India, and (2) that this has been aggravated by the popularity of the "take-off" theory and by the tendency of some of the modern writers to treat the subject not as an academic discipline but as an adjunct to making out a persuasive general case for increasing international economic aid to the underdeveloped countries.

I

When the sociological writers questioned the applicability of economics to the underdeveloped countries on the ground that people there do not behave like the "economic man," they were questioning

3. For a fuller development of this argument, see my book, *The Economics of the Developing Countries* (London: Hutchinson, 1964).

the "realism" of economic theory. It is not difficult to meet this type of criticism by showing that, with suitable adaptations to take into account local circumstances, the demand and supply analysis can be made to explain the behavior of individuals in the market and the prices and quantities bought and sold, etc., in the under-developed countries as well as in the advanced countries. For instance the much-cited case of the "backward-bending" supply curve of labor in the underdeveloped countries (even if it really exists) can be explained in terms of the demand and supply appara-tus, not to speak of refinements such as the "income effect" and the "substitution effect." Similarly, even the reaction of the "subsistence sector" to the impact of the exchange economy can be dealt with by extending the concept of "retained" demand and supply and the factor-proportions analysis of the international trade theory.[4] But this type of defense does not impress some of the modern critics who are questioning the "relevance" of economic theory to the underdeveloped countries. They are not really concerned with the question whether the basic tools of economic theory, such as the demand and supply analysis, can explain economic behavior in a wide range of underdeveloped countries. What they are concerned with is whether it is *important* for the underdeveloped countries to give a central place to the study of the market mechanism and how far the theory of the optimum allocation of resources, which goes with this approach, is relevant for countries seeking rapid economic development.

Now, the discussion would have been much simpler if the critics had simply concentrated on this suggestive line of attack. We could then go on to discuss the usefulness, or otherwise, of the concept of the static optimum for economic development. But what they usually tend to do is, first, identify the existing "orthodox" theory with the laissez faire approach; next, argue that the free play of market forces in the underdeveloped countries will not lead to an optimum allocation of resources, because the conditions of perfect

4. See my "The 'Classical Theory' of International Trade and the Under-developed Countries," below, Chapter 5.

competition, such as perfect mobility and divisibility of resources
and perfect knowledge, are lacking; and, finally, emerge with the
twin conclusions that both the existing economic theory and the
laissez faire policy are inapplicable to the underdeveloped countries.
This type of argument tends to obscure a number of issues.

First, consider perfect competition. It may be taken for granted
that the ideal conditions required by it will not be fulfilled in any
real-life situation, whether in the advanced or the underdeveloped
countries. What is more interesting is to find out how far these two
types of country suffer from the same types of market imperfection
and how far the existing theories of imperfect competition arising
out of the problems of the mature industrial economies are relevant
to the underdeveloped countries at a much earlier stage of development in market institutions. Further, given the important differences
in population pressure, the over-all size of the economy, and the
general stage of development, etc., among the underdeveloped countries, it would be interesting to find out how far the different types
of underdeveloped country suffer from different types of market
imperfection. But many critics have been distracted by the easy
target offered by the perfect-competition model from making a
"realistic" exploration of how the market mechanism actually works
or fails to work in the different types of underdeveloped economic
framework.

This has an interesting consequence on current writings on "planning" in the underdeveloped countries. On the one hand, we have
the rejection of the perfect-competition model. On the other hand, it
is quite fashionable to formulate "pure" planning models (with given
target figures of outputs, given production functions with constant
sectoral capital-output ratios, and given supplies of resources) and
to make a great show of testing the formal consistency of the plan.
Such a plan is supposed to cover the economy as a whole, but the
fact that most governments of the underdeveloped countries control
a relatively small part of their GNP (say 10 to 20 per cent) through
taxation is used as evidence that there is a larger scope for the
expansion of the state sector rather than as evidence of a need for

a more systematic analysis of how the private (including the subsistence) sector will react to government policy. Although some lip service is paid to the role of the fiscal, monetary, and commercial policies of the government, the attention is focused mainly on the "quantifiable" aspects of the plan. Thus, much in the same way as the perfect-competition model fails to tell us how the market mechanism will actually overcome the existing immobility of factors and, particularly, the existing imperfect knowledge, the "pure" planning model fails to tell us how the state mechanism will actually perform these tasks in the given administrative and institutional framework of an underdeveloped country. The substitution of the phrase "planning agency" for the "market mechanism" merely glosses over the actual problems of the mobilization and allocation of resources according to the plan and, above all, the problems of co-ordination and flexible readjustments. Thus, the failure to study systematically how the economic forces work in the private sector of the underdeveloped countries, which produces the bulk of their GNP, has contributed to the failure to develop a satisfactory analysis of the "mixed economy" in the underdeveloped countries.

Next, take the optimum. Much confusion has been caused by the habit of identifying the laissez faire approach with the theory of the optimum allocation of resources. Although there is a historical association, there is no necessary logical link between the two. Thus it is possible to accept and work on the basis of an optimum allocation of resources without accepting the laissez faire policy; for instance, welfare economics is mainly concerned with correcting the market forces to get closer to the optimum. Conversely, it is equally possible to reject the concept of the optimum as being too "static" and yet advocate a laissez faire policy. The case for laissez faire can then be made on other economic grounds, such as that it is likely to impart a "dynamism" to the economy by stimulating enterprise, innovation, and investment. Thus, in criticizing the working of the market mechanism in the underdeveloped countries, it is necessary to distinguish clearly whether we are concerned with its defects as the means of attaining the (accepted) norm of the optimum allocation of resources or whether we are concerned with the inadequacy of the concept of the optimum itself for the purposes of promoting the economic development of these countries.

Few critics have done this. Instead, they tend to bring out further objections against the market mechanism in the underdeveloped countries, objections that are also used as the arguments against the applicability of the existing conventional economic theory to these countries. These various arguments may be grouped under four main lines of attack on the market mechanism.

1. The first type of criticism runs in purely relative terms.[5] It is argued that the market mechanism works *more* imperfectly in the underdeveloped than in the advanced countries for various reasons, such as a greater degree of immobility, indivisibility of resources, and imperfect knowledge. Thus free-market forces will lead to larger deviations from the optimum, requiring a correspondingly greater degree of state interference in the underdeveloped countries compared with the advanced countries. This type of criticism implies that the market imperfections in the advanced and the underdeveloped countries differ in degree rather than in kind and that the existing theory of the optimum and the deviations from the optimum may be usefully extended and adapted to deal with the problems of the economic development in the latter countries.

2. The second type of criticism is based on the view that the most important problem facing the overpopulated underdeveloped countries is that they suffer from a surplus of labor and a shortage of other factors, namely, capital and natural resources. It is argued that this fundamental disequilibrium in factor proportions cannot be corrected merely by improving the allocative efficiency of the market mechanism on the basis of *given* resources, techniques, and pattern of consumers' demand.[6] So long as these structural determi-

5. Most critics have put forward this argument at one time or another. For a clear exposition of this view, see T. Balogh, "Economic Policy and the Price System," *United Nations Economic Bulletin for Latin America,* March, 1961.
6. For example, see R. S. Eckaus, "The Factor-Proportions Problem in the Underdeveloped Countries," *American Economic Review,* September, 1955.

nants of the economy remain unchanged, perfect competition, even if it were attainable, would merely bring out this problem sharply: According to the logic of the optimum theory, since labor is redundant relative to given wants and technology, it should have zero wages. This type of criticism implies a rejection of the concept of the static optimum. But, unfortunately, in the absence of a thorough-going dynamic theory, many exponents of this view revert to the conventional methods of correcting the deviations from the static optimum. This can be illustrated best by the argument that the manufacturing sector of an underdeveloped country should be subsidized or protected because it has to pay positive wages to labor whose social-opportunity cost in agriculture is zero.[7]

In this connection it may be noted that current writings tend to restrict the market mechanism too narrowly to its role of allocating given resources, neglecting its possible longer-term effect on the supply of factors, particularly capital.[8] Private savings may increase through improvements in the market for finance or through a rise of a capitalist class ploughing back profits. Even if it is decided that savings should increase only through public channels, such as taxation, marketing boards, and the issue of government securities, the success of such a policy will still depend considerably on the market factors including the stage of development of the exchange economy and the development of a capital market.

3. The third type of criticism is based on the view that the underdeveloped countries are trapped in a very stable low-income equilibrium and that they can be jerked out of this only through a "balanced growth" development program big enough to overcome the smallness of the domestic markets and to take advantage of the economies of scale and complementarities. It is argued that, at its

7. For example, see W. A. Lewis, "Economic Development with Unlimited Supplies of Labour," *Manchester School,* May, 1954, p. 185.
8. In international trade theory there has been some discussion of how far the expansion of primary exports of the underdeveloped countries tends to aggravate the initial "skewness' of their factor endowments. See C. P. Kindleberger, *Foreign Trade and the National Economy* (New Haven, Conn.: Yale University Press, 1962), chap. iii.

best, the market mechanism can only make one-at-a-time "marginal" adjustments, whereas an effective development program requires large "structural" changes introduced by a simultaneous expansion of a wide range of complementary industries.

Without going into all the different versions of the "balanced-growth" theory, it is sufficient to point out that we can adopt at least two different attitudes toward the role of the optimum allocation of resources in economic development, depending on the version of the theory we favor: (a) One version emphasizes the over-all size of the investment program, which must be large enough to overcome technical indivisibilities and the smallness in the size of domestic markets caused by the low levels of purchasing power in the under-developed countries.[9] Those who adopt this version tend to attach a greater importance to the problem of the aggregate level of invest-ment and effective demand than to the problem of better allocation of resources at a given level of economic activity. A. O. Hirschman has justifiably described this as "a variant of the Keynesian analysis of the slump."[10] Many of the "balanced-growth" economists of this school would, for instance, be willing to put up with the possible distortion in the allocation of resources through inflationary methods of financing development rather than cut down the over-all size of the investment program. (b) This may be contrasted with the other version of the "balanced-growth" theory which stresses the inter-relationships between investment in different sectors of the economy and the need for a government "planning agency" to co-ordinate the investment plans so as to achieve an optimum allocation of resources.[11] Those who adopt this version believe that the market

9. The most notable exponent of this version is P. N. Rosentein-Rodan. Contrast, however, his early paper, "Problems of Industrialization of Eastern and South-Eastern Europe," *Economic Journal,* 1943, with his "Notes on the Theory of the 'Big Push,' " in *Economic Development of Latin America,* ed. H. S. Ellis (London: Macmillan, 1951).

10. *The Strategy of Economic Development* (New Haven, Conn.: Yale University Press, 1958), p. 5.

11. For example, see T. Scitovsky, "Two Concepts of External Economies," *Journal of Political Economy,* LXII, April, 1954, 143–51; and H. B. Chen-

mechanism is ineffective in the underdeveloped countries, not because the people there do not behave like the "economic man" in responding to its signals, but because the market signals themselves are defective and cannot accurately forecast what the future economic situation would be, after a complex of large-scale interrelated projects has been carried out. Thus, far from belittling the importance of the optimum, this second group of "balanced-growth" theorists have made important contributions to the theory of the optimum involving complex interrelations between investment in different sectors of the economy over a period of time.

4. Finally, there is the criticism which is based on the view that the free play of market forces tends to fossilize or exaggerate the existing market imperfections and the inequalities in income and bargaining power that are to be found in many underdeveloped countries.[12] The idea of the cumulative disequalizing forces has been applied both to the international economic relations between the advanced and the underdeveloped countries and to the internal economic relations between the "advanced" and the "backward" sectors or groups of people within each underdeveloped country. This type of criticism attempts to break sharply away from the conventional ideas of a stable equilibrium and the optimum and to focus attention on the concept of the "dualism" in the economic structure of the underdeveloped countries which underlies most other types of criticism of the working of market mechanism in these countries.

Although the ideas contained in this line of attack are suggestive, they have not been satisfactorily formulated so far. The concept of "dualism" needs more systematic study, and the theoretical mechanism of how the cumulative disequalizing factors work has been

---

ery, "The Interdependence of Investment Decisions," in *The Allocation of Economic Resources,* ed. Moses Abramovitz (Stanford, Calif.: Stanford University Press, 1959).

12. For example, see T. Balogh, "Static Models and Current Problems in International Economics," *Oxford Economic Papers,* June, 1949; see also my "An Interpretation of Economic Backwardness," below, Chapter 3; and Myrdal, *op. cit.,* chap. iii.

sketched out in a rather impressionist manner. For instance, while the fragmentation of an economy into an "advanced" and a "backward" sector will lead to a deviation from the optimum in a static sense, might not "dualism" have certain dynamic advantages enabling the "leading" sector to drag the "lagging" sector in its wake? Following the trend of thought suggested by Hirschman's "unbalanced-growth" approach, might not an attempt to impose a deadpan uniformity and equality between the different sectors of the economy lead to the elimination of "growth points" and dynamic tensions for further economic development? These questions bring us to the difficult problem of choice between economic equality and rapid economic development. Here the critics are not always clear whether they object to the free play of market forces because they want to prevent economic inequality for its own sake or because they think that this inequality will in its turn inhibit the growth of the economy as a whole.

II

The relations between the four main types of criticism of the market mechanism in the underdeveloped countries and the theoretical approaches they suggest for development economics may be summed up schematically as shown in Figure 1.

We are now in a position to appraise the criticisms directed against

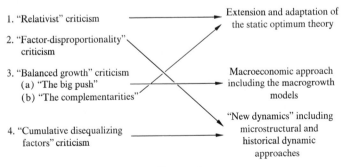

Figure 1

economic theory (as distinct from those directed against the market mechanism) in the context of the underdeveloped countries. There can be no serious quarrel with those critics who stress the need to increase the "realism" of economic theory by taking into account the various social, historical, and institutional differences between the advanced and the underdeveloped countries. If anything, our analysis has suggested the need also to take into account the differences between the underdeveloped countries themselves with respect to the degree of population pressure, the over-all size of the economy, the general level of economic development and institutional framework, and various other factors that may be expected to introduce significant differences in the structure and texture of their economic life. In particular, we have suggested that a failure to study systematically how the market forces actually work or fail to work in the different types of underdeveloped frameworks has contributed to the failure to develop a satisfactory analysis of the "mixed economy" in the underdeveloped countries. A study of the different patterns of market imperfections in different types of underdeveloped country is a largely unexplored subject.[13]

The argument of those critics who question the "relevance" of "Western" economic theory (in particular, the relevance of the "orthodox" static theory of the optimum allocation of resources to the underdeveloped countries) is more debatable. In the light of the criticisms 2 and 4 in Figure 1, few will question the need for a thoroughgoing "new" dynamic approach to economic development involving changes in the supplies of factors, techniques of production, and the "transformation" of the whole organizational structure of the economy. It may be that such a new approach means widening the scope of conventional economics to take into account the broader sociological factors that made up "political economy" in the classical sense. But there is no need to argue about this since orthodox opinion has never imposed a methodological interdict on

13. For a pioneer effort in this field, see Morton R. Solomon, "The Structure of the Market in Underdeveloped Economies," *Quarterly Journal of Economics,* August, 1948.

such a process. As A. Marshall wrote: "Each economist may reasonably decide for himself how far he will extend his labour over that ground."[14]

What is really at stake is how far we should discard the existing static optimum theory before we have time or are clever enough to build up a satisfactory "dynamic" approach to the underdeveloped countries. That is to say, how far are we to follow Myrdal's advice to the "young economists in the underdeveloped countries" to "throw away large structures of meaningless, irrelevant and sometimes blatantly inadequate doctrine and theoretical approaches."[15] There are a number of considerations against following this advice, if this means throwing away the static optimum theory.

The first and most powerful is that the underdeveloped countries are too poor to put up with the burden of preventable waste that arises even within the static framework of given wants, techniques, and resources. As Galbraith has suggested in his *Affluent Society*, only the richer advanced countries can afford to take an indulgent view toward the misallocation of resources. There is a real danger that in searching for newer approaches and more advanced techniques of analysis, the economist (particularly if he is a visitor) in the underdeveloped countries may easily overlook quite glaring sources of wastage through misallocation, whether due to spontaneous market imperfections or inept state interference.

To give an example of the latter: After her independence, Burma followed a policy of cutting out all private middlemen from her rice-marketing board operations and opening numerous state buying stations all over the country to purchase rice directly from the peasant-producers. Until very recently, the government also insisted on paying the same fixed price all the year round, to cut out "the speculators." It also insisted on paying the same fixed price to all inland rice cultivators, irrespective of their distance from the main

14. *Principles of Economics* (4th ed.; London: Macmillan), p. 780; see also L. Robbins, *Nature and Significance of Economics* (2d ed.; London: Macmillan), p. 150.
15. Myrdal, *op. cit.,* p. 101.

seaports (on grounds of regional justice). The consequences of conducting a marketing board on the basis of zero rate of interest, zero storing costs, and zero transport cost are apparent from elementary optimum theory. As it happened, the rice crop, which normally took about four to six months to be cleared under free-market conditions, now had to be cleared almost at once, since no one had any incentive to hold the rice stocks. This would have wrecked a very much more efficient marketing machinery than the government had been able to provide. The wastage and deterioration of the rice through bad storage, for instance, fire, rain, theft, mixing of different grades, etc., was enormous. Further, the more remote regions that previously grew rice for local consumption now sold their crop to the state buying center; from there it was sent down to seaports for export so that consignments of milled rice from the seaports had to be sent back to those remote regions to prevent food shortages, entailing two useless journeys on the country's limited transport system. Yet, many economists visiting Burma during this period characteristically overlooked this "simple" but extremely wasteful misallocation of resources in their preoccupation with the more elaborate development plans, including the expansion of investment in "infra-structure." It is hard to believe that this is an isolated instance.[16]

If the underdeveloped countries are too poor to put up with the waste from preventable misallocation of resources, they are presumably too poor to forego immediate sources of relief from poverty for the sake of larger benefits promised in the future. Here, the

16. See, however, A. C. Harberger, "Using the Resources at Hand More Effectively," *American Economic Review,* May, 1959. Harberger argues that for economies like Chile, Brazil, and Argentina, reallocating resources with existing production functions "would raise national welfare by no more than 15 per cent." He considers that this, although substantial, is relatively small compared with the large potential dynamic gains to be obtained from technical improvements raising labor productivity. One may reply that any source of gain is likely to appear small compared with the gains from technical improvements; but, from the point of view of this paper, Harberger's article remains an interesting attempt to apply the optimum analysis in a quantitative manner to the underdeveloped countries.

time preference that the critics have adopted on behalf of the under-developed countries shows a curious kink. In arguing for more international aid, they stress the urgent need to do something to give immediate relief to the underdeveloped countries; but in other contexts, they tend to adopt a much lower valuation of the present in favor of the future. Thus they generally stress the longer-run social benefits from various forms of development expenditure to justify their immediate cost to the developing countries. Also, as against the orthodox presumption that the underdeveloped countries should choose less capital-intensive methods of production with quicker returns, some of the critics would defend capital-intensive methods on the ground that these are necessary for a higher rate of economic growth in the future. Thus the critics may be regarded as exercising the same pattern of time preferences in the choice of theoretical techniques when they urge that the existing static theory should be discarded in favor of a new dynamic theory which is rather sketchy at present and which promises to yield results in the somewhat indeterminate future. There are strong reasons to be worried about the future of the underdeveloped countries, but there are equally strong reasons to be worried about their present poverty, and the former should not be stressed almost to the exclusion of the latter. If it is urgent to give immediate relief to the underdeveloped countries by stepping up international aid, it is equally urgent to find out how far they can help themselves by stopping obvious sources of waste through misallocation of resources. The significance of the conventional static theory of the allocation of scarce resources to the underdeveloped countries can be properly appreciated only in this perspective.

So far we have been concerned with criticisms 2 and 4. Let us now turn to criticism 3a, which may be regarded as the Keynesian criticism of the orthodox economics. The tendency in the writings on the underdeveloped countries to neglect the problem of allocating scarce resources has been aggravated by the "backwash" effect of the Keynesian revolution. In the early postwar years, at least, the Keynesian reaction against orthodox economics was automatically extended from its original context in the advanced countries to the underdeveloped countries. The Keynesian approach was enthusiastically adopted both as a basis of economic planning at a macroeconomic level and also as an argument for the deficit financing of development plans. Since then there has been an increasing realization of the need to probe below the macroeconomic approach into the "structural" and "frictional" factors in the underdeveloped countries. Nevertheless, the point raised by criticism 3a, namely, how far we should put up with the possible distortion effect of inflation on the allocation of resources before cutting back the overall size of the investment program, still remains a live issue dividing the expansionist and the orthodox economists. But even here an important change is noticeable. In the earlier days, the case for deficit financing of economic development was made mainly at the macroeconomic level. Thus it was argued that the investment expenditure financed by pure credit creation would expand the money incomes but keep them stabilized at a certain level according to the multiplier theory. Thus the increase in physical output from the newly created capital goods would have a chance to catch up with the increase in money incomes until at last prices were restored to the initial level and inflation destroyed itself.[17] More recently, however, the structural and allocative factors have been brought into the forefront. It is now argued that a mere negative elimination or ending of the inflationary pressure will not lead automatically to an optimum allocation of resources and that what is really needed are "carefully discriminatory policies" designed to correct the structural imbalance and market imperfections in the underdeveloped countries.[18] One can follow up this point by asking how far the government of an underdeveloped country will, in fact, be in a position to pursue such discriminatory policies effectively and consistently

17. Lewis, *op. cit.,* p. 165. Lewis himself points out "the usual objections against applying multiplier analysis to inflationary conditions, namely the instability of the propensity to consume, the effect of secondary investment and the dangers of cost inflation."

18. Balogh, "Economic Policy and the Price System," *op. cit.,* p. 53.

after the inflationary pressure and balance-of-payments difficulties have gone beyond a certain point.[19] But for our present purpose it is sufficient to point out the shift of emphasis from the Keynesian approach to the optimum approach.

We can now pull together the threads of our argument so far. As shown in Figure 1, the various criticisms of the working of the market mechanism in the underdeveloped countries have suggested three types of theoretical approach to these countries: (1) the extension and adaptation of the existing static theory of the optimum allocation of scarce resources; (2) the extension of the Keynesian macroeconomic approach, including the macrogrowth models of the Harrod-Domar type; and (3) the introduction of a new thoroughgoing dynamic approach that is capable of dealing with the changes in the long-run supplies of factors of production and with changes in the techniques of production involving the "transformation" of the whole organizational structure of the underdeveloped economies. In the postwar writings on the underdeveloped countries there has been some progress made in the application of the optimum theory to development economics, particularly on the problems of complementary investment and of optimization over a given plan period.[20] Nevertheless, the optimum approach to the underdeveloped countries has been unduly neglected by the critics of the "orthodox" economics, partly because they identify this with the laissez faire type of liberal economics, partly because they feel that anything short

19. For example, the differential advantages offered by tariff protection to "infant industries" are likely to be swamped under random short-term speculative rises in prices of the non-protected imports when successive rounds of quantitative import restrictions have to be imposed because of a balance-of-payments crisis. For a fuller treatment, see my "Infant Industry Arguments for Assistance to Industries in the setting of Dynamic Trade Theory," below, Chapter 6.

20. For example, H. B. Chenery, op. cit., and "Comparative Advantage and Development Policy," American Economic Review, Proceedings, March, 1961; also A. K. Sen, The Choice of Techniques (Oxford: Blackwell, 1961); and O. Eckstein, "Investment Criteria for Economic Development and Intertemporal Welfare Economics," Quarterly Journal of Economics, February, 1957.

of a thoroughgoing, dynamic approach should be discarded, and partly because of the "backwash" effect of the Keynesian revolution. While fully admitting the need to develop a new dynamic approach to the underdeveloped countries, we have tried to show (1) that the orthodox static theory of allocation of scarce resources remains as "relevant" to these countries as any other part of economic theory so long as they suffer from serious misallocations of resources which they can ill afford, and (2) that the optimum approach can be made more fruitful by a "realistic" study of how the market forces actually work or fail to work in the different settings of the different types of underdeveloped country.

III

Some critics have attributed the lack of "realism" in the current writings on the underdeveloped countries to the tendency of the Western economists to generalize from the "special case" of the advanced countries.[21] But this is only half the trouble; the other half must be traced to the tendency to generalize about all underdeveloped countries from the "special case" of a particular type of underdeveloped country. This latter tendency has been aggravated by the tendency to treat the whole subject as an adjunct to making out a persuasive case for increasing international aid. It is no accident that the theory of economic development of the underdeveloped countries should come to be dominated by a "conventional" model that most closely resembles India, since the case for increasing international aid to the underdeveloped countries is strongest when we have a country like India.

Given India's acute population pressure on natural resources and material poverty, the case for increasing aid to her on purely humanitarian grounds is obvious. Given her low ratio of foreign trade to national income, she cannot hope to earn enough foreign exchange through the expansion of her exports even if the market

21. For example, Seers, *op. cit.*, pp. 79–83 and *passim.*

prospects for them were brighter and, when she has reached the limits of borrowing on commercial terms, there is little alternative but to rely on aid. One further consequence of a low ratio of foreign trade to national income is that foreign exchange shortage cannot be overcome by increasing domestic saving. Again, given the very large over-all size of her economy, it is reasonable to suppose that she will be able to reap the economies of scale from setting up a large and interrelated industrial complex, including a capital-goods sector oriented toward the domestic market. Finally, whatever our views about India's chance of ultimate success in achieving economic development through integrated economic planning, it is widely admitted that her general institutional framework and her administrative and planning machinery are well in advance of other developing countries. Thus in India's case both the need to receive material aid and the ability to absorb aid for successful economic development are stronger than in most other underdeveloped countries. Only Mexico and Brazil, at about the same stage of general development as India but without her population pressure, seem to have a comparable capacity to absorb material aid.

There is nothing wrong with concentrating on such a type of underdeveloped country, provided it is clearly recognized as a very "special case." The danger arises in trying to generalize from the Indian case and, in particular, in trying to apply to other underdeveloped countries the standard Indian model of development planning. Here are some of the more obvious limitations of this "special case." (1) Although population is growing very rapidly over all the underdeveloped world, there are still many sparsely populated countries, covering most of Latin America, considerable parts of Africa, and most of Southeast Asia, where the Indian type of extreme population pressure on natural resources does not apply. The concept of "disguised unemployment" has limited application for these countries, and their problem is how to make the best use of the available elbow room of natural resources before plunging into the more heroic measures of development required by the Indian situation. (2) Even among the overpopulated countries, the overall size of the population and area of India has no peer except for China. Many of the overpopulated countries are much smaller countries, which, unlike India, have a high ratio of foreign trade to national income and which, because of their smallness, cannot hope to imitate the Indian model of industrialization based on a substantial capital-goods industry and oriented mainly toward the domestic market. Short of organizing themselves into larger common-market units for which they are not politically ready, exports (particularly exports of primary products) must continue to play an important part in their economic development. In this respect the position of the smaller overpopulated countries, some of them overcrowded islands, is harder than that of a big overpopulated country like India with a domestic market potentially large enough to yield the economies of scale. While a few small countries like Hong Kong and Puerto Rico may have found an escape route in the export of "simple manufactures" and/or emigration, this is not likely to be open to the others because of various obstacles, partly of their own creation and partly created by the advanced countries. (3) Above all, it should be stressed that the underdeveloped countries are at widely varying stages of general social, political, and economic development. At one end of the scale are a few countries like India, Mexico, and Brazil which have reached a stage of development where they may be considered to be within a reasonable striking distance of the "take-off." The rest of the underdeveloped countries are at different substages of the "pre-take-off" phase, tailing off into a considerable number of countries that are hard put to maintain even the minimum of law and order, political stability, and public services, and that clearly do not yet possess the necessary institutional framework to carry out elaborate economic development planning.

Given the popularity of the conventional Indian model of economic development, however, most underdeveloped countries have tried to fulfill the first and the second of Rostow's conditions for the take-off: "(a) a rise in the rate of productive investment from (say) 5 per cent or less to 10 per cent of national income (or net national product); (*b*) the development of one or more substantial manufacturing sectors, with a high rate of growth." But in their preoccupation with quantitative planning and target figures, they have neglected his third elusive condition: "(*c*) the existence or quick emergence of a political, social and institutional framework which exploits the impulses to expansion in the modern sector and the potential external economy effects of the take-off and gives to growth an on-going character."[22] It turns out that condition (*c*) is the most important of the three in the sense that unless it can be fulfilled it is not possible to keep the two other conditions fulfilled for long. It is also the most important factor determining an underdeveloped country's capacity to absorb aid productively.

Yet, in spite of the fact that the majority of the underdeveloped countries are either just emerging from the "traditional society" or are somewhere in the "pre-take-off" stage, the discussion of this earlier phase is perhaps even more unsatisfactory than the rest of the take-off theory.[23] The central problem of these countries is not how to plan for an immediate take-off but how to compress the pre-take-off phase into a few decades instead of "a long period up to a century or conceivably more" [24] which the Western countries are said to have taken. Here, one may agree that if these countries are not yet ready for the final "big push" into take-off, they need not rely solely on the unaided working of the market forces to shorten the preliminary period. In the past, even the so-called laissez faire colonial governments encouraged the growth of the exchange economy, particularly through the provision of better transport and communications. But beyond this, analysis has not proceeded very far.

For instance, the success of a policy of concentrating on "infrastructure" investment will depend on the various economic factors

22. W. W. Rostow, "The Take-off into Self-Sustained Growth," *Economic Journal,* March, 1956, p. 32, and *The Stages of Economic Growth* (New York: Cambridge University Press, 1960), p. 39.
23. See S. Kuznets, "Notes on the Take-off," in W. W. Rostow *et al., Economics of Take-off into Sustained Growth* (London: Macmillan, 1963).
24. Rostow, "The Take-off into Self-Sustained Growth," *op. cit.,* p. 27.

determining the structure and behavior of the "subsistence sector" and on the question of how far its persistence is due to the limitations on the demand side, that is, lack of marketing facilities and outlets and how far it is due to limitations on the supply side, that is, lack of a marketable surplus. Yet there is little systematic study of the mutual interactions between the "subsistence sector" and the "money economy" (including the government sector) in the different types of underdeveloped country, taking into account the differences in the degree of population pressure, the nature and extent of the export production, and the urban manufacturing sector. In this context, we may also ask how far the more sophisticated monetary policy of deficit financing is really suitable for the earlier stages of the development in the money economy when we should be concerned with encouraging the people from the subsistence economy to use money, not only as a medium of exchange, but also as a unit of account for a rational economic calculus and as a store of value. Recently there has been a shift of interest from investment in material "infra-structure" to "investment in human capital," particularly in education. Yet, so far, this line of approach has been limited by too much emphasis on what the government should do in the way of a "crash program" in education combined with too little analysis of the demand and supply factors affecting the market for skilled labor at various stages of economic development.[25]

All this is merely another way of stating our argument that we need to have a more systematic study of how the market forces actually work or fail to work in the different types of underdeveloped country. Applied to the majority of the underdeveloped countries at the earlier "pre-take-off" stages of economic development, this now assumes a special significance. The degree of effective control that the government of such a country can exercise over the rest of the economy depends more clearly than elsewhere on

25. For further discussion, see my papers, "The Universities of Southeast Asia and Economic Development," below, Chapter 9, and "Social Flexibility, Social Discipline and Economic Growth," *International Journal of Social Science,* 1964.

the growth of suitable monetary, fiscal, and market institutions through which it can extend its control. Thus, we may reasonably suggest a more systematic study of the market forces in such an underdeveloped country even to the most planning-minded economist.

To sum up: Current writings on the underdeveloped countries have been vitiated not merely by the tendency to generalize from the "special case" of the advanced countries but also by the tendency to generalize from the "special case" of a particular type of underdeveloped country, notably India. This in its turn has been aggravated by the popularity of the idea of development planning based on the "take-off" theory and by the tendency to treat the subject, not as an academic discipline but as an adjunct to making out a persuasive general case for increasing international aid to the underdeveloped countries. The new crusading spirit has rendered a valuable service in getting the idea of giving aid to these countries firmly established in the advanced countries. But now that the general good will toward these countries seems to have outstripped an accurate knowledge of how the economic systems of these countries really function, one may venture to urge the revival of the traditional academic approach to the subject.

2 | Economic Theory and Development Policy

Both economic theory and development economics are getting highly specialised nowadays. A specialist in a branch of economic theory cannot hope to keep up with the highly technical development in other branches of economic theory. Similarly, a specialist in a particular aspect of economic development or on a particular group of underdeveloped countries cannot hope to keep up with the vast outpouring of publications in other fields of development economics. The proliferation and sub-division of development economics is most dramatically shown by the many periodicals which devote themselves entirely to some particular aspect of the subject, such as development finance, development agriculture and so on.

But, it seems to me that precisely because of this trend towards specialisation, there is some need, in the universities at least, for a general practitioner to act as a middleman between different specialised fields of development economics and also between development economics and general economics. Such an economist should try to acquire a good working knowledge at least, of the broad economic dimensions and the basic features of the situation, in a

The text of an inaugural lecture given at the London School of Economics on December 1, 1966.

From *Economica*, May 1967, pp. 117–30. Reprinted by permission.

wide range of underdeveloped countries. His aim should be to try to apply the existing economic theory in a more realistic and fruitful way to suit the varying conditions of the different types of under-developed country. An equally important part of his job would be to try to prevent serious misapplications of economic theory, whether of the orthodox type or the newer modern theories, to the under-developed countries.

This way of looking at a general development economist as a middleman between the tool-makers and the tool-users brings me face to face with the perennial controversy: how far are the existing tools of economic theory applicable to the underdeveloped countries? There are many distinguished economists [1] who would be impatient with my proposal to start from the existing theoretical framework and try to improve its applicability to the underdeveloped countries in the light of accumulating experience and factual knowledge. They would say that the existing "Western" economic theory is so in-timately bound up with the special conditions, problems and pre-conceptions of the industrially advanced countries that large por-tions of it have to be abandoned before we can come to grips with the problem of the underdeveloped countries.

These economists have advanced three main types of criticism against the existing economic theory.

First, they question the "realism" of trying to apply the standard models of theoretical analysis meant for the advanced countries to the different economic and institutional setting of the underdeveloped countries. I have no quarrel with this line of criticism. In fact I shall be giving illustrations of other types of lack of realism in apply-ing economic theory to the underdeveloped countries which are not mentioned by the critics. But it seems to me that this is not an argument for abandoning existing economic theory but merely an argument for trying to improve its applicability.

1. For example, G. Myrdal, *Economic Theory and Underdeveloped Regions,* London, 1957; also his *An International Economy,* London, 1956; D. Seers, "The Limitations of the Special Case," *Bulletin of the Oxford Institute of Economics and Statistics,* May 1963.

Second, the critics question the "relevance" of the static neo-classical economics concerned with the problem of allocating given resources within an existing economic framework to the problem of promoting economic development in the underdeveloped countries, which is concerned with increasing the amount of available resources, improving techniques and generally with the introduction of a dynamic self-sustaining process of economic change, disrupting the existing framework. Here again I agree that we do not possess a satisfactory dynamic theory for studying development problems. In fact, I would go further and say that the recent developments in the theory of dynamic economics in terms of the growth models are not very relevant and are not meant to be relevant for the underdeveloped countries.[2] But I do not accept the conclusion which the critics have drawn, viz. that the static theory of efficient allocation of given resources is irrelevant for the underdeveloped countries. I shall come back to this point.

Third, the critics maintain that the orthodox economic theory is inextricably bound up with preconceptions and biases in favour of the orthodox economic policies of *laissez-faire*, free trade and conservative fiscal and monetary policies. They believe that these orthodox economic policies are generally inimical to rapid economic growth, which can be promoted only by large-scale government economic planning, widespread protection, import controls and deficit financing of development programmes, if sufficient external aid is not available. Thus they propose that large chunks of existing economic theory, particularly the orthodox neo-classical theory, should be abandoned to pave the way for the adoption of these new development policies.

There are two questions here. The first is the general question whether the new policies are always more effective than the orthodox policies in promoting economic development in the underdeveloped countries. The second is the more specific question whether there is an unbreakable ideological link between orthodox economic theory

2. Cf. Sir John Hicks, *Capital and Growth*, Oxford, 1965, p. 1.

and orthodox economic policies so that if we wish to adopt the new development policies we must necessarily abandon much of the existing theory.

The underdeveloped countries vary widely among themselves and I, therefore, find it difficult to accept the general presumption that the new policies will always be better for their economic development whatever their particular individual situation. Later, I shall give some examples where the orthodox type of economic policies have in fact been more effective in promoting economic development than the new-style development policies. However, I have chosen as the subject of this paper, not the general debate on the rival merits of the orthodox and the new development policies but the relation between economic theory and development policy. I have done this partly because I feel that such a general debate without reference to a concrete situation generates more heat than light and partly also because it has been rapidly overtaken by events. Whether we like it or not, it is no longer an open question whether the underdeveloped countries should choose the orthodox or the new type of development policies. One after another, they have already made their choice in favour of the new policies which have now become a part of conventional economic wisdom. Accepting this as one of the facts of life, the more immediately relevant question seems to be the second question, viz. whether large parts of orthodox economic theory have now become obsolete because the underdeveloped countries wish to plan for rapid economic development.

I shall argue that this is not so; that on the contrary, the orthodox economic theory assumes a greater significance in the context of the new "progressive" development policies. I shall show that even if development planning is to be regarded as new and radical policy, the *theory* underlying development planning is, technically speaking, quite orthodox and conventional. Similarly, I shall show that the orthodox theory of international trade can be made to support more liberal and generous trade and aid policies towards the underdeveloped countries, if we choose to use it in this way. What I am saying is not new. It is merely a restatement of the familiar doctrine that economic theory is "ethically neutral" and can be made use of in the more efficient pursuit of the economic objectives to be chosen by the "value judgments" of the policy maker.

However, let us start from a closer look at the question of "realism" in applying existing economic theory to the underdeveloped countries. Some critics speak of "existing theory" as though it were contained in a modern textbook like Samuelson. Properly speaking, it should include the whole corpus of Western economic theory, offering a wide choice of theoretical models, ranging from those of the older economists writing at earlier stages of economic development to the highly complex and abstract models of contemporary economic theory. To my mind, a very important cause of lack of realism arises from the wrong choice of theoretical models to be applied to the underdeveloped countries. In much the same way as the governments of the underdeveloped countries succumb to the lure of the "steel mills" embodying the most advanced and capital-intensive type of Western technology, many development economists have succumbed to the lure of the intellectual "steel mills" represented by the latest and most sophisticated theoretical models. This is where I believe the greatest mischief has been done. This is why I have always maintained that a good development economist should also be something of an applied historian of economic thought.

If it is unrealistic to apply highly sophisticated theoretical models meant for the complex economic structures of the advanced countries to the simpler economic structures of the underdeveloped countries, has this been corrected by the new theories of development and underdevelopment which are specially meant for the underdeveloped countries? Looking at these new theories which became popular during the 1950s, such as the "vicious circle," the "take-off" or the "big push," it does not seem to me that these have stood up any better to the test of realism. The weakness of these new theories is that they try to apply to all the underdeveloped countries a composite model of *the* underdeveloped country incorporating in it certain special features of some one or other type of underdeveloped country. The "vicious circle" theory assumes poverty and stagnation caused by severe population pressure on resources; the "take-off" theory assumes the pre-existence of a fairly high level of development in the political, social and institutional framework; the "big push" theory assumes both and also an internal market large enough to support a domestic capital-goods sector. By the time we have incorporated all these special features into a composite model, the number of the underdeveloped countries to which this model might apply becomes severely limited to one or two countries such as India and possibly Pakistan.

The limitations of these new theories of development, particularly the "vicious circle" theory, can be illustrated by looking at the broad dimensions of the economic performance of the underdeveloped countries during the decade 1950–60. During that decade, compared with the 4 per cent average annual growth rate for the advanced Western countries, the gross domestic product of underdeveloped countries as a group has grown at the average annual rate of 4.4 per cent, giving them a growth in *per capita* incomes of a little over 2 per cent per annum.[3] This may or may not be very much, but the really interesting thing is that some underdeveloped countries have been growing at a faster rate than the average, say between 5 and 6 per cent, while others have been barely able to keep up with their population increase. Thus instead of the earlier *simpliste* view according to which all underdeveloped countries are caught up in a vicious circle of stagnation and population pressure, we are led to the question why some underdeveloped countries grow faster or slower than others.

When we try to answer this question, we become greatly aware of the differences between the underdeveloped countries in size, in the degree of population pressure on natural resources, in the conditions of world demand for their exports and in their general level of economic development and political stability. These differences by themselves will explain quite a lot of the differences in the growth

3. United Nations, *World Economics Survey,* 1963, Part I, p. 20.

rates among different underdeveloped countries. If in addition we want to say something about the influence of development policies, we shall have to choose a fairly uniform group of countries where the basic social and economic differences are small enough for us to isolate the effect of economic policy.

To illustrate, let me take the concrete example of the post-war economic development of Southeast Asia. This will also serve to illustrate the dangers of generalising about development policies, particularly the danger of assuming that the new "progressive" development policies will always promote faster economic growth than the orthodox economic policies.

The five countries I have chosen, Burma, Thailand, the Philippines, Indonesia and Malaya, form a fairly homogeneous group. In contrast to India or China, they are not only much smaller but also do not suffer from any great pressure of population. They do not have to contend with food shortage and have much more elbow room in respect of natural resources to allow for the working of economic incentives. They are also similar in the general level of social and economic development and moreover have common exports such as rice, timber and rubber. Yet the rapid post-war economic development of Thailand, the Philippines and Malaya contrasts sharply with the economic stagnation of Burma and Indonesia. By 1960, both Thailand and the Philippines doubled their pre-war gross national product (in real terms) combined with a considerable growth in import-substituting industries, while the gross national product of Burma and Indonesia rose by a bare 11 per cent above the pre-war level, much slower than their rate of population growth during the same period. Malaya, starting at a somewhat higher *per capita* level than the others, has also enjoyed economic prosperity which compares favourably not only with Burma and Indonesia but also with Ceylon to which her economic structure is similar in many aspects.

These large differences in the rates of economic growth are closely related to the rate of expansion in the exports of the two groups of countries and, since they have common exports sharing the same world market conditions, the differences in their export performance must be traced largely to the domestic economic policies which have affected the supply side of their exports. Here, broadly speaking, the first group of countries with the faster rates of economic growth, viz. Thailand, Malaya and the Philippines, have pursued the more orthodox type of economic policies with a greater reliance on market forces, private enterprise and an outward-looking attitude to foreign trade and enterprise; while Burma and Indonesia lean heavily on economic planning and large-scale state intervention in economic life combined with an inward-looking and even hostile attitude towards foreign trade and enterprise.

More specifically we may note the following. (1) Thailand and the Philippines have very successfully used market incentives to encourage their peasants to bring more land under cultivation and expand production both of export and domestic food crops, while the Burmese peasants have been depressed by the operation of the state agricultural marketing board which has used peasant agriculture simply as a milch cow for government investment in state enterprises in manufacturing industry and social overhead capital. (2) Thailand and the Philippines have encouraged their domestic entrepreneurs to set up new manufacturing industries through protection and subsidies, while Burma and Indonesia have tried to do this by state enterprises which have failed, amongst other reasons, because of a shortage of entrepreneurial ability among the civil servants. Here it may be noted that all these Southeast Asian countries suffer from the fear of being dominated by the Chinese or the Indian entrepreneurs who are or were prominent in small or medium scale enterprises in light manufacturing industries. Thus one may say that Burma and Indonesia have chosen to substitute Indian and Chinese private enterprise by indigenous state enterprise while Thailand has absorbed the Chinese entrepreneurs into her own business class and the Philippines have successfully substituted Filipino private entrepreneurs for them. This problem has yet to be solved in Malaya. (3) Malaya, Thailand and the Philippines have offered a stable economic climate to Western enterprises both in the traditional plantation and mining sectors and in the new manufacturing sector and have benefited from a considerable inflow of private foreign capital, while Burma and Indonesia have discouraged fresh inflow of private investment by nationalization and other hostile policies. (4) Malaya and Thailand have pursued conservative monetary and fiscal policies and their currencies have been strong and stable, and the Philippines tackled her balance-of-payments disequilibrium successfully by devaluation in 1962. In contrast Burma and Indonesia have tried to solve their balance-of-payment problems arising out of deficit financing and domestic inflation through an intensification of inefficient and hurtful import controls, which, combined with pervasive state interference at all levels of economic activity, have throttled most of the promising infant industries.[4]

It is not for me to judge the ultimate rightness or wrongness of the economic nationalism and the anti-Western attitude of Burma and Indonesia contrasted with the more pro-Western attitude of Malaya, Thailand and the Philippines. But at the conventional level at which economists judge development policies, it seems to me that in the case of Southeast Asia at least the orthodox type of economic policies have resulted in a more rapid rate of economic development during the post-war period than the newer "progressive" development policies. How far is the Southeast Asian experience applicable to other underdeveloped countries outside the region? I think that it may be of some relevance to the other smaller and less densely populated export economies, notably in West Africa. There, also, expansion in the exports of primary products still offers the most promising engine of economic development both as a source of foreign exchange earnings to finance the new import-substituting industries and, even more important, as the method of drawing the under-utilised natural resources of the subsistence sector into the money economy. But these conclusions in favour of

4. For a fuller treatment, see "The Inward and the Outward-Looking Countries of Southeast Asia," reprinted as Chapter 12 below.

the orthodox policies are likely to become weaker as we try to extend them to less similar types of country, particularly to large overpopulated countries like India. But conversely it would be equally unrealistic to try to apply the Indian model to the smaller export economies.

Let me now conclude my remarks on the "realism" of applying economic theory to the underdeveloped countries by drawing attention to the dangers of trying to be too different from the standard models of economic analysis. These arise from selecting the "queer cases" in the standard Western models of analysis and in taking it for granted that these exceptions to the standard case must automatically apply to the underdeveloped countries because they are so different from the advanced countries in social values and attitudes and institutional setting. Such for instance is the famous case of the "backward-sloping supply curve" of labour attributed to the underdeveloped countries by many writers, who nevertheless speak also of the "demonstration effect" and "the revolution of rising expectations." Such also is the belief that the people of the underdeveloped countries, being more communally minded, will take more easily to co-operative forms of economic organization, despite the fact that writers on the co-operative movement in the underdeveloped countries frequently complain about the lack of co-operative spirit and the excessive individualism of the people. Yet another example is the generalisation that the people of the underdeveloped countries naturally lack entrepreneurial ability, irrespective of the economic policies followed by their governments. Here, if one were to tell the politicians of the underdeveloped countries that their people are lazy, stupid, lacking in initiative and adaptability, one would be branded as an enemy: but if one were to rephrase these prejudices in another way and say that they lack entrepreneurial capacity, one would be welcomed for giving "scientific" support for economic planning. To take just one more example, there is the hoary belief that peasants in the underdeveloped countries do not respond to economic incentives, while agricultural economists have been accumulating abundant evidence to show that peasants do respond to price changes by switching from one crop to another or by bringing more land under cultivation. The real problem is how to introduce new methods of cultivation which will raise productivity: this is a difficult practical problem, but in principle it is little different from, say, the problem of introducing new methods to raise productivity in British industry.

This is where I think that a closer co-operation between economics and other branches of social studies is likely to prove most useful, both in getting rid of questionable sociological generalizations and also in tackling the more intractable problems of analysing social and economic change.

I now turn from the "realism" to the "relevance" of the existing economic theory to the underdeveloped countries. The problem of promoting rapid economic development in these countries may ultimately lie in the realm of social and economic dynamics of the sort we do not at present possess; and there is nothing in my argument to prevent anyone from launching into new dynamic theoretical approaches to the underdeveloped countries. But in the meantime it is dangerously easy to underestimate the significance to the underdeveloped countries of the orthodox static theory of the allocation of given resources. The affluent Western economies with their steady rates of increase in productivity may be able to take a tolerant attitude towards misallocation of resources. But the underdeveloped countries are simply too poor to put up with the preventable wasteful use of their given meagre economic resources. In particular, they can ill afford the well recognized distortions of their price system such as the excessively high levels of wages and low levels of interest rates in their manufacturing and public sectors compared with those in the agricultural sector, and the over-valuation of their currencies at the official rates of exchange. Having to bear the brunt of low earnings and high interest rates discourages the expansion of agricultural output both for export and for domestic consumption and this in turn slows down the overall rate of growth of the economy. Higher wages attract a large number of people from the countryside to the towns but only a small proportion of this influx can be absorbed because of the highly capital-intensive methods adopted in the modern import-substituting industries. This aggravates the problem of urban unemployment and the problem of shanty towns which increases the requirements for investment in housing and social welfare. The scarce supply of capital tends to be wastefully used both in the government prestige projects and in private industry because of the artificially low rates of interest. This is aggravated by the over-valuation of currencies and import controls in favour of capital goods which positively encourage the businessmen who are fortunate enough to obtain licences to buy the most expensive and capital-intensive type of machinery from abroad.

These then are some of the glaring sources of waste which can be reduced by a better allocation of resources. Now I should point out that just because the orthodox neo-classical theory is concerned with the efficient allocation of *given* resources, it does not mean that the theory becomes unimportant in the context of aid policies to increase the volume of resources available to the underdeveloped countries. On the contrary, a country which cannot use its already available resources efficiently is not likely to be able to "absorb" additional resources from aid programmes and use them efficiently. That is to say, a country's absorptive capacity for aid must to a large extent depend on its ability to avoid serious misallocation of resources. A similar conclusion can be drawn about an underdeveloped country's ability to make effective use of its opportunities for international trade. If we find that a country is not making effective use of its already available trading opportunities, because of domestic policies discouraging its export production or raising the costs in the export sector, then we should not expect it to benefit in a dramatic way from the new trading opportunities to be obtained through international negotiations.

This is a part of the reason why I have suggested that orthodox economic theory, instead of becoming obsolete, has assumed a greater significance in the context of the new "progressive" policies for promoting economic development in the underdeveloped countries. Let me illustrate this argument further by examples from development planning theory and from recent discussions about the appropriate trade and aid policies.

I think that a great deal of confusion would have been avoided by clearly distinguishing the *policy* of development planning and the economic *theory* which underlies development planning which is, as we shall see, only an application of the traditional theory of the optimum allocation of the *given* resources. This confusion was introduced during the 1950s when it was the fashion to try to make out the case for development planning mainly by attacking the orthodox equilibrium and optimum theory. At the macroeconomic level, there were theories of deficit financing trying to show how economic development might be accelerated by forced saving and inflation or by making use of "disguised unemployment" for capital formation. More generally, the theories of the "vicious circle," the "big push" or "unbalanced growth" tried to show, in their different ways, the desirability of breaking out of the static equilibrium framework by deliberately introducing imbalances and disequilibria which would start the chain-reaction of cumulative movement towards self-sustained economic growth. Ironically enough, when the underdeveloped countries came to accept the need for development planning and asked how this might be done efficiently, is turned out that the economic theory required for this purpose was basically nothing but the traditional equilibrium and optimum theory.

Thus according to the present day textbooks on development planning,[5] the first task of the planner is to test the feasibility of the plan at the macroeconomic level by making sure that the aggregate amount of resources required to carry out the plan does not

5. See, particularly, W. A. Lewis, *Development Planning,* London, 1966; A. Waterson, *Development Planning: Lessons of Experience,* Oxford, 1966; and W. B. Reddaway, *The Development of the Indian Economy,* Cambridge, Mass., 1962.

exceed the aggregate amount of resources available. That is to say, deficit financing and inflation are to be avoided and this is to be checked at the sectoral level by seeing to it that the projected rate of expansion of the services sector does not exceed the possible rate of expansion in the output of commodities by a certain critical margin. The next task of the planner is to test the consistency of the plan at the sectoral and microeconomic level to make sure that the demand and supply for particular commodities and services are equated to each other and that there is an equilibrium relationship between the different parts of the economy, not only within any given year, but also between one year and another during the whole of the plan period. Finally, if the plan is found to be both feasible and consistent, the task of the planner is to find out whether the plan adopted is an optimum plan in the sense that there is no alternative way of re-allocating the given resources more efficiently to satisfy the given objectives of the plan.

If this standard formulation of development planning is accepted, then there is no fundamental theoretical difference between those who aim to achieve the efficient allocation of the available resources through the market mechanism and those who aim to achieve it through the state mechanism. Both accept the optimum allocation of resources as their theoretical norm and their disagreements are about the *practical* means of fulfilling this norm. In any given situation, they will disagree how far planning should be "indicative" or "imperative," that is to say, how far the task of allocating resources should be left to the decentralised decision-making of the market or to the centralised decision-making of the state. But technically speaking they are using the same type of economic theory, viz. the extension of the othodox neo-classical theory, in the pursuit of their different practical policies.

From a theoretical point of view the great divide is between those who believe on the one hand that economic development of the underdeveloped countries can be promoted in *an orderly manner* by a more efficient allocation of the available resources which are assumed to be steadily expanding between one period and another through good management of domestic savings and external aid, and those who believe, on the other hand, that only sudden disruptive and *disorderly* changes such as social revolutions and technical innovations can bring about economic development. Now this second revolutionary approach to economic development may well be the correct approach for some underdeveloped countries. But it is difficult to see how this can be incorporated into the planning approach. Development planning is by definition an orderly approach: on the other hand, genuinely far-reaching and disruptive social changes cannot be turned on and turned off in a predictable way and incorporated into the planning framework. Those who advocate the necessity of breaking out of the static equilibrium framework by deliberately introducing imbalances and tensions are in effect advocating at the same time the need to break out of the planning framework. Thus one may advocate social revolution now and planning later, but one may not advocate social revolution and planning at the same time without getting into serious contradictions. Further, it should be pointed out that the revolutionary approach to economic development is by no means the monopoly of the critics of the private enterprise system. The case for *laissez-faire* can be made, not on grounds of static allocative efficiency, but on the ground that it imparts a "dynamism" to the economy by stimulating enterprise, innovation and savings. Schumpeter's picture of the disruption of the existing productive framework through a process of "creative destruction" by innovating private entrepreneurs is a well-known illustration of this type of revolutionary approach to economic development.

Let me conclude by illustrating how the orthodox theory of international trade may be used in support of more liberal or generous trade and aid policies towards the underdeveloped countries. There is still a considerable amount of prejudice against the export of primary products in the underdeveloped countries. To some extent this has been overlaid by the more pro-trade views which have gained ground since the United Nations Conference on Trade and Development. The views which are now accepted by most underdeveloped countries may be summarised as follows. (1) While the underdeveloped countries should be allowed to protect their domestic manufacturing industries in any way they think fit, they should have preferential treatment or freer access to the markets of the advanced countries for their exports of primary products, semi-processed products and fully manufactured products. (2) More aid should be given to supplement the trade concessions, but there should be less tying of aid to imports from the donor country and also less tying of aid to the specific projects chosen and managed by the donor country.

Now it is possible to find a variety of opinions among the orthodox-minded economists on the question of giving aid to the underdeveloped countries. There are some who are against aid-giving either because they fear that this would lead to a misallocation of the world capital resources or because of the various undesirable political and sociological side effects of aid. For instance, Professor Bauer has recently argued that the material benefits which an underdeveloped country might obtain from aid would be swamped by the deleterious sociological and political effects, such as the development of a beggar mentality and the growth of centralised power which would pauperise the aid-receiving country.[6] On the other hand, not all orthodox economists are against aid-giving. In this connection, I should mention the name of the late Professor Frederic Benham who wrote what I consider to be the best book stating the case for aid-giving.[7] These individual views aside, the standard orthodox economic theory would say something like this on the subject: how much aid the rich countries should give the poor countries should be decided by "value judgements" based on moral and political considerations which are beyond the scope of economic analysis. But once it is agreed that a certain amount of aid, say 1 per cent of the national income of the rich countries, should be given, economic analysis can be used to show how this given policy objective can be carried out in the most efficient way. By a familiar

6. Barbara Ward and P. T. Bauer, *Two Views on Aid to the Developing Countries,* Institute of Economic Affairs, Occasional Paper 9, 1966.
7. F. Benham, *Economic Aid to Underdeveloped Countries,* London, 1961.

process of reasoning, orthodox theory would say that this could be most efficiently carried out by free trade for both the aid-givers and the aid-receivers. For the aid-givers, the more efficient allocation of their resources through free trade would enable them to spare the 1 per cent of their income they are giving away with the least sacrifice. For the aid-receivers, free importation of goods at cheaper prices than could be produced at home would maximise the value of the aid they received. Further, if the aid resources are to be invested, the more efficient choice of investment opportunities under free trade would raise the returns from investment.

Thus from the point of view of orthodox trade theory the one-way free-trade plus aid for which the underdeveloped countries are asking is less efficient than two-way free trade plus the same amount of aid. This is likely to be so even when the need to protect the "infant industries" has been conceded.[8] But if the underdeveloped countries insist on adopting what it considers to be the less advantageous option, then the orthodox trade theory can still say something useful within this restricted framework: and what it has to say is in support of opening the markets of the advanced countries more freely to the products from the underdeveloped countries and in support of the untying of aid.

Take the rather protracted debate about "reciprocity," on the question whether the advanced countries should give trade concessions to the underdeveloped countries without getting back some *quid pro quo*. In support of one-way free trade the champions of the underdeveloped countries usually appeal to moral considerations

---

8. For one thing, the import controls practised by the underdeveloped countries are too indiscriminate and bound up with short-run balance-of-payments considerations to give selective protection to the promising infant industries; for another, the correction of the distortions due to the imperfections of the domestic market may require other forms of government intervention than protection. See my paper (ch. 7) in R. Harrod and D. C. Hague (eds.), *International Trade Theory in a Developing World,* London, 1963, reprinted below, Chapter 6; and H. G. Johnson, "Optimum Trade Intervention in the Presence of Domestic Distortions," in *Trade, Growth and the Balance of Payments,* Economic Essays in Honor of Gottfried Haberler, Amsterdam, 1965.

such as not having the same rule for the lion and the lamb and the need for a double moral standard when dealing with unequal trading partners. The advanced countries, on the other hand, tend to argue that while they do not expect "reciprocity" from the underdeveloped countries, they would like other advanced countries to give similar concessions to the underdeveloped countries before they commit themselves. Professor Harry Johnson [9] has recently reminded us that these arguments, based on the mercantilistic view of trade, have entirely overlooked the point that according to the theory of comparative costs the gains from trade consist in having cheaper imports. By allowing free imports from the underdeveloped countries, the consumers in the advanced countries already would have gained from trade by being able to buy these imports more cheaply: thus there is no need to ask for a further *quid pro quo*.

Basing himself entirely on the orthodox trade theory, Professor Johnson has argued that the United States would gain by a unilateral removal of trade barriers to the products from the underdeveloped countries without waiting for other advanced countries to follow suit. Similarly, he has shown that the official figures for the United States aid to the underdeveloped countries would be very appreciably reduced if the goods and services given under tied aid, notably aid in the form of agricultural surpluses, were revalued at world market prices under free-trade conditions.

These seem to me to be very good illustrations of how orthodox trade theory can be used in support of more liberal trade and aid policies, if we choose to do so. What has given flexibility to the theory is the much-maligned postulate of the "ethical neutrality" of economic theory. The champions of the underdeveloped countries tend to look upon it with great suspicion as a sign of an underdeveloped social conscience on the part of those who adopt it. But I hope that I have shown it to be no more objectionable than the notion of a constrained maximum.

Finally, the question of how far aid should be tied to the specific

9. H. G. Johnson, *U.S. Economic Policy Towards the Less Developed Countries,* Washington, D.C., 1967.

projects to be chosen and managed by the donor country raises fundamental issues of how far we consider the underdeveloped countries to be competent to run their own affairs without a benevolent supervision from the advanced country. Here we come at last to the "presumptions" and "preconceptions" of the orthodox economists which conflict sharply with those of the planning-minded economists. One important presumption of the liberal orthodox economists which I believe in, is that the underdeveloped countries can best educate themselves for economic development by being allowed to make their own mistakes and learning from them, and that without this painful process of self-education and self-discipline they are not likely to acquire the degree of competence required for economic development. I think this runs contrary to the implicit or explicit philosophy of the present-day administrators of aid. They would like to make up for the underdeveloped countries' lack of "absorptive capacity" for aid by insisting upon tighter planning and supervision of their economic affairs by economic and technical experts from the advanced donor countries. Ultimately, then, we have two philosophies about aid-giving to the underdeveloped countries. The liberal orthodox view is to give an agreed amount of aid to the underdeveloped countries and then to leave it to them to use it freely in any way they think fit, to learn from their mistakes and to take the consequences of their action. According to this view the advanced countries can only guarantee the amount of aid but not the rate of economic development of the underdeveloped countries which must to a large extent depend on how they use the aid. One further implication of this view is that, since the underdeveloped countries differ so much in their circumstances and capacity to benefit from mistakes, it would be unrealistic to expect an equally fast rate of economic development for all the underdeveloped countries. The alternative view which pervades thinking at present is that the advanced countries should take the responsibility of guaranteeing a politically acceptable target rate of economic growth for all underdeveloped countries and, if this cannot be achieved by the latter countries' own efforts, the advanced countries should be prepared

II | Trade and Development

examining the current fashion of including not only the natural resources but also the so-called "human resources" under the generic
heading of "underdeveloped resources," which seems to imply that
the two terms we have distinguished really overlap. But is it merely
a matter of taste or tact whether we choose to speak of "backward
people" or of "underdeveloped human resources"? On a close
examination it will be seen that each term has its own hinterland of
associated ideas and the two cannot be superimposed on each other
without creating a number of serious logical difficulties.

In common-sense terms, a "backward people" may be defined as
a group of people who are in some fashion or other unsuccessful in
the economic struggle to earn a livelihood. Thus we are starting
from a Classical or Marshallian distinction between man, on the one
hand, and his environment on the other: only then can we think of
a group of people as being successful or otherwise in adapting
themselves to their environment. Further, the idea of "backwardness" inevitably implies a comparison of different degrees of success
in this economic struggle: some groups of people are less successful
or "backward" compared with other more successful or "advanced"
groups. Thus the nature of backwardness would lose much of its
significance if applied to a homogeneous group of people without
international economic relations. It is when a self-sufficient primitive
or medieval economy has been opened up to outside economic forces
and its people come into contact with other economically more
"advanced" people that the idea of backwardness suggests itself.

This way of approach at once raises a number of issues. Firstly,
we shall have to make a more systematic analysis of the continuous
process of mutual adaptation between wants, activities, and environment which we have described as "economic struggle." Secondly,
in order to make a valid comparison of the varying degrees of success
in the economic struggle of different groups of people we require
the assumption that these different groups are in fact pursuing the
same or comparable sets of ends. This is a big assumption which
will have to be examined closely. Finally, we shall have to consider
whether it is sufficient to measure the degree of "backwardness" or

"advancement" of different groups of people merely in terms of the relative distribution of final incomes among them; or whether the pattern of distribution of economic activity among the different groups and the different roles they play in economic life might not in the long run offer a more significant clue to the future potential development of each group.

These will be discussed at a later stage (section IV). For the purpose of a preliminary contrast, however, it is sufficient to note that when we adopt the approach in terms of "backward people" we are by definition making their failure in the economic struggle the centre of the problem and that this involves: (*a*) a fundamental contrast between them (the "backward people") and the natural resources and the economic environment of their country, and (*b*) a deliberate concentration of attention on their share of incomes or economic activity either within their own country or in relation to the world at large as distinct from the total volume of output or economic activity.

When we turn to the approach in terms of "underdeveloped resources," however, we are led to quite a different set of ideas. To treat "human resources" on exactly the same footing as natural resources as part of the common pool of "underdeveloped resources" is to abandon the older man-against-environment approach in favour of the modern "allocative efficiency" approach. We are then concerned, not with the success or failure of a given group of people in their struggle against their economic environment (including other groups of people), but with the allocation of given "resources" among alternative uses as determined by the price system or by the central planner or by a mixture of both. The aim of this allocative process is to maximize total output, and "underdevelopment" becomes a species of deviation from the productive optimum defined in some sense or other.

We can now see that although, physically speaking, the same people are involved when we speak of "backward people" and of "underdeveloped human resources," the standpoint adopted in each case is different. From the first standpoint, these people are regarded as actors (even if unsuccessful ones) in the economic struggle. From the second, they are regarded as impersonal units of "underdeveloped" resources not distinguishable from units of other types of underdeveloped resources except by the degree of underdevelopment defined in some functional sense. Thus we are not specially concerned with "human resources" more than with other types of resources except in so far as it could be shown that "developing" the human resources would in fact increase the total output by a greater extent than by developing other "material" resources.

The difference between the "backwardness" and the "underdevelopment" approach becomes very clear when we exclude human resources from the definition of "underdeveloped resources" and confine it entirely to natural resources. This is by no means an unusual or deliberately contrived "strong case" to boost our distinction. As a matter of fact, much of the thinking on the subject is still influenced by the idea of "underdeveloped countries" as those which (whatever their "human resources") possess a greater amount of potential natural resources waiting to be developed compared with the "developed countries" whose natural resources have already been fully brought into use. We may also note how the use of such expressions as "underdeveloped countries," "underdeveloped areas," "underdeveloped regions," &c., tends to foster this belief in the existence of potential natural resources.

Here, once we have excluded the human beings from the "underdeveloped resources," a number of propositions emerge. Since they will recur again in the course of our argument, they may be summarily stated at this stage. (1) "Underdevelopment" of natural resources and "backwardness" of people are two distinct phenomena and they need not even always coexist: thus the inhabitants of the "overpopulated" countries which admittedly have very little natural resources left for further unaided development are also generally "backward." (2) When "underdeveloped" natural resources and "backward" people coexist, they mutually aggravate each other in a "vicious circle"; but this mutual interaction is an essentially dynamic and historical process taking place over a period of time and may be too complicated and qualitative to be easily fitted into the formal quantitative framework of optimum allocation of resources (including capital resources) suggested by the pure "underdevelopment" approach. (3) Although the "underdevelopment" of natural resources may cause the "backwardness" of the people, it does not necessarily follow that any efficient development of natural resources resulting in an increase in total output will always and *pari passu* reduce the backwardness of people. On the contrary, the problem of economic backwardness in many countries has been made more acute, not because the natural resources have remained "underdeveloped," but because they have been as fully and rapidly developed as market conditions permitted while the inhabitants have been left out, being either unable or unwilling or both to participate fully in the process.

II

Let us now turn to the logical difficulties which arise from attempts to superimpose the "backwardness" and the "underdevelopment" approach on each other. These can be best illustrated by examining some of the typical arguments in favour of increasing the flow of investment from the "advanced" to the "underdeveloped" countries.

Advocates of plans for the international economic development of the underdeveloped countries generally start by saying that the case for alleviating the poverty and discontent, ill health and ignorance of the peoples of these countries can be made whether we approach the subject from a humanitarian standpoint or purely in self-defence to ease the storm-centres of international relations. At this stage therefore the problem seems to be set out in terms of human misery and discontent, in terms of "backwardness" rather than in terms of "underdevelopment" of resources. Indeed, the existence of "underdeveloped" natural resources at least, far from creating a "problem" in the relevant sense, may be regarded as part of the means of solving it. When, however, we pass from this initial statement of the problem to the later parts of the economic develop-

ment plans which contain a more technical treatment of the proposals and "target figures" for investment, we generally encounter a
shift from the "backwardness" to the "underdevelopment" approach.
The existence of "underdeveloped" natural resources is no longer
regarded as the means of solving the problem; it has become the
problem itself. The argument then proceeds as though the phenomenon of the "backwardness" of the people can be satisfactorily
accounted for purely in terms of the "underdevelopment" of the
resources and deviations from the optimum allocation of world's
capital resources (cf., for example, United Nations Report, *Measures
for the Economic Development of Underdeveloped Countries,* ch.
viii).

It is now time to consider the meaning of "underdeveloped resources" more closely. In the language of optimum theory, it seems
to describe two types of deviation: (1) less than optimum amounts
of these "underdeveloped" resources have been used in producing
final output, and (2) less than optimum amounts of capital have
been invested to augment the quantity and improve the quality of
these "underdeveloped" resources. Where the first occurs by itself
it would be possible to increase the total output of the underdeveloped countries without outside investment merely by reorganizing
their own existing resources by such measures as legal and administrative reforms, the mobilizing of domestic savings, and so on. In
current discussion, although this possibility is admitted, it is considered that as a rule the two types of deviation occur simultaneously,
the first caused by the second. That is to say, the scope for a more
productive reorganization or "development" of the resources of the
underdeveloped countries is limited without first removing the basic
cause of "underdevelopment," viz. an insufficient flow of investment
from the "advanced" countries.

The typical arguments in favour of increasing investment in the
underdeveloped countries may now be examined. They may be
classified according to the degree of optimism concerning the richness
of the "underdeveloped resources."

1. The most optimistic type of argument assumes that as a rule

underdeveloped countries possess *natural* resources capable of being developed by private investors on a purely commercial basis and this process will automatically help to raise the standard of living of the people of these countries. "Underdevelopment" is therefore caused by "artificial" obstacles and restrictions to the free international movement of private capital. Whatever our views about the richness of potential natural resources, this type of argument serves to illustrate a sharp clash between the "underdevelopment" and the "backwardness" approach. For, on a closer examination, it turns out that the only type of investment which private investors are willing to undertake in the underdeveloped countries is the exploitation of raw materials, e.g. petroleum, and it is precisely in this field that the governments of the underdeveloped countries are frequently unwilling to admit private foreign capital because they fear that this "nineteenth-century type of investment" will merely develop the natural resources and not the people and will result in "foreign economic domination" aggravating the economic "backwardness" of their peoples. This is a genuine deadlock to which no satisfactory answer can be given in terms of the simple "underdevelopment" approach. And to dismiss the whole thing merely as irrational economic nationalism seems suspiciously like throwing the baby away with the bath water (see section VI below).

2. The next type of argument may be regarded as an attempt to retrieve the "underdevelopment" approach by introducing the Pigovian concept of the "social" productivity as distinguished from the "private" productivity of investment. Here it is argued that although the underdeveloped countries may not possess (or are unwilling to make available) resources which can be developed by private enterprise, they can nevertheless very profitably absorb large sums of international investment in the form of public enterprises using a broader criterion of "social" productivity. These enterprises would include public utilities, transport, hydro-electric and irrigation schemes, &c., which offer economies of large scale and scope for complementary investment and where only a public agency can collect the diffused social returns by means of taxation. A good

example of a direct application of this argument may be found in
the United Nations Report on *National and International Measures
for Full Employment*. Here the authors, after recommending that
the International Bank for Reconstruction and Development should
be used as the main channel of inter-governmental lending to reduce
political risks on both sides, lay down the following conditions:

The criteria of worthwhileness for the loans should be their effect on
national income, taxable capacity and export capacity. The Bank should
not in general lend, unless it is convinced that in consequence of the
loan, the borrowing country's current balance of payments will improve
sufficiently to permit interest and amortisation payments to be made.[2]

Development loans should be made at interest rates uniform for all
borrowing countries.' (*Op. cit.,* pp. 93–94.)

These two conditions may be regarded as the logical limits to
which the investment policy towards the underdeveloped countries
can be liberalized on the basis of the Pigovian concept of "social"
productivity of investment. It may be noted that fairly substantial
amounts of capital can still be absorbed by some of the underdeveloped countries within these limits. But comparing this view with
the general run of discussions on the subject, it soon becomes
apparent that many advocates of international development plans
would consider the Pigovian conditions as too restrictive to be
regarded as a serious basis of investment policy towards the underdeveloped countries. There are two possible ways out of this im-
passe. The first, which we shall recommend in the later part of this
paper, is to make a clean break with the whole "underdevelopment"
approach and to adopt a more direct approach to the problem of
economic backwardness of the people. The second and more popular alternative is to try to broaden the "underdevelopment" approach
still further; and this brings us to the third type of the under-investment argument.

3. The argument at this stage consists in attempts to stretch the

2. We are not concerned here with the question how far this rule can be
reconciled with the authors' practical proposals for stabilizing longer-term
lending by fixing target figures. Cf. also A. E. Kahn, "Investment Criterion
for Development Programmes," *Quarterly Journal of Economics,* Feb. 1951.

concept of "social productivity" or "desirability" by invoking (*a*) the principle of "needs," and (*b*) the dynamic principle of trying to stimulate further rounds of loan investment by "productive" grants to "improve social capital," particularly in the fields of public health, education, and communications. A good example of this may be found in a later United Nations Report on *Measures for the Economic Development of the Underdeveloped Countries.*

Here the authors argue:

(*a*) that "the amount that can be profitably invested at a 4 per cent rate of interest depends on the amount which is being spent at the same time on improving social capital; and especially on public health, on education and on roads and communications. There is much to be done in this way in the underdeveloped countries before they will be in a position to absorb large amounts of loan capital" (para. 269);

(*b*) that the underdeveloped countries "cannot borrow" for these purposes, presumably because "they could not meet the full burden of loan finance" (paras. 270 and 277);

(*c*) that, therefore, grants-in-aid should be made to the underdeveloped countries, but purely for "productive" purposes (paras. 271 and 276).

The authors do not, however, hesitate to invoke the principle of needs. Thus:

The principle that the better off should help to pay for the education, the medical services and other public services received by the poorer classes of the community is now well established within every Member nation of the United Nations. The idea that this principle should also be applied as between rich and poor countries is relatively new. It has however been put into practice on several occasions. [Para. 272.]

How far are these attempts to stretch the idea of "social" productivity successful?

To begin with, there is an important shift in the basic definition of the "underdeveloped countries" which is not as clearly stated as it might be. Up to now the main burden of the argument has been on the proposition that "underdeveloped countries" possess a greater amount of "underdeveloped" resources than the developed countries and that therefore the "social" productivity of investment is higher in the former than in the latter. From now on the emphasis has shifted to the fact that the underdeveloped countries have lower *per capita* incomes and therefore suffer from greater needs than the developed countries.

The introduction of the principle of needs does not create any difficulties provided we are prepared to keep it clearly apart from the principle of productivity. Then loans should continue to be made strictly on the productivity principle while grants should be made *separately* on the need principle.

This, however, results in somewhat unpalatable conclusions. (*a*) When we are allocating loans, our main conern is to maximize the total world output and not to equalize international incomes. Thus the social productivity curves of investment must be constructed objectively, and independently of our value judgements concerning needs. This means that capital should not be diverted in the form of low interest loans or grants to the poorer countries simply because they are poor. A more *economic* way of reducing inequalities in the international distribution of income is to allocate the world capital resources in uses where its social productivity is highest even if it happens to be in the richest countries, and to redistribute the resultant output after first ensuring that it is maximized. (*b*) Conversely, when we are allocating grants, our concern is with a more equitable international distribution of incomes and not with their effects on total output. Thus grants should be made in the form of final consumers' goods and services, directed not only towards the poorer countries but also towards the poorer sections within each country. The principle of need in its strict form is an argument for diverting final incomes from the richer to the poorer countries for consumption purposes and not an argument for diverting capital grants for "productive" purposes.

These conclusions are not without relevance to the practical issues of economic policy in the underdeveloped countries. Thus critics of the unsuccessful developmental ventures of the British Overseas

Food Corporation and the Colonial Development Corporation may reasonably maintain that the root cause of the failure lies not as much in the wrong choice of men and inefficient methods of administering the ventures but in the vagueness of the mandate itself which tries to compromise between the principle of obtaining economic returns and the principle of needs. They may say that rather than waste huge sums of money by investing in projects which cannot be justified on the strict productivity principle, it were better to distribute them as free gifts of consumers' goods and services among the poor of Africa. Again, individuals and governments in underdeveloped countries sometimes find themselves with large sums of money which they cannot profitably or safely invest locally; and then, following the strict productivity principle and the need to protect their capital, they have found it wiser to invest it in the most developed countries such as the U.S.A. or the U.K.

The last example, however, brings out the unsatisfactoriness of trying to apply the static rules of the productive optimum to the problem of the underdeveloped countries. This, however, is rather damaging to the conventional definitions of the "underdeveloped" countries both in terms of "underdeveloped" resources and in terms of low *per capita* incomes. For now it begins to transpire: (*a*) that if we take the productivity curves of international investment on the basis of existing economic conditions in the "developed" and the "underdeveloped" countries, more often than not capital is likely to be more productive in the former than the latter and the Pigovian distinction between "social" and "private" product will not appreciably change the broad picture; (*b*) that therefore if we were to allocate capital according to the existing productivity curves, even taking a generous view of "social" productivity, this would still result in relatively greater quantities of capital being invested in the "developed" than in the "underdeveloped" countries, accentuating the unequal rate of economic development between the two types of country; and (*c*) that a policy of a more equal redistribution of international incomes based on the pure principle of needs, although it may relieve the burden of cumulative unequal rates of economic development, does not touch the heart of the problem; for fundamentally the problem of the "underdeveloped" countries is not merely that of low or unequal distribution of final incomes but also that of unequal participation in the processes of economic activity.

Faced with these considerations, those who wish to retain the "underdevelopment" approach are obliged to "dynamize" it and to refer to social productivity in the *longer run* as distinct from the *present* social productivity of investment.

We are now in a position to examine the argument of the authors of the United Nations Report on the *Measures for the Economic Development of the Underdeveloped Countries.* It will be seen that the crux of their argument lies in the question how far "improving social capital" in public health, education, and communications, whether financed by grants or loans, can successfully stimulate further rounds of loan capital. Thus the authors' appeal to the principle of need in para. 272 (also implicit earlier on, e.g. para. 248) turns out to be a side-issue. It is a confusing side-issue at that because the requirements for creating incentives for further investment and those for promoting economic equality do not always conveniently coincide in the same policy as the authors have implied. On the contrary, there are many instances where the incentives for further investment can be created only by pursuing relatively disequalizing policies, such as control of domestic wages, tax exemptions to new (foreign) enterprises, &c. (Cf., for instance, "Industrialisation of Puerto Rico," *Caribbean Economic Review,* Dec. 1949, by Prof. A. Lewis, one of the authors of the Report.)

Turning to their main argument, the extent to which further rounds of loan investment can be effectively stimulated by a policy of "improving social capital" by grants must depend on a wide variety of circumstances which vary from country to country and about which no definite generalizations can be made. We are no longer in the static world where "under-investment" in a particular line can be deduced in principle by an inspection of the *given* social marginal productivity curves and where there is a definite functional relationship between the quantity of capital invested and the quantity of "returns" in the form of final output. Thus given favourable circumstances, a small amount of "investment" in social capital might start a chain-reaction and yield "returns" in the form of secondary rounds of investment out of all proportion to the initial investment. On the other hand, if circumstances are not favourable, even a larger amount of initial investment might not successfully start these secondary rounds of activities, and there is no real guarantee that increasing the amount of the initial investment still further would induce the desired results. In reply to such objections, the authors can only appeal to the general presumption that if average incomes per head or expenditure per head in the type of social services they have chosen is low, then longer-run social productivity of investment in "social capital" is likely to be high. This general presumption is not as strong as it appears, and there are two general arguments which may be advanced against it.

The first is clearest in the case of education and technical training although it can be applied also to other types of "social capital." It is the fairly common experience of the underdeveloped countries to find themselves, not merely with an overall shortage of educated people, but also with a relative shortage of those regarded as "socially productive," such as engineers and doctors, combined with a relative abundance of those regarded as less socially productive, such as lawyers and clerks. The reason for this is, of course, that with the existing social and economic organization of these countries there is a relatively greater market demand for the latter type of person than the former. This would seem to suggest that the problem of creating and organizing demand for trained personnel in the underdeveloped countries may even be more important than the problem of creating the supply by investment in "social capital." Given the demand, the supply of trained personnel of most types (including those trained abroad) would seem to respond more automatically and to a greater extent than is usually allowed for. On the other hand, there is less indication that the demand can be effectively stimulated merely by creating the supply without simultaneously introducing far-reaching changes into the economic structure. Thus most underdeveloped countries can provide numerous instances of graduates from technical and agricultural colleges who cannot be absorbed, because the existing economic structure cannot be changed quickly enough to absorb them, although in terms of broad averages the amount of money spent per head of education and technical training is quite modest. The common fate of these people is to suffer a form of intellectual "disguised unemployment" by taking up appointments as clerks and ordinary school teachers (cf. J. S. Furnivall, *Colonial Policy and Practice,* pp. 380–82). Thus there is a genuine tendency for a great deal of investment in "social capital" to be wasted, although the full extent of this wastage is concealed because expenditure on education and technical training is classed under the head of social services and not subject to the strict profit-and-loss accounting of other types of state enterprises.

This leads us to the second argument, which is rather disconcerting to the economic theorist. The application of fairly sophisticated economic theory involving concepts of social productivity and induced investment tends to create the impression that we have now opened up new possibilities of investment in the underdeveloped countries which were unappreciated and unexplored by the governments and administrators of these countries. This, however, overlooks two circumstances. Firstly, a substantial part of capital inflow into the underdeveloped countries was in the form of government borrowing even in the heyday of private investment. Secondly, the governments of the newly-opened-up countries have always been impelled by a powerful "self-interest" to try to obtain adequate revenues to meet the expanding costs of administration. Thus, untutored as they may be in economic theory, they have been obliged by practical necessity to borrow and deploy their loans and grants in ways not so different from the recommendations of the present-day economic experts.[3] The moral of this argument is not merely

3. In some cases, however, there may be an important divergence between the social productivity of investment to the community and the "private" productivity to the government interpreted narrowly in terms of quick revenue receipts. Sometimes governments may actually discourage new domestic industries to protect their vested interests in customs and excise duties.

that there is less scope for the deployment of "productive" loans and grants (as distinct from those social service expenditures which are frankly based on the principle of need) than appears at first sight. There is a further consideration which cuts across the whole of the "underdevelopment" approach. For, as we shall see, ironically enough, where the governments of the underdeveloped countries have been successful in stimulating private (foreign) investment, the result has frequently been too great and rapid an expansion in a few lines of primary production for export which further aggravated the problem of the adjustment of the indigenous peoples of these countries to outside economic forces. Thus again, we are led back from the consideration of the total quantity of investment and the total volume of output and economic activity to a consideration of the type of investment and the distribution of economic activities and economic roles between the backward peoples and the others.

This is a convenient point at which to pause and summarize our argument so far. (1) The problem of the so-called "underdeveloped countries" consists, not merely in the "underdevelopment" of their resources in the usual senses, but also in the economic "backwardness" of their peoples. (2) Where it exists, the "underdevelopment" of *natural* resources and the backwardness of people mutually aggravate each other in a "vicious circle." (3) While (2) is very important, it needs to be handled with care, for it is liable to distract our attention from the real problem of economic backwardness. Thus, impressed by the connexion between the "backwardness" of the people and the "underdevelopment" of the resources, many have sought to superimpose these two concepts on each other and to explain the former entirely in terms of the latter. In doing so, however, they are continually obliged to stretch and shift the basis of their argument: from the "underdeveloped" *natural* resources to the "underdeveloped" *human* resources; from the "private" to the "social" productivity of investment; from the principle of "productivity" to the principle of "need"; and finally, from the static idea of the optimum allocation of investible resources to the dynamic idea of stimulating further rounds of investment by "productive" grants. It is fair to say that, in spite of all these contortions, the real issues of

cannot be regarded as the cause of backwardness; rather it is a manifestation of the maladjustment of backward peoples to outside economic forces at the physical level. Nor need this maladjustment always take the form of overpopulation. In some cases of extreme backwardness the size of the backward populations has been known to diminish to the point of extinction. Finally, the degree of overpopulation depends, not only on the relation between the physical quantity of natural resources and the size of population, but also on the level of technical and economic development of the people. Thus advanced industrial countries can usually maintain a denser population at a higher standard of living than the backward agricultural and pastoral countries. Further, in the past the advanced countries have absorbed very large increases in population without lowering their standard of living; indeed, many would maintain that these increases were a necessary part of their even greater rates of expansion in output and economic activity.[4] Thus to try to account for economic backwardness purely in terms of population pressure is to leave unanswered the question why the economically backward peoples have been unable to increase their productivity to match the increase in their population while the economically advanced people have managed to increase their standard of living on top of large increases in population.

The second possible line of approach is in terms of the deliberate and legalized political, economic, and racial discriminations imposed on the "backward" peoples by the "advanced" peoples. Here again, although this appears to be a major factor in certain countries, notoriously in Africa, it does not explain why the indigenous peoples of other countries who are not subject to such obvious discriminations to the same extent should also be similarly backward. Here, of course, the definition of the nature and extent of discriminations raises very formidable difficulties which we must frankly by-pass if we are to get farther on with our analysis. We shall thus content ourselves with drawing a somewhat crude working distinction be-

4. Cf. J. R. Hicks, *Value and Capital,* Oxford, 1939, p. 302 n.

tween the deliberate and therefore directly remediable causes of
backwardness in the form of open and legalized *discriminations* and
the more fortuitous and intractable *disequalizing factors* which may
operate even where there is a perfect equality of formal legal rights
between different groups of people in their economic relations with
each other (cf., however, section V below).

We are now able to sketch the general outlines of our problem.
When the backward countries were "opened up" to economic relations with the outside world, their peoples had to face the problem
of adapting themselves to a new environment shaped by outside economic forces. In this, whatever their degree of cultural advance in
other spheres, they seem to have been conspicuously unsuccessful
or "backward" compared with the other groups of economically
"advanced" people—whatever their degree of cultural advance in
other spheres. Our problem is to explain this gap, to explain why
the backward people cannot stand on a "competitive footing" with
the advanced people in this "economic struggle." The problem is
further complicated by the fact that the gap between the advanced
and backward peoples instead of being narrowed has been frequently
widened by the passage of time. Thus an inquiry into the causes of
economic backwardness essentially consists in searching for those
disequalizing factors which instead of being neutralized are cumulatively exaggerated by "the free play of economic forces."

In order to isolate these disequalizing factors, we can adopt a
"model" of a backward country which has the following broad
negative specifications. (1) Initially the country started with a fairly
sparse population in relation to its potential natural resources; so
it cannot be said to have been suffering from "overpopulation" to
begin with. (2) Its natural resources are then "developed," usually
in the direction of a few specialized lines of primary production for
export, as fully as the world market conditions permit. This process
of "development" is generally carried out by foreign private enterprise under conditions of *laissez-faire;* but frequently the process
may be aided by a government policy of stimulating expansion in
investment, export, and general economic activity motivated by a

desire to expand taxable capacity. So the country's natural resources cannot be said to be obviously "underdeveloped." (3) Whatever its political status, its native inhabitants at least enjoy a perfect equality of formal legal rights in their economic relations with other people, including the right to own any type of property and to enter into any type of occupation; so they cannot be said to suffer from obvious discriminations in economic matters.

To those who are firmly wedded to the conventional explanations of economic backwardness this may seem like assuming away the entire problem. But when we turn and survey the different types of backward countries, it will be seen that there is a large group, for example those in south-east Asia, British West Africa, Latin America, which approximates more to our model than to any models of obvious "underdevelopment," "overpopulation," or "discrimination" or a combination of all of them, if the first and the second can in fact be combined. Further, even in the other groups of backward countries where these conventional explanations are obviously very important, our model is still useful in turning attention to the residual causes of backwardness which may turn out to be by no means negligible.

IV

Before we consider our "model" further let us examine the concept of economic backwardness more closely. We may begin by distinguishing between the "backward country" as an aggregate territorial and economic unit and the "backward people" who frequently form merely a group within it confined to certain sectors of the economy. Now the disequalizing factors which we are seeking must be considered as operating, not only between the backward and the advanced countries as aggregate units, but also between the backward and advanced groups of peoples within the same backward country itself. Obviously a complete analysis of economic backwardness must take into account both sets of disequalizing factors which are closely interrelated with each other. Even so, we shall come to realize that the familiar "countries A and B" approach of the conventional theory of international trade is seriously inadequate for our purpose and that to study the actual impact of outside economic forces on the backward people we shall have to go behind these macro-economic units to those disequalizing factors which operate within the backward country itself.

But much still remains to be done even in terms of the conventional approach, using these versatile letters A and B to denote the "advanced" and the "backward" countries respectively. It is only recently that the general run of economists have turned their attention to the long-run problem of unequal rates of economic growth and productivity among the different countries participating in international trade. But even so, it is fair to say that this has somewhat shaken the belief in the adequacy of the static theory of comparative costs to deal with the essentially dynamic process of growth of the international economy. Thus it is now increasingly admitted that the existing ratios of comparative costs are by no means immutable and rigidly related to the original natural resources of the countries but may be influenced to a great extent by such factors as education, experience, technical skills, and so on, which arise out of the process of international trade itself and may exert a cumulatively disequalizing influence against the countries which have a later start. Following on from this, it would seem that the gains from international trade cannot be adequately measured merely in the form of the conventional "terms of trade" and the distribution of final incomes among the participating countries; we must also take into account the distribution of economic activities, in the form of induced investment and secondary rounds of employment, growth of technical knowledge and external economies, and all those dynamic stimuli which each participating country receives as a consequence of a given increase in the volume of its trade (cf. H. W. Singer, "The Distribution of Gains between Investing and Borrowing Countries," *American Economic Review,* Papers and Proceedings, May 1950). Although different views may be held about the practical policies most likely to induce these secondary rounds of investment and economic activity, there is little doubt that the concept of "induced" investment affords great theoretical insight into the nature of economic backwardness. In a sense, one might say that the difference between the "advanced" and the "backward" country lies in the fact that the former, subject to the powerful "accelerator" effect, can generate its own trade-cycle while the latter merely receives the fluctuations transmitted to it from outside, although of course the size of the impact need not be smaller for that reason.

Having said this, however, it is necessary to add that an approach to backwardness which stops short at this level will be seriously inadequate and that many of the discussions on the subject have been vitiated precisely because they are couched in terms of such geographical aggregates as "countries," "areas," "territories," &c. A natural consequence of this is a preoccupation with such macro-economic quantities as the aggregate and *per capita* national income, total volume of exports, total and average amount of investment, &c. Whence follow those economic development plans which aim to increase either the total or the *per capita* national income by a certain percentage by means of target figures for investment calculated on the basis of average capital requirements per head of population.

This type of macro-economic model of economic development may be suitable for the advanced countries,[5] but there are a number of reasons why it cannot be satisfactorily extended to the backward countries. To begin with, the advanced country, by definition, is in the middle of a self-generating process of economic growth characterized by a steady rate of technical innovation and increase in productivity. Thus it seems reasonable to rule out diminishing returns and assume that a given rate of net investment will, on the whole, result in a corresponding rate of increase in total output or productive capacity. Further, certain basic ratios, such as the propensity to consume, are not obviously unstable and may be used as constants for the process analysis. When we turn to the backward country, however, these assumptions are no longer plausible. The problem

5. Cf., however, T. Wilson, "Cyclical and Autonomous Inducements to Invest, "*Oxford Economics Papers,* March 1953.

here is not to trace the working of the process of economic growth on the basis of certain constant proportions but to try to start that process itself. We cannot stop short at thinking in terms of overall rates of net investment and increase in total output because the two rates are no longer connected in a determinate manner by a stable average ratio of capital to output.[6] Indeed, even if we could assume constant average productivity of capital, this will not be sufficient for the purpose of many economic development plans because they rely to varying degrees on the assumption of "external economies" and increasing returns to scale. Further, none of the basic ratios required as constants for the process analysis can be assumed to be stable for the relevant long period. Under the impact of outside economic forces, most of these ratios, such as propensity to consume and import, population growth, &c., have been changed or are in the process of changing. Here again it is the accepted task of economic development policy, not merely to accept these ratios as given, but to try to change them in directions considered to be favourable for development. This is not to say that all economic development plans based on macro-economic analysis will always fail. It is merely to say that it is not sufficient to stop short at this level and assume as a matter of course that, provided the required supply of capital[7] is forthcoming, the process of economic growth will work itself out automatically as it does in the advanced countries. Thus the very nature of our problem, which is to start this process of economic growth, obliges us to go behind the macro-economic units and investigate the actual structure and "growing-points" of the backward economy. For the same reason, we cannot treat the changes in the basic ratios and propensities as "exogenous" changes in data but must inquire into their nature and causes.

So far we have been concerned only with the mechanical difficul-

6. "The law of large numbers" is unconvincing when applied to the industrial sector of backward economies, where instead of n number of firms in full working order the State is trying to start a few odd new industrial units.
7. Including "productive" grants to stimulate investment. Cf. section II above.

ties of applying the macro-economic models to the backward countries. Even more serious difficulties are encountered when we inquire
into the meaningfulness of macro-economic quantities such as the
aggregate national income or the *per capita* income to the peoples
of the backward countries. These arise in addition to the complication already noted—that "backward peoples" normally form only
a sector of the economy of their "countries"—so that the fortunes
of the "country" and the "people" cannot be closely identified.

Even in the advanced countries, such concepts as the increase in
national income or aggregate output capacity create serious problems
of interpretation once we drop the static assumption of given and
constant wants and enter the real world of a continual stream of new
wants and commodities and improvements in the quality of existing
goods. We can, however, put aside these "index-number" problems
in favour of a "common-sense" interpretation, since we can assume
that the "measuring rod of money" and physical productivity are
meaningful to the individuals concerned and broadly approximate
to the social goals they are pursuing as groups in a fairly simple and
straightforward manner. When we come to the backward countries,
however, this assumption has to be carefully re-examined. The
peoples of backward countries have had shorter periods of contact
with the "money economy" so that the habits of mind and the sym-
bolism associated with monetary accounting may not be deep rooted
in their minds.[8] Further, as groups, they are subject to complex
pulls of nationalism and racial status, so that there may not be a
simple means–end relationship between the increase in national
output and the achievement of their social goals. Thus, in many
backward countries, people seem to desire up-to-date factories and

8. Cf. S. H. Frankel, *Some Conceptual Aspects of International Economic
Development of Underdeveloped Countries* (Princeton, May 1952), now
reprinted in *The Economic Impact on Underdeveloped Societies* (Blackwell,
Oxford, 1953). My debt to my colleague Professor Frankel cannot, however, be adequately expressed in terms of specific points, for I have had
the benefit of discussing with him the fundamental issues of the subject for
several years. I cannot, of course, claim his authority for the particular
conclusions I have arrived at in this paper.

other trappings of modern industrialism, not so much for the strictly material returns they are expected to yield as for the fact that they are in themselves symbols of national prestige and economic development. Following Veblen, one might describe this as a case of "conspicuous production."

There is then a greater need in the study of backward countries than in that of the advanced countries to go behind the "veil" of conventional social accounting into the real processes of adaptation between wants, activities, and environment which we have described earlier on as the "economic struggle." When we do this we shall see that the "problem" of the backward countries as it is commonly discussed really has two distinct aspects: on the subjective side it might be described as the economics of discontent and maladjustment; on the objective side it might be described as the economics of stagnation, low *per capita* productivity and incomes. In principle the latter should be a counterpart to the former and provide us with quantitative indices of it. In practice there is a real danger of the macro-models of economic development "running on their own steam" without any reference to the fundamental human problems of backwardness on the subjective side.

To illustrate this, let us begin by considering the backward country as a stationary state. In terms of the objective approach this is a standard case of economic backwardness and "overpopulation" popularly attributed to the Classical economists.[9] In terms of the subjective approach the situation may not appear so gloomy. Many of the backward countries before they were "opened up" were primitive or medieval stationary states governed by habits and customs. Their people might live near the "minimum subsistence level" but that, according to their own lights, did not appear too wretched or inadequate. Thus in spite of low productivity and lack of economic progress, there was no problem of economic discontent and frustration: wants and activities were on the whole adapted to each other and the people were in equilibrium with their environment. This is

9. Cf., however, Ricardo's *Principles*, Sraffa ed., Cambridge, Eng., 1951, p. 99 and p. 100 n.

not to say that everything was idyllic: there may have been frequent tribal wars and insecurity of life and property. But on the whole it is fair to say that there was no "problem" of backward countries in the modern sense and that the situation perhaps resembled J. S. Mill's picture of the stationary state more than that of his predecessors (cf. Mill, *Principles,* bk. iv, ch. vi).

Now consider the second stage particularly in the second half of the nineteenth century and the beginning of the twentieth century when these stationary backward societies were opened up to the outside economic forces. Here we can see why the term "backward" which we have been obliged to use for lack of a better alternative is so loose and liable to different interpretations. For at this stage, and to a certain extent even today, the economic backwardness of a society was simply measured by the lack of response of its members to monetary incentives. This in effect meant measuring the backwardness of a people, not by their inefficiency and inaptness in satisfying their given wants or in pursuing their own social goals, but by their tardiness in adopting new Western standards of wants and activities. Measures for "economic development" then consisted mainly in attempts to persuade or force the backward people into the new ways of life represented by the money economy—for example, by stimulating their demand for imports and by taxing them so that they were obliged to turn to cash crops or work in the newly opened mines and plantations. Whether it was meaningful or not to the people, the accepted yardstick of economic development of a "country" was its export and taxable capacity.

"Backwardness" in the sense of economic discontent and maladjustment does not fully emerge until the third stage of the drama when the natural resources of the backward countries have been "developed" to a large extent, usually by foreign private enterprise, and when the backward peoples have been partly converted to the new ways of life. Here the irony of the situation lies in the fact that the acuteness of the problem of backwardness at this stage is frequently proportional to the success and rapidity of "economic development" at the second stage. To begin with, it becomes apparent that the backward peoples can be only too successfully converted to new ways of life on the side of wants and aspirations while this cannot be matched by a corresponding increase in their earning capacity. We then have a progressive maladjustment between wants and activities, the former outstripping the latter at each round of "education" and contact with the outside world. (This may spread from the individual to the national level when at the fourth stage the independent national governments of the backward countries find their resources insufficient to carry out ambitious schemes of economic development and social welfare.) Further, the backward peoples now find that they cannot successfully adapt themselves to the new economic environment shaped by outside forces and that they lag behind in the "economic struggle" with other economically advanced groups of people who have initiated the "opening-up" process. Thus they find themselves with a relatively smaller share of the economic activities and the national incomes of their countries although these may be rapidly increasing in the aggregate (at least up to the limits set by the diminishing returns in the new lines of the primary production for export). Here then we have the problem of economic backwardness in its full efflorescence charged with the explosive feeling of discontent and grievance against "lop-sided economic development," "foreign economic domination," "imperialistic exploitation," and so on.

We can now see why it is so unsatisfactory to approach the problem of the backward countries as the source of international tension purely at the macro-economic level of the conventional development plans. Aggregates such as the total national income and volume of exports are very unsatisfactory as indices of economic welfare of a "plural society" made up of different groups of people such as that which exists in many backward countries. Here the well-known maxim of static welfare economics, that the economic welfare of a country is increased if some people can move to a better position while leaving the others exactly as they were before, must sound somewhat galling to the backward peoples who frequently happen to be those left "exactly as they were before."

Nor is *per capita* income very satisfactory as an index of "poverty." The sort of maladjustment between wants and earning capacity which we have been describing may occur even if *per capita* incomes are rising. Indeed a greater amount of discontent may be created where incomes rise enough to introduce new commodities into the consumers' budget and then fluctuate and decline (a common experience in export economies) than where incomes per head remain stationary or decline slowly. Further, we should note that the degree of discontent depends, not as much on the absolute level of *per capita* incomes as in their *relative* ranking. Thus motives of "conspicuous consumption" and the external diseconomies of consumption of higher income groups associated with Veblen and more recently with Professor J. S. Duesenberry should be taken into account (cf. Ragnar Nurkse, *Some Aspects of Capital Accumulation in Underdeveloped Countries*, Cairo, 1952, Third Lecture).

It is important to point this out since low income per head has now crystallized into the definition of backward countries. Some have even tried to put it on a "scientfic" basis by arguing that since the existing low incomes of the backward peoples are insufficient to provide them with the minimum nutritional requirements, their physical efficiency and productivity is lowered, thus creating a "vicious circle." While this may be an important long-run factor, it is a dangerous over-simplification of the complex motivations and aspirations of the backward peoples both at the individual and national levels to assume that Communism can be "contained" by calories. Even in the backward countries, perhaps particularly there, men do not live by bread alone. Thus as a *Times* correspondent has recently written about the wage claims in the African Copper Belt:

Another factor which drives the African to make demands is his increasing needs. He is beginning to buy smarter clothes; to eat foods he never did before; to drink wine and English beer instead of native liquor. It is, indeed, an almost impossible task to-day to compile a reasonable family budget because of this transitional stage in African 'consumer' requirements. This, too, however much people may disapprove of the elaborately dressed up African 'spiv' with his cowboy hat, sunglasses, and new bicycle, is a healthy trend; it is obviously essential if the African is to be weaned from a subsistence to a cash economy that he should develop the needs that create incentive. [*The Times* 19 January 1953.]

If the backward peoples as individuals desire those commodities one associates with the "American way of life," at the national level they seem to desire the latest models of social security schemes associated with the "British Welfare State." It would thus be a crowning-point of irony if some backward countries were to turn towards Communism through an excessive fondness for the American and British ways of life.

V

In the light of what has been said above, the study of the "disequalizing factors" at work against the backward peoples within the economies of their countries emerges as an essential link between the two aspects of the problem of backwardness: the economics of discontent and maladjustment on the one side and the economics of stagnation or relatively slow rates of growth in total or *per capita* national income and productivity on the other.

When we consider these "disequalizing factors" we shall see that the exclusion of the "obvious" explanations in terms of "under-development," "overpopulation," and "discrimination" still leaves us with a great variety of residual causes of backwardness. To analyse them in detail is beyond the scope of this paper. For our purpose of obtaining a general interpretation of the nature of back-wardness it is sufficient to point out certain broad patterns of backwardness in which the initial differences in experience, opportunities, capital supply, &c., between the economically backward and advanced groups of people seem to have been "fossilized" or accentuated by the "free play of economic forces." We shall illustrate these patterns with reference to the backward peoples in their typical roles as unskilled workers, peasant producers, and borrowers of capital which between them cover most types of economic contacts between the backward and the advanced peoples.

In order to do this we shall introduce three characteristic features of the "opening-up" process into our "model" of the backward economy.

1. The first concerns the nature of "specialization" for the export market. Now it is commonly realized that "specialization" does not merely mean moving along the given "production-possibility" curve of the textbook; and that in practice it involves an irreversible process whereby much of the resources and the productive equipment, e.g. transport and communications, of the backward economy have been moulded and made "specific" to satisfy the special requirements of the export market. (Hence the well-known argument for diversification.) But the habit of thinking in terms of "countries" or "areas" leads to the inadequate appreciation of one further fundamental fact: in spite of the striking specialization of the inanimate productive equipment and of the individuals from the economically advanced groups of people who manage and control them, there is really very little specialization, beyond a natural adaptability to the tropical climate, among the backward peoples in their roles as unskilled labourers or peasant producers. Thus the typical unskilled labour supplied by the backward peoples is an undifferentiated mass of cheap manpower which might be used in any type of plantation or in any type of extractive industry within the tropics and sometimes even beyond it.[10] This can be seen from the range of the primary industries built on the immigrant Indian, Chinese, and African labour. Thus all the specialization required for the export market seems to have been done by the other co-operating factors, the whole production structure being built around the supply of cheap undifferentiated labour.

When we turn to the backward peoples in their role as peasant producers, again the picture is not appreciably changed. Some backward economies "specialize" on crops which they have traditionally produced, and thus "specialization" simply means expansion along the traditional lines with no perceptible change in the methods of production (e.g. rice in south-east Asian countries). Even where

10. Cf. S. H. Frankel, *Capital Investment in Africa,* London, 1938, pp. 142–46.

a new cash crop is introduced, the essence of its success as a *peasant* crop depends on the fact that it does not represent a radical departure from the existing techniques of production [11] (e.g. yams and cocoa in West Africa). Thus as a historian has said about the palm-oil and ground-nuts trade of West Africa: "They made little demand on the energies or thought of the natives and they effected no revolution in the society of West Africa. That was why they were so readily grafted on to the old economy and why they grew as they did" (A. McPhee, *The Economic Revolution of West Africa*, pp. 39–40). Here again one is tempted to say that much of the "specialization" seems to have been done by nature and the complementary investment in transport and processing. On the side of productive activities, the fact that the crop is sold for the export market instead of for domestic consumption is an accidental detail. It is only on the side of wants that disturbing changes seem to have been introduced, including a decline of skills in the domestic handicraft industries now no longer able to compete against the imported commodities. To prevent misunderstanding, it should be added that frequently the peasant methods are found to have lower costs than the "modern" scientific methods, and that is the reason why peasant production has been able to withstand the competition of the plantation system in some countries. But at the best this merely means the survival of old skills rather than a steady improvement in the methods of production through "specialization" for the export market.

Thus, paradoxically enough, the process of "specialization" of a backward economy for the export market seems to be most rapid and successful when it leaves the backward peoples in their unspecialized roles as unskilled labour and peasant producers using traditional methods of production.

2. The second characteristic feature of the "opening-up" process is the monopoly power of varying degrees which the foreign busi-

11. If this condition is not fulfilled, the peasant system soon gives way to the plantation system or the peasant is so supervised and controlled that he is reduced to the status of a wage-earner except in name (cf. J. H. Boeke, *The Evolution of Netherland Indies Economy*, New York, 1946, p. 11).

ness concerns exercise in relation to the backward economy. Here again the actual process of the growth of trade between the advanced and the backward countries differs from the textbook picture of two countries coming into trading relations with each other under conditions of perfect competition. Indeed, if we were to insist on applying the rules of perfect competition to foreign enterprises, very few backward countries would have been "developed." The process of opening up a new territory for trade is an extremely risky and costly business, and it is only by offering some sort of monopolistic concessions that foreign business concerns can be induced to accept the risks and the heavy initial costs, which include not only those of setting up transport and communications and other auxiliary services but may also include the ordinary administrative costs of extending law and order to places where it does not exist. Hence the age-old method of economic development by chartered companies. In the case of mining this is reinforced by the technical advantages of large-scale enterprise.

Even where there is no formal concession of monopoly power, as in a peasant economy, conditions are generally very favourable for its growth. To begin with, only fairly big firms with large enough reserves to meet the heavy initial costs and risks may venture into the new territory. Further, although there may be no restriction to free entry, potential competitors may be put off by the "economies of experience" which give a great differential advantage to the pioneers. Thus there are usually a small number of fairly big export-import firms engaged in a "cut-throat" competition with each other in their effort to increase their turnover and spread their heavy overhead costs. This need not be limited to "horizontal" competition among the export-import firms; it may also result in a "vertical" competition between the export-import firms and the steamship companies which control the trade routes. After some time this trade war generally results in "pools" and "combinations" both of the horizontal and vertical types,[12] for "the small trader

12. This "vertical integration" may also spread downwards towards a greater supervision and control of peasant producers resulting in a "mixed" system between peasant and plantation systems (cf. Boeke, *op. cit.,* ch. i).

must grow to greatness, either in himself, or in combination with others. The alternative is his failure and ultimate disappearance. In fact, economic conditions of England are exhibited on an intenser scale in West Africa, where businesses grow, decay and combine with mushroom rapidity." (McPhee, *op. cit.*, p. 103; cf. W. K. Hancock, *Survey of British Commonwealth Affairs*, vol. ii, part 2, ch. iii, sec. iii; also J. S. Furnivall, *Colonial Policy and Practice,* pp. 95–97 and pp. 197–98.)

Thus in a typical process of "development," the backward peoples have to contend with three types of monopolistic forces: in their role as unskilled labour they have to face the big foreign mining and plantation concerns who are monopolistic buyers of their labour; in their role as peasant producers they have to face a small group of exporting and processing firms who are monopolistic buyers of their crop; and in their role as consumers of imported commodities they have to face the same group of firms who are the monopolistic sellers or distributors of these commodities.

3. The third characteristic feature of the "opening-up" process is the growth of the middlemen between the big European concerns and the economically backward indigenous populations. They are the necessary adjuncts to any process of rapid economic development and fill in the gaps between the highly specialized Western economic structure and the relatively unspecialized roles of the backward peoples. Although they may operate in the labour market, they are more important in their activities as collectors of produce from the peasant farmers, as distributors of imported articles to the indigenous consumers, and, most important of all, as money-lenders. In most backward countries they seem to owe their special position to their longer contact with Western economic life; frequently they may start as immigrant labour and work their way up as small traders and money-lenders. The racial distribution of the middlemen groups among the backward countries is familiar: thus we have the Indians and Chinese in south-east Asia, Indians in East Africa, Syrians and "Coast Africans" in West Africa, &c. Thus the economic hierarchy of a typical backward country is generally a

pyramid with Europeans on top, then the middlemen, and lastly the indigenous people at the bottom.

Each of the characteristic features outlined above tends to reduce the relative share of the national incomes of the backward countries accruing to the indigenous peoples. But, as we have said before, the nature of economic backwardness cannot be fully appreciated until we go beyond the distribution of incomes to the distribution of economic activities: for "it is to changes in the forms of efforts and activities that we must turn when in search for the keynotes of the history of mankind" (Marshall, *Principles*, p. 85.)

When we consider the backward peoples in their role as unskilled labour, it is important to ask, not merely why their wages have remained low but why they have been frozen into their role of cheap undifferentiated labour with little vertical mobility into more skilled grades. Here, apart from the monopsony power of the employers, various complex factors are at work to stereotype their role; out of these we may select three as being fairly typical (cf. Wilbert E. Moore, *Industrialization and Labor*, ch. v, for a more systematic analysis).

The first is the very high rate of turnover of indigenous labour, partly because the backward peoples are unused to the discipline of the mines and plantations, and partly because they have one foot in their traditional tribal and village economies which make them look upon wage labour not as a continuous permanent employment but as a temporary or periodical expedient to earn a certain sum of money. Given this rapid rate of labour turnover, there is no opportunity to acquire the experience and skill for promotion to skilled grades. If this were the only cause, one might assume that this is a transitional problem which would gradually disappear with the breakdown of the traditional social institutions and the spread of money economy. But unfortunately there are other obstacles.

This brings us back to the difficulties which we by-passed when defining the nature and extent of "discrimination" against backward peoples. Here, with reference to the lack of vertical mobility of indigenous labour, we must frankly admit that our distinction between "discrimination" and "disequalizing factor" wears very thin in many backward countries. Even where there is no official colour bar, unofficial industrial colour bar is fairly widespread (for example, say, the Rhodesian copper-mines). Even where "discrimination" has not hardened into a "bar" of any sort, the natural and frequently unconscious tendency of the white employers to mark off "native" or "coloured" occupational categories irrespective of individual differences in ability and skill can be very damaging to the backward peoples; for the educational effect of apprenticeship and promotion to skilled grades in ordinary economic life is more far-reaching than huge sums of money spent on educational institutions.

The third factor which has contributed to the fossilization of the "cheap labour" convention is the additional supplies of labour which mines and plantation can draw, either from the breakdown of tribal societies (e.g. the Ashanti Wars in West Africa) or from the human reservoirs of India and China. Importation of immigrant labour has been blessed by liberal economic policy as contributing to the international mobility of labour; and it may be freely admitted that "economic development" and the rapid growth of output of tropical raw materials could not have been achieved without it. But as a solution to the problem of human backwardness it has been somewhat unhappy. It has not appreciably relieved the population pressure in the donating countries; and in the receiving countries, apart from the complex social problems it has created, it has robbed the indigenous people of the chance to acquire vertical mobility in the labour market through the automatic operation of the laws of supply and demand and the principle of substitution.

Let us now turn to the backward peoples in their role as peasant producers in relation to the middlemen and the big export-import firms. Here we have the familiar disequalizing factors, such as the peasants' ignorance of market conditions, which are extremely unstable, their lack of economic strength to hold out against middlemen and speculators, and their need to borrow money at high rates of interest, which have reduced the relative share of incomes accruing to the backward peoples. It may also be freely admitted that this has been helped by their well-known "extravagance" and lack of thrift which are after all the logical consequences of too successful a policy of creating economic incentives for the production of cash crops. The formal framework which offers perfect equality of economic rights offers no protection, and the result of the "free play of economic forces" under conditions of fluctuating export prices is the well-known story of rural indebtedness, land alienation, and agrarian unrest (cf. Furnivall, *Colonial Policy and Practice,* passim). Here again we should go beyond the distribution of incomes to the distribution of economic activities. We shall then see that the real damage done by the middlemen lies not in their "exploitation," considerable as it may be in many cases, but in the fact that they have put themselves between the backward peoples and the outside world and have robbed the latter of the educating and stimulating effect of a direct contact (cf. Hancock, *op. cit.*, pp. 225–27). As a consequence, even after many decades of rapid "economic development" following the "opening-up" process, the peoples of many backward countries still remain almost as ignorant and unused to the ways of modern economic life as they were before. On the side of economic activities they remain as backward as ever; it is only on the side of wants that they have been modernized, and this reduces their propensity to save and increases their sense of discontent and inequality (cf. Ragnar Nurkse, *Some Aspects of Capital Accumulation in Underdeveloped Countries,* 1952, Third Lecture).

Finally, we may comment briefly on the backward peoples in their role as borrowers. Here, when we inquire closely why they are obliged to borrow at very high rates of interest from the moneylenders, we frequently find that high risks and the difficulties of finding suitable outlets for liquid funds may be more important than an overall shortage of saving. It is true that the rigid sterling exchange standard of some backward countries (which works like the gold standard) may have a deflationary bias, particularly during periods of rapid extension of the money sector. But, in spite of this, it is difficult to establish that there is an overall shortage of saving for the backward economy as a whole. In the "advanced" or Western sectors at least, big business concerns can raise loans on the international market on equal terms with the borrowers from the advanced countries and the banks generally tend to have a very high liquidity ratio.

This leads us to the problem which is apt to be obscured by the "under-investment" approach which stresses the overall shortage of capital supply. It is the problem of organizing the *distribution* of credit as distinct from the problem of increasing the total supply of saving. The "retail distribution" of credit among peasant producers is beyond the capacity of the ordinary commercial bank and, in spite of the rise of the co-operative movement, still remains one of the unsolved problems of the backward countries which may have greater long-run significance than the more spectacular projects for economic development. Further, there is a great need to extend credit facilities not only to the peasant producers but also to the growing class of small traders and business men among the backward peoples who would like to enter into the traditional preserves of the middlemen. Here many would-be business men from the backward groups frequently complain of the "discrimination" against them by the commercial banks when the truth of the matter is that they are simply caught up in a vicious circle of lack of business experience resulting in a lack of credit-worthiness. The banks, far from discriminating, are playing strictly according to the "rules of the game," but these rules tend to put the heaviest handicap on the weakest players.

That the real "bottleneck" may frequently lie in the difficulties of organizing the distribution of credit and finding suitable outlets for existing savings, rather than in the overall shortage of saving, may also be seen from the fact that domestic saving even where it exists in sizeable amounts is normally used for money-lending on the basis of land and jewellery mortgage since this yields a very much higher rate of return to the savers than any other available form of "productive" investment.

VI

The idea of economic backwardness put forward in this paper may
be better appreciated in terms of the deviations, not from the static
concept of the allocative optimum, but from the dynamic presumption concerning the beneficial effects of free trade held by the older
generation of liberal economists. For it will be remembered that
the Classical case for free competition was based, not as much on
the purely static considerations of allocative efficiency as on dynamic
considerations of economic expansion. Thus it was believed that
the growth of individualism and economic freedom would encourage
initiative and enterprise, thrift, industriousness, and other qualities
favourable to the dynamic expansion of the economy both horizontally, through the international division of labour and the extension of the market, and vertically, through capital accumulation and
technical innovations. (Cf. L. Robbins, *The Theory of Economic
Policy*, p. 16; also H. Myint, *Theories of Welfare Economics*, ch. iv.)

This line of thought is worth pursuing. The Classical economists
did not claim that the free play of economic forces would necessarily lead to a more equitable distribution of wealth; as a matter
of fact, they believed that inequalities of incomes (on the basis of
equal opportunities) were necessary to provide the incentives for
economic expansion: thus a redistribution of incomes from the
rich to the poor might discourage saving, and poor relief (whether
on a national or an international scale) might aggravate the population problem. As a corollary to this, they denied that the free play
of economic forces would set up disequalizing factors which would
ultimately inhibit the expansion in the total volume of output and
economic activity.

As is well known, this Classical vision of harmonious economic
growth through free enterprise has been shattered by two major
factors: the growth of monopoly and imperfect competition, and the
growth of unemployment. These did not, however, immediately
lead to a reconsideration of the long-run theory of economic devel-

opment on the Classical lines, for many economists have been too preoccupied with the purely static effects of imperfect competition, as in much of modern welfare economics, or with purely short-run problems, as in much of modern Keynesian economics. It is only fairly recently that the tide has turned, and the economics of backwardness, apart from its practical interest, may now come to occupy an important position in its own right as an essential element in the new theory of long-run economic development.

One of the most interesting developments in the long-run theory of economic development is Professor Schumpeter's well-known argument that the growth of monopoly, which from a static view would result in a maldistribution of resources, might actually favour technical innovations and economic development (J. Schumpeter, *Capitalism, Socialism and Democracy*, chs. vii and viii). We have already seen a parallel case of this argument when we were led to the conclusion that monopoly was an essential element in the "opening-up" process of the backward countries to international trade. The question then arises: can the Schumpeter argument be extended to the backward countries or is there a fundamental difference in the operation of monopoly in the backward countries as compared with the advanced countries?

Recently Professor J. K. Galbraith has put forward a theory which seems to provide a part of the answer. He maintains that the growth of monopoly in the advanced countries, particularly in the U.S.A., has been accompanied by a growth of "countervailing power" on the opposite side of the market, e.g. trade unions, retail chain stores, co-operative societies, farmers' unions, &c. The growth of monopoly increases the gains from building up the countervailing power and induces its growth and this provides a new self-regulatory mechanism to the economy in a world of monopoly (J. K. Galbraith, *American Capitalism*, "The Concept of Countervailing Power"). In Professor Galbraith's terminology, then, economic backwardness may be described as a phenomenon which arises because the process of "economic development" has been too rapid and the initial conditions too unfavourable to give rise to an effective "countervailing power" to check the "foreign economic domination" of the backward peoples. One remarkable thing about Professor Galbraith's argument is that although he is concerned with the economically most advanced country in the world, the U.S.A., the sectors of the economy which he regards as being particularly in need of the countervailing power—agriculture, consumers' goods markets, and the labour market—are exactly paralleled in the backward countries with their export-import monopolies and large scale mining and plantation businesses (cf. Galbraith, *op. cit.*, chs. x and xi).

Now if we were merely concerned with the problem of backwardness in its subjective aspect as the economics of discontent it would be sufficient to show how the working of the disequalizing factors set up by the free play of economic forces in the absence of countervailing power has resulted in the present situation. But we must go on to the other side of the problem and investigate the relation between the disequalizing factors and economic stagnation or the slow rate of growth in total output and economic activity (apart from the unfavourable effects of political and social unrests, both on present production and future investment).

Here, as we have noted above, we must be on guard against the convenient supposition that the requirements of economic equality and economic development always work in the same direction. Bearing this in mind, when we consider the typical process of "economic development" of most backward countries there seem to be prima facie reasons for thinking that the disequalizing factors have affected not merely the distribution but also the rate of growth in the total volume of output and economic activity.

The fundamental assumption of liberal economics is that the free play of economic forces would lead to the maximum development of *individual* talents and abilities; whereas in practice the free play of economic forces in backward countries has resulted, not in a division of labour according to individual abilities, but in a division of labour according to stratified groups. The accurate selection of the different types and qualities of natural resources by the automatic market mechanism contrasts dramatically with its lack of selectivity concerning human resources which has resulted in the "fossilization" of the backward peoples in their conventional roles of undifferentiated cheap labour and unspecialized peasant producers. Thus, unless we are prepared to subscribe to the doctrine of inherent racial inferiority of the backward peoples, there seems to be a strong presumption that the potential development of the backward countries has been inhibited by this waste of human resources, leading to a stultification of the possible "growing-points" of the economy. Nor can the loss of educational opportunities be adequately remedied by "investment in human capital" as is frequently assumed. Mere increase of expenditure on technical training and education, although it may offer a partial relief, is really too weak and unselective to be an active countervailing force to the deep-seated disequalizing factors. Too great an emphasis on the "under-investment in human capital" therefore tends to confuse the issues and distract attention from the more potent disequalizing factors.

Further, the disequalizing factors work not only on the supply side but also on the demand side, and unequal distribution of incomes and of activities combine with each other to inhibit economic development. One of the most important reasons why the backward countries have been prevented from enjoying the stimulating effect of manufacturing industry is not the wickedness of foreign capitalists and their exclusive concern with raw material supplies but merely the limitation of the domestic market for manufactured articles (cf. Ragnar Nurkse, *Some Aspects of Capital Accumulation in Underdeveloped Countries*, First Lecture).

When we were discussing the concept of "social productivity" towards the end of section II above, we remarked on the tendency of economic practice to forestall economic theory. So also here, with the concept of "countervailing power." Long before the economists were aware of the problem, practical administrators and economic historians of the backward countries were impressed by the fact that the peoples of these countries seem to need some sort of countervailing power to enable them to stand up against the "free play of economic forces." Some have sought the countervailing power in the preservation of the traditional social institutions and, in extreme cases, have even toyed with the idea of a retreat into the self-sufficiency of the traditional stationary state. Others, more forward-looking, have tried to foster countervailing power in the form of co-operative societies and, more recently, by means of trade unions and marketing boards for the peasant produce. Above all this, the disequalizing forces themselves have generated a fierce nationalism among the backward peoples which is the most powerful source of countervailing power in the present times. So we are already in a position to learn a few lessons about the nature and limitations of the countervailing power in the backward countries.

The first lesson is that some sources of countervailing power, like the co-operative societies, themselves need a fairly high degree of business-like behaviour and "economic advance" and can only be fostered very slowly in the backward countries. The second lesson is that it is easier to redistribute existing incomes than to redistribute and stimulate economic activity by the use of countervailing power. The governments of some backward countries are now able to obtain a larger share of the income from the exploitation of the natural resources, either by striking better bargains with foreign mining concerns or by means of marketing boards in the case of peasant produce; but they are still faced with the problem of reinvesting the money in a directly productive way as distinct from increasing expenditure on general social services. It is difficult enough to find outlets for productive investment in backward countries; it is far more difficult to find those outlets which will increase the direct participation of the backward peoples in the processes of economic activity. It is important to stress this point because the governments of the backward countries, in their desire to have rapid and spectacular economic development, may be tempted to embark on those large-scale projects which, even if they were successful as business concerns, might not appreciably increase the

participation of their peoples in the new economic activities.[13]
Apart from its failure as a business concern, the fundamental weakness of the famous "Ground Nut Scheme" of the British Overseas
Food Corporation was that in an attempt to have rapid results on
a large scale the Corporation was obliged to minimize the African
participation in it.

The final lesson to be learnt is the danger of an excessive use of
the countervailing power combined with an extreme economic nationalism. As a counter-measure to the disequalizing forces at the
international level, discriminatory and protective measures to change
the existing terms of comparative costs and foster the national
economies of the backward countries have their place. In certain
circumstances, they may even have a favourable effect on the volume
of international trade in the long run. But, on the other hand,
the dangers of an excessive nationalist policy should not be under-
rated. The loss to the backward countries in this case is not merely
consumers' loss through having to pay a higher price or through
having to put up with poorer qualities of commodities substituted
for imports; a far heavier loss may lie in the sphere of economic
activities when cut off from the stimulating contact with the outside
world. This is also true of trade unions. In some backward countries trade unions have the very important function of breaking the
industrial colour bar; but in others they may become a crippling
burden on the economy and inhibit economic progress (cf. *Report
on Cuba*, by the Economic and Technical Mission of the International Bank for Reconstruction and Development, pp. 138–59).

These considerations should not, however, blind us to the genuine-
ness of the disequalizing factors working against the backward
peoples and their real need for countervailing power. From the
point of view of these peoples this is where the real rub lies. It is,
however, precisely on this point that economists, both of liberal and
of central-planning persuasion, have shown the least sympathy and
understanding. The liberal economist is apt to believe that the

13. In some countries excessive central planning may give rise to a new class
of "middlemen" in the guise of government agents or officials.

disequalizing factors do not exist and that all attempts to use the countervailing power are the result of "irrational economic nationalism." The central planner is apt to seek a solution of the essentially distributive and structural problems of economic backwardness in terms of bigger and better aggregative economic development plans. Thus the study of the disequalizing factors at work against the backward peoples has never really been allowed to emerge from the intellectual underworld of extreme economic nationalism.

4 | The Gains from International Trade and the Backward Countries

In this paper we shall examine the existing theory of the distribution of the gains from international trade in relation to the process by which some of the backward countries were opened up to international trade and foreign investment.

The countries with which we are concerned here are those which started off "semi-empty" with sparse populations in relation to their natural resources and which have, therefore, been able to expand their export production on such a scale as to be called the "export economies." They are to be found in various parts of the economically backward areas of the world, including South-East Asia, West Africa and Latin America. But their rapid rate of economic expansion raises awkward problems, both for the theory of the backward countries and for the theory of international trade. To begin with, this rapid rate of economic expansion would not have been possible without an equally rapid utilisation of their available land, mineral and forest resources. Thus it is difficult to accept the view that the people of these countries are poor because their

I should like to thank Professor S. H. Frankel, Mrs. U. K. Hicks and Mr. H. G. Johnson for their comments and criticisms of this paper.

From *The Review of Economic Studies,* Vol. XXII(2), No. 58 (1954–55), pp. 129–42. Reprinted by permission.

natural resources are "underdeveloped"[1] or have been developed too slowly or inadequately in the past. Nor is it satisfactory to account for their poverty simply in terms of rapid population growth. For, once the opening-up process had got into its stride, these countries generally experienced long waves of economic expansion, lasting for at least two or three decades, but frequently for longer periods. During these periods, the rate of expansion in their export production was far in excess of any possible natural population growth.[2]

1. See my paper, "An Interpretation of Economic Backwardness," above, Chapter 3, for a further discussion of this argument in relation to the differences between the "private" and the "social" productivity of investment. Here we may note that even at the height of the *laissez-faire* era in the late nineteenth century, the development of these countries was not left entirely to private enterprise. There has always been a considerable amount of government encouragement of export production with a view to increasing the revenues to finance the development of "social capital" in the form of modern administration, transport, health and education services, etc.

2. For instance, the total value of Burma's exports, covering years of high and low prices, seem to have been increasing at a constant proportional rate of 5 per cent per annum from 1870 right up to the Great Depression of the 1930's (cf. J. S. Furnivall, *Colonial Policy and Practice,* Cambridge, Eng., 1948, Appendix I, for some interesting abstracts from Burma's trade returns; for the development of Indonesia's foreign trade, see J. H. Boeke, *The Structure of Netherlands Indian Economy,* New York, 1942, p. 184). It may be noted that, with the possible exception of Indonesia, the countries in South-East Asia do not as yet suffer from a serious population pressure. The rapid increase of population in Java has become a classic illustration of the population-pressure argument; but then Indonesia still has vast regions of sparsely populated areas in the Outer Islands. For the countries in West Africa, which were opened up at a much later date, foreign trade figures are available only from 1900. Here we must be on guard against exaggerating the increase in export production by basing our calculations on too early a date at which the volume of output was very small. If, however, 1905 can be taken as a "fair" base year, the cocoa production of the Gold Coast and Nigeria seems to have increased over forty times from 1905 to 1939. See also a chart prepared by J. W. Williams in the *Conference Papers,* Economic Section, Achimota, April, 1953, for a characteristic growth curve of cocoa production in the Gold Coast since 1900. Similar rates of increase can be observed elsewhere (cf. W. K. Hancock, *Survey of British Commonwealth Affairs,* London, 1940, Vol. II, Part II, Appendix C, and A. McPhee, *The Economic Revolution of West Africa,* London, 1926, Appendix A).

A part of this expansion might have been at the expense of the subsistence and the domestic sectors, but it is clear that the bulk of it was in the form of net additions to output made possible by the utilisation of *new* resources. Thus, contrary to popular views on population pressure, it seems quite probable that the total (territorial) output of these countries was increasing at a faster rate than their population growth for fairly long periods in their modern economic careers. Thus we are led to examine with special interest the process by which these countries were opened up to international trade, the role which foreign capital and enterprise played in their rapid economic development and the distribution of the gains from this process between the "domestic" and the "foreign" factors of production.

The question whether or not the people of the backward countries received their "fair" share of incomes under the "nineteenth century" or the "colonial" system of international trade is a formidable subject with a long and bitter controversy behind it. It is obvious that we cannot hope to arrive at clear-cut conclusions on the complex issues involved, particularly with our present rudimentary knowledge of the economic history of these countries. But we cannot, on that account, avoid entering into these thorny questions for, particularly with the rise of the new national governments in these countries, beliefs concerning the past are bound to have great influence in shaping their future international trade policies. To appraise these policies, therefore, we shall discuss in this paper how far the conventional approach to the subject really comes to grips with the problem of the distribution of the gains from international trade to the people of the backward countries and how far their share of these gains can be satisfactorily accounted for in terms of the existing theories. We shall then draw a few tentative conclusions concerning their future international trade policy.

I

From the outset, it is apparent that for our purpose the existing theory of the distribution of the gains from international trade suffers from two general limitations.[3] (1) It is largely based on the static or the "cross-section" view of international trade at a moment of time with the given wants and resources of the trading countries, whereas we are concerned with the process of the development of international trade over a period of time involving new wants and new resources. (2) It is still largely influenced by the assumption of immobility of factors between different countries, whereas our problem arises from the existence of foreign investment and immigrant labour.

Let us consider the effect of these limitations starting with the familiar apparatus of the indifference curves and the terms of trade. The method of the indifference curves requires the assumption that trade takes place on the basis of the given and constant wants of the two trading countries. This assumption may be applicable to the early and limited form of international trade in some backward countries in which primitive tribesmen bartered ivory and gold dust for beads and guns. But it becomes highly unrealistic when we turn to the development of the modern form of international trade in the backward countries based on the spread of the money economy and involving large quantities of the export staples. Here it is clear that the rapid expansion of export production would not have been possible without an equally rapid development of new wants for the imported manufactured goods on the part of the people of the backward countries, frequently assisted by taxation methods designed to increase their propensity to work for money wages and grow cash crops. Thus the assumption of constant wants has to be rejected, not merely because wants are likely to change in the fairly long periods with which we are concerned, but also because the development of the new wants is an essential mechanism of the development of international trade in the backward countries. This means that we are debarred from the use of the elaborate apparatus of the modern welfare economics and have to be content with the more common-sense Pigovian approach to economic welfare in terms of "the measuring rod of money." However, the jump

3. Cf. J. H. Williams, "The Theory of International Trade Reconsidered," *Economic Journal,* June, 1929.

from levels of money incomes to levels of economic welfare is particularly treacherous in the context of the backward countries, and it must be admitted that, even when we have made all the possible corrections to allow for the transitional effects of the spread of the money economy, our procedure is still liable to serious objections.[4] But we really have no other alternative and our only consolation is that, even without the special complications of the backward countries, any attempt to draw welfare conclusions in a realistic situation of international trade is bound to be based to some extent on common-sense presumptions rather than on logically stringent demonstrations.

Let us now consider the idea of the terms of trade which occupies such a prominent position in the theory of the distribution of the gains from international trade. From our standpoint, we shall have a somewhat different perspective of it. For the terms of trade (whether we take the "price" or the "income" version) are a satisfactory measure of the gains from international trade accruing to the people of a country only in so far as they receive the whole of the earnings from the exports of that country as a territorial unit. In the backward countries, however, due to foreign investment and immigrant labour, a substantial part of these earnings has had to be remitted abroad in the form of export surpluses on the trade account. Since these export surpluses are frequently as large as a quarter to a half of the total value of the exports, and since they continue for decades,[5] the question of sharing the earnings from the total (territorial) volume of exports looms larger than the question of the changes in its purchasing power. In such a setting, it is possible for the external terms of trade of a backward country to be improving, while the relative share of incomes or the *per capita* income

4. Cf. S. H. Frankel, *The Economic Impact on Underdeveloped Societies,* Oxford, 1953, Essays III and IV, and also his paper in *Income and Wealth,* Series III, pp. 156–67. See also S. Kuznets, *Economic Change,* London, 1954, Essays 7 and 8. See J. Viner, *Studies in the Theory of International Trade,* London, 1937, Chapter IX, particularly p. 593, for a defence of the common-sense approach in international trade theory.
5. See footnote 15.

accruing to its indigenous population is falling.[6] Conversely, during a phase of rapid development, the deterioration in the terms of trade of a backward country may be consistent with (and the result of) the economic betterment of its people. Further, while the backward countries as territorial units are compensated, sometimes handsomely, for the unfavourable terms of trade during slumps by favourable terms of trade during booms, this compensatory movement is less noticeable with the export surpluses. These continue through both booms and slumps, and in spite of the variations in the total value of the exports, their ratio to the totals appears to be more stable over the trade cycle. This suggests that, while the terms of trade may be a useful concept to trace the cyclical variations in the purchasing power of the share of the incomes accruing to the people of the backward countries, it can only very imperfectly reflect the underlying long-term forces which determine the size of that share. To consider this, we are obliged to go behind the external terms of trade to the internal terms of co-operation between the "domestic" and the "foreign" factors of production in the backward countries.

It may be noted that this need to probe the internal economic relationships is not diminished even if we were concerned mainly with the external terms of trade of the backward countries. Given the role which the inflow of foreign resources played in the opening-up of the backward countries, it is not possible to approach their terms of trade as though they were uniquely determined by the tastes and resources of these countries. In the text-books, the terms of trade are usually depicted as being determined by the reciprocal

6. This may well have been the situation in Burma from the 1870's to the 1920's, during which there was a general upward trend in the price of rice (the chief peasant export) and a downward trend in the price of cotton goods (the chief import) (cf. J. S. Furnivall, op cit., Chapter III and IV, particularly p. 100, and W. K. Hancock, *Wealth of Colonies,* Cambridge, Eng., 1950, pp. 29–30). Where the improvement in the terms of trade is due to a rise in the price of non-peasant export, such as minerals, this would have no effect on the economic position of the indigenous population provided their wages remain constant.

demand curves or the offer curves which are directly derived from their respective indifference maps. This frequently tends to push the tastes and demand factors into the foreground to the relative neglect of the supply and cost factors. For our purpose, however, the emphasis has to be reversed. For although, as we have seen, the wants of the backward countries developed rapidly, the main forces determining the terms of trade are to be found on the supply side, in the vast expansions in their output induced by foreign investment. Further, foreign investment in the backward countries frequently took place in a direct form (as distinct from portfolio investment) and under conditions which diverged from the ideal competitive norm due to monopolistic concessions, zoning of spheres of influence, "economies" of experience and contacts combined with the institutional rigidities and monopsonistic elements in the labour market. Given these imperfections, it is not sufficient to dismiss the complications introduced by foreign investment by appealing to the theory of "normal profits." On the contrary, in the typical situation where foreign enterprises in the backward countries are large enough to be monopsonistic buyers of labour and peasant produce, their behaviour may depress the terms of trade. Thus they may meet the pressure of competition in the world market by cutting prices rather than output and by pressing down on the internal incomes of the backward countries while maintaining their "normal" profit on an unreduced volume of output. But at this stage, however, we have clearly passed from the external factors determining the terms of trade to the internal factors arising from the domestic economic structure of the backward countries.[7]

7. Thus a recent attempt by Drs. Singer and Prebisch to show that there has been a long-term deterioration in the terms of trade of the backward countries has to fall back on the internal factors at a crucial stage in the argument. It is maintained that while wages in the advanced countries rise during the upswings of the trade cycles, they are extremely resistant to cuts during the downswings, whereas in the backward countries, due to monopsony and less powerful trade unions, wages and incomes do not rise as much during upswings and are certainly more easily cut during the downswings. Thus with each trade cycle, the costs and prices of the manufactured goods are irreversibly jerked upwards relatively to the costs and prices of the raw

Before we leave the subject of the terms of trade, let us briefly glance at a recent variant called the "internal" or the "up-country" terms of trade. The procedure here is to take the ratio of the price of the produce which the peasants receive from the marketing board (instead of its export price f.o.b.) to the "up-country" price they pay for imported goods (instead of the import price c.i.f.). This clearly gives us a better indication of the economic position of the peasants, provided there is a significant divergence in the movements of the internal and the external terms of trade persisting for fairly long periods such as that which might occur under a marketing board system. But when we turn to study the long-term pattern of the distribution of the gains from international trade to the people of the backward country, it is doubtful whether any special advantage can be claimed for the concept of the internal (price) terms of trade. This is so, because under *laissez-faire* conditions one might reasonably expect the middlemen dealing with the peasants to charge normally more or less constant rates of profits on the external prices of exports and imports. If they did that, then however high the rate of their profits and, therefore, however small the share of the gains from international trade accruing to the peasants, this would not be reflected in a divergence between the internal and the external terms of trade. With a possible time-lag, the long-term movements of the two indices would be parallel and the

---

materials. (Cf. R. Prebisch, *The Economic Development of Latin America and Its Principal Problems*, New York, 1950, pp. 12–14; the United Nations Report on *Relatives Prices of Exports and Imports of Underdeveloped Countries*, New York, 1949; and also H. W. Singer, "The Distribution of the Gains between the Investing and the Borrowing Countries," *American Economic Review, Paper and Proceedings*, May, 1950.) It may be noted that the United Nations Report is an attempt to measure the commodity terms of trade between the raw materials and the manufactured products and not the terms of trade between the backward and the advanced countries. As its authors recognise, there are many difficulties in jumping from the movement of the terms of trade between large aggregate groups of *commodities* to conclusions about changes in the share of gains from international trade accruing to the people of particular backward countries.

former would be subject to the same limitations as the latter.[8] However, for the study of the short-term or cyclical disturbances to the normal pattern of income distribution between the "domestic" and the "foreign" factors, the internal terms of trade will come into their own. Here, if sufficient information were available, it would be extremely interesting to find out how far the internal terms of trade fluctuate more than the external terms of trade and how far, therefore, the middlemen have been able to shift the burden of cyclical adjustments onto the peasants.

II

Turning now to our main subject-matter, let us consider the broad features of the process by which the backward countries were opened up to international trade and their effect on the internal terms of co-operation between the "domestic" factors and "foreign" factors of production. We shall start with the "domestic" factors of the backward countries in their role as unskilled labour, particularly in the non-peasant sectors. The text-book account of the impact of international trade on the internal income distribution of a country

8. These limitations may be overcome by constructing the internal *income* terms of trade. But even if that is statistically possible, it is conceptually hardly distinguishable from the approach suggested here, viz. to go directly to the internal terms of co-operation between the "domestic" and the "foreign" factors in the backward countries instead of being side-tracked by the conventional terms of trade approach. To prevent possible mis-understandings, it should be pointed out that our argument is directed not against the concept of the terms of trade as such, but against the mechanical application of it to the problem of the distribution of the gains from inter-national trade to the people of the backward countries. This has distracted attention from more fruitful and statistically less elaborate lines of approach to the problem, e.g. (1) the long-run and the cyclical behaviour of the export surpluses; (2) the long-run changes in the composition of exports produced by the peasant sectors and the "western" sectors; and (3) the long-run changes in the composition of imports, i.e. of consumers' goods destined for the indigenous market and construction and capital goods destined for the "western" sectors (cf. J. S. Furnivall, op. cit., and J. H. Boeke, *The Evolution of the Netherlands Indies Economy*, New York, 1946, Chapter II).

is worked out mainly in terms of different factor proportions in the different industries. Thus, if a country specialises in the export of primary products which require more land to labour than its domestic industries, then we should expect rents to rise relatively to wages. This, however, assumes that the resources of the country are given and constant, and that it can increase export production only by withdrawing resources from the domestic industries. This assumption will have to be dropped when we consider the opening-up process of the backward countries. A part of the resources used for their export production may have come from the domestic and the subsistence sectors. But as we have seen, this "substitution" effect was clearly swamped by the "expansion" effect, since the bulk of the increase in their export production was in the form of net additions to output made possible by the utilisation of the new natural resources. How would this affect the relative scarcity of labour? On the demand side, as the hinterlands of these "semi-empty" countries were being rapidly opened up, large quantities of labour would be required; firstly, for the initial clearing of land and construction work and, secondly, for working on the land thus cleared. This increase in demand would take place both in the peasant and non-peasant sectors. In the non-peasant sectors it would take the form of an increase in the fund available for "the advances to labour" in the classical sense. How far there was a similar financing of the peasants will be discussed later. However, it is true to say that, with the possible exception of mining, the bulk of the foreign investment made during the opening-up process took the form of circulating capital rather than of fixed capital. On this basis, therefore, we should expect the rate of increase in the demand for labour to be roughly the same as the rate of increase in the total volume of export production during the period in which the expansion process was in full swing, and this usually lasted for at least two or three decades. On the supply side, the possible sources of extra labour were the shrinkage of the domestic and subsistence sectors, the natural growth of population and the release of labour through the introduction of modern transport. This last item may have been quite important, particularly in African countries, where the porterage system existed on a large scale. But we must balance this against the fact that, initially, large quantities of labour would be required for the construction of roads and railways as the interior districts were opened up in successive stages. Now as we have seen earlier,[9] the characteristic rates of expansion of the export economies were very high and sustained for fairly long periods. Thus, if the demand for labour increased at the same rates, it would seem almost impossible that the domestic supplies of labour could have kept up with them without an upward trend in wages. Considering the rates of expansion involved, this upward trend in wages should have been sharp enough to be clearly observable, even allowing for the limitations in our knowledge of the economic history of these countries and for the possibility that a part of this trend may have been masked by the imperfect spread of the money economy.[10] But it is fair to say that, contrary to what we might expect from the laws of supply and demand, the wages of the unskilled labour appear to have been fossilised at their "customary level" even during periods of very rapid economic expansion.

At the start of the opening-up process, we should expect the wages to be very low due to the initial lack of experience and the rawness of labour just emerging from the tribal and village communities. Further, this "transition" stage had two unfortunate features which encouraged the development of the "cheap labour policy." Firstly, the turnover of labour was high due to its "migrant" nature and individual workers did not stay long enough in their jobs to acquire

9. See footnote 2.
10. E.g., frequently only a part of the wages is paid in cash; the rest is paid in the form of free food and living quarters. Thus we cannot generalise from the movements of cash wages only. But on the other hand, this practice of paying in kind may have itself contributed to wage rigidity. Further, in the African countries, where labour is locked up in tribal economies, the pressure of demand may show itself, not by a rise in wages, but by an increase in the stresses and strains on the tribal organisation. But it is important to note that the pressure to detach labour from the tribal economies appears frequently to take the "negative" form of taxation and compulsion rather than the "positive" form of incentives.

whatever little skill might be attached to them. Secondly, at this stage, those who offered themselves for wage labour still retained a foothold in their tribal and village societies and looked upon it as a subsidiary source of income. Thus they were willing to accept very low wages which might have little relation to their productivity but which confirmed their employers' belief that "the native can live on a handful of rice." But once established, the "customary" wage rate became frozen at the initial level in spite of subsequent increases in the demand for labour and in spite of the breakdown of the tribal and village societies, which threw the workers more and more upon their wage labour as the chief means of livelihood. It is this continuance of the conventional level of low wages, even where the "transition phase" has passed, which is difficult to explain purely in terms of rational economic factors and gives substance to the discontent with the "nineteenth century" pattern of economic development. The convention of low wages may even have partly "justified" itself subsequently by preventing a rise in potential labour efficiency or by pulling efficiency down to its level. But the attempt to rationalise it as the necessary and inevitable pattern, given the initial social and economic conditions of the backward countries, does not appear to stand up to a critical examination on a number of points.

First, consider the prevalent belief that the supply curve of labour in these countries is backward sloping so that raising the wage rate would merely reduce the quantity offered. This is usually taken to be "proved" by the fact that labour in the backward countries can be made to work more by lowering wages, since they need a certain minimum sum to pay taxes or debts or simply to live on. But this merely means that the supply curve of their labour is forward falling in the downward direction, which does not prove that it is also backward sloping in the upward direction. Indeed, in the downward direction, such behaviour could be induced from unskilled labour anywhere provided that the employers could press down the wages low enough without restraint from the government or trade unions. The real point, therefore, is whether the wants of the people of the backward countries are so fixed that they would prefer not to earn more above a certain sum. Now this may have occasionally happened in the short-run in the face of a sudden and transient rise of wages. But considering the rapid development of new wants in the backward countries, which we have noted earlier, it seems difficult to believe that the supply curve of labour in these countries would be backward sloping over the *long period* with which we are concerned. Those who favour this doctrine are fond of giving examples from the behaviour of the remote tribes in Africa who are still on the fringe of the money economy, forgetting the fact that the bulk of the people in the backward countries, particularly the export economies, have been in contact with the money economy and imported goods for many generations. Indeed, it has now become apparent that an important obstacle to their economic development may arise from the fact that their wants for the new imported goods are "overdeveloped" rather than "underdeveloped."

Whatever its logical validity, the doctrine of the backward sloping supply curve had far-reaching consequences in shaping the labour policy practised in the backward countries. Firstly, it encouraged the use of negative or compulsive methods of obtaining labour through taxation and administrative pressure. This resulted in a high cost of supervising labour and gave rise to an additional reason for not raising wages. Secondly, and with graver consequences, it gave a ready-made justification to the employers for importing immigrant labour once no more labour was available at existing wage rates. Thus in the latter half of the nineteenth century, immigrant labour from India and China was introduced, not only to the neighbouring countries in South-East Asia, but also into others, such as Fiji, the West Indies and parts of East and South Africa. The amount of immigrant labour was frequently large even in relation to the total population of the receiving countries and far larger still in relation to the working population. As Professor Knowles has said, there were, in fact, three "mother countries" of the British Empire in the nineteenth century: the United Kingdom, India and China.[11] The

11. L. C. Knowles, *The Economic Development of the British Overseas Empire,* London, 1928, Vol. I, p. viii and pp. 182–201.

introduction of immigrant labour is generally defended on the ground that without it the rapid economic development of the export economies would not have been possible.[12] This is true enough when we are thinking purely in terms of the total territorial volume of export production. But when we turn to the share which the people of the receiving country obtained out of this process of economic development we have a very different picture. For, in the latter half of the nineteenth century, immigrant labour, particularly from India, may really be regarded as an internationally traded commodity having a uniform price rather than as a factor of production. Wherever it was imported, it decisively pulled down wages and incomes in the "semi-empty" countries to the very low level appropriate to the over-populated countries instead of giving them a chance to rise a part of the way towards the high wage levels of the "empty" continents of North America and Australia. Thus, in this context, the Heckscher-Ohlin approach in terms of the "original endowments of the factors" has to be completely suspended. It may be noted, further, that out of this process of "the equalisation of factor rewards," the people of the "semi-empty" backward countries could at best hope only for indirect benefits.[13] Directly, they consumed very little or none of the raw materials which the immigrant labour had helped to export cheaply.

Let us now turn to a more complicated defence of the cheap labour policy (with or without immigrant labour) based on interrelated considerations of capital scarcity, the poor quality of the indigenous labour and the expensiveness of skilled European labour and management. To begin with, the capital-scarcity argument in

12. Frequently, the introduction of immigrant labour is defended on the semi-ethical ground that the people of the "semi-empty" backward countries have no exclusive rights to their natural resources. But if this means that all the world's resources should be equitably shared among the world's population, then the rich "empty" continents of North America and Australia should take the largest amount of immigrant labour from India and China.

13. If we can accept the conclusions of the United Nations report on *Relative Prices of Exports and Imports of Underdeveloped Countries,* these indirect benefits may be smaller than is generally assumed.

the popular form may be rejected outright, since the foreign firms in the export sectors were normally able to borrow capital on equal terms with firms of comparable credit-worthiness in the advanced countries (cf. J. Viner, op. cit., pp. 95–96). But there were real obstacles in less recognised forms. The attempt to switch over from the cheap labour policy to a policy of higher wages and a more intensive use of labour usually involved taking decisions about "lumpy investments," both in the form of plant and machinery and in the form of camps and villages, where it was necessary to change over from casual labour to a permanent labour force. Given the unstable conditions of the raw materials market (and perhaps also a desire to make profits as quickly as possible and get out) employers were naturally unwilling to take the risk of locking-up their capital in this way. Further, during the booms, output had to be expanded as quickly as possible along existing lines and there was no time to wait for the fruits of a longer term labour policy; during the slumps, it would be difficult to raise capital for this purpose. This is an understandable account of why the cheap labour policy continued. But it also shows that, given the discontinuities in investment and cyclical factors, private business firms cannot or will not make an attempt to weigh up accurately the relative productivities and costs of using labour more intensively and on a permanent basis compared with using it extensively and on a casual basis. Indeed, particularly in mining, there is some evidence that the cheap labour policy was continued long after it was recognised as uneconomic (cf. W. M. Macmillan and others, *Europe and West Africa,* Chapter III, particularly pp. 48–50).

Next we have the argument that the quality of the indigenous labour is so poor that, whatever its scarcity, it would not be economic to use it more intensively. Admittedly, a long time-lag may be necessary before the raw labour emerging from the tribal and village societies can be trained to be used more intensively. But this time-lag may be unnecessarily prolonged by the cheap labour policy itself creating a vicious circle of low wages and low efficiency. Those who favour the "qualitative approach" tend to ignore this. Further, in considering the profitability of labour-saving methods, the relevant "quality" is the efficiency of labour *relatively* to its wages. Thus, if it is true, as is frequently maintained, that the indigenous labour is "expensive" because, although its wages are low, its efficiency is lower still, then this should be an argument for and not against using labour-saving methods. In this context, it is interesting to quote Taussig, who believed that it was the low initial efficiency of immigrant labour, combined with the convention of high wages, which led to the rapid adoption of labour-saving machinery in the United States.

His [the American entrepreneur's] own energy and the ingenuity and attention of his engineers and inventors and mechanics have been directed to devising machinery that will almost run itself. Here the newly-arrived immigrant can be used. So far as the American can do this sort of machine making to peculiar advantage, so far can he pay wages to the immigrants on the higher American scale and yet hold his own against the European competitor who pays lower wages to the immigrant's stay-at-home fellow. But it is on this condition only that he can afford to pay the green hand wages on the American scale or on some approach to it: he must make the total labour more effective. The main cause of greater effectiveness in the dominating industries is to be found, under the economic conditions of the recent times, not so much in the industrial quality of the rank and file as in that of the technical and business leaders. [*Some Aspects of the Tariff Question,* p. 43.]

The upshot of Taussig's analysis is to turn our attention towards the subject of skilled labour and management. If the low ratio of capital to labour in the non-peasant sectors is not due to the higher cost of borrowing then it must be largely accounted for by the expensiveness of the complementary skilled labour and management which is required for the adoption of labour-saving methods of production. This subject is sometimes too easily dismissed by saying that the skilled European labour in the tropics is "one of God's most expensive creatures on earth." But precisely because of this it is important to inquire what are the obstacles to the substitution of this expensive labour by the cheaper local personnel. The shortage of skilled, local labour in the backward countries is generally attributed to the lack of educational and technical facilities. But this explanation is only partly satisfactory. For, in many backward countries, we can observe the curious phenomenon of a general shortage of trained personnel combined with a relative abundance in such professions as law, where there is free entry. This would suggest that, given the demand, the supply of skilled labour, including those trained abroad, responds to the market conditions more quickly and automatically than is generally assumed. Thus, apart from the obstacles on the supply side, one of the reasons for the shortage of skilled local labour seems to be a lack of effective demand for it. To a considerable extent this must be attributed to the conventional pattern of the "vertical" division of labour into "non-competing" racial groups. This again arises from the cheap labour policy and tends to reinforce it. Given the cheap labour policy, there is no vertical mobility of labour into skilled and managerial grades, which keeps these factors at a premium. Hence, it is not possible to introduce labour-saving methods of production which require these expensive factors in a greater proportion. Unfortunately, this institutional pattern of "non-competing groups" is not confined only to those countries in Africa with an official or unofficial industrial colour bar. In some degree or other, it can be found wherever European capital and enterprise have opened up the backward countries to international trade.

III

Let us now turn to the share of the gains from international trade accruing to the "domestic" factors of the backward countries in their role as peasant producers. Here, the characteristic features of the peasant sectors, such as the prevalence of large foreign firms exercising monopolistic powers, both in buying the produce from the peasants and in selling imported goods to them, the peasant's need to borrow at high rates of interest and his indebtedness to the money lenders, etc., are too familiar to be described again.[14] We shall,

14. Cf. J. S. Furnivall, op. cit. *passim,* also above, Chapter 3.

therefore, concern ourselves mainly with the pattern of the balance of trade of the peasant economies which is at variance with accepted ideas on the subject and gives some substance to the older idea of the "colonial drain." According to the conventional theory, the balance of trade of a backward country receiving foreign investment should fall into two phases. In the first phase, during which outside capital is flowing into the backward country, we should expect it to have an import surplus on its trade account. It is only in the second phase, when profits and interest charges on past investment exceed the new investment, that we should expect the backward country to have an export surplus. When we turn to the trade statistics of the tropical countries, however, this conventional pattern is clearly observable only in purely mining countries, such as Northern Rhodesia. Where peasant production played an important part in the export production unexpected results were obtained. Thus, except for one year of slight import surplus in each case, both Burma and Indonesia have had a consistent and heavy export surplus right from the start of the opening-up process in the 1860's and '70's to the Second World War.[15] The Gold Coast and Nigeria appear to have arrived at the second phase of normal export surplus by the early 1920's without ever going through the first phase of import surplus, for before that time they had small alternating export and

15. Thus Burma's export surplus averaged one-third of the total value of her exports from 1870 to the First World War and rose to one-half of the total value of exports during the inter-war period. During this period, the remittances of the Indian immigrant labour have been estimated at Rs. 30 million out of an average annual export surplus of Rs. 250 million. (Cf. J. S. Furnivall, op. cit., Appendix I, and J. R. Andrus, *Burmese Economic Life,* Stanford, 1947, p. 182.) Indonesia's export surplus averaged one-third of the total value of her exports from 1876 to 1939. Here, however, estate production is more important relatively to peasant production than in Burma or West Africa. In particular, western commercial interests tend to gain control of peasant production to such an extent that the peasant "becomes a wage earner in all but name." (Cf. J. H. Boeke, *The Structure of Netherlands Indian Economy,* New York, 1942, p. 184, and *The Evolution of Netherlands Indies Economy,* pp. 10–11 and Chapter II.) Export surpluses ranging from a third to a quarter of the total value of exports can be found in African countries after 1920.

import surpluses which roughly cancelled out. It is not possible to explain this in terms of the cost of building-up "immaterial capital" in the form of a modern administration and social and economic services. For, whatever the benefit of these, their actual cost, in salaries and pensions of civil servants and technical experts, formed only a part, frequently a small part, of the total value of the export surpluses. Allowing for other items, such as the remittances of immigrant labour, we are still left with the larger part of the export surpluses in the form of profits of foreign companies. How can we account for these profits when there is no evidence of a previous inflow of capital in the form of import surpluses? Pending further research, the following explanation seems the most probable: (*a*) Foreign investment, if it took place at all, was mainly in the form of short-term trade capital in the peasant sectors which could be turned over within the one-year period on which trade statistics were compiled. (*b*) In spite of this short duration of investment, profits were large enough not only to lead to a sizeable net outflow, but also to cover all other foreign investment in the form of durable capital goods which would otherwise have appeared as import surplus. (*c*) Trading profits on such a scale must arise partly from the strategic position occupied by the big export-import firms which exercised varying degrees of monopoly power both in the buying of the produce from the peasants and in the selling of the imported goods to them. Frequently, these profits have been defended on the ground that they were merely the returns on capital which had a genuine economic function of "financing" peasant production during the waiting period before the harvest. But this argument is not entirely satisfactory. A large part of the peasants' subsistence fund generally consisted of locally produced consumers' goods, so that it is difficult to say how much of their need for "finance" was due to a genuine shortage of domestic real resources to tide over the waiting period before the harvest and how much of it was due merely to defects in the organisation of rural credit.

Much interesting light has been thrown on this question by the post-war experiments with marketing boards in various countries, including West Africa and Burma. Firstly, it appears that there is little or no connection between the profits of these marketing boards and the financing of the peasants. Thus the West African peasants appear to be mainly self-financing (though boom conditions may have helped), while the Burmese Government's advances to the peasants form only a small fraction of the annual profits of the rice marketing board. Secondly, even staunch supporters of the marketing boards must admit that at present they are mainly agencies for redistributing incomes and have little or no productive functions of their own. Yet the ease with which these marketing boards have been able to step into the shoes of the private firms without any serious disruption in the productive organisation of the peasant sectors seems to suggest that, by the time of the change-over at least, the profits of the firms were as little connected with indispensable productive functions as are the present profits of the marketing boards.[16]

IV

So far, we have been concerned with the distribution of the gains from international trade in the direct sense in the form of the final incomes of the "domestic" factors of the backward countries. It is now time to turn to the question of the "indirect," or the "dynamic," gains from international trade, and here we have to switch our

16. Recently it has been suggested that the price policy of the marketing boards may have a depressing effect on the long-run trend of output. Later we shall touch briefly on the question how far past outputs under *laissez-faire* conditions can be regarded as "optimal" and how far, therefore, the marketing boards tend to introduce divergences from the optimum. For the moment it is sufficient to say that the economic functions of the trading firms could not have been so vital or urgent if their suspension has led merely to slight changes in the long-term trend of output which, even if they exist, are small enough to be a subject of dispute among statisticians (cf. P. T. Bauer and F. W. Paish, "The Reduction of Fluctuations in the Incomes of Primary Producers," *Economic Journal,* December, 1952; Miss P. Ady's comments in the same journal in 1953; also E. Hawkins, "The Terms of Trade of Nigeria," *Review of Economic Studies,* Vol. XXII(1), No. 57, 1954–55.

attention from the defenders to the critics of the "nineteenth century" system of international trade. Thus there is a considerable body of opinion that, given this system under which the advanced countries specialised in manufacturing and the backward countries specialised in raw materials production, the former was bound to get the larger share of the dynamic or indirect gains from international trade in the form of secondary rounds of economic activities and a general stimulus to economic growth. This thesis is put forward on two main arguments. The first is that while an increase in demand for manufactured products leads to a further increase in demand for the durable capital goods required to produce them, thus creating secondary rounds of activities through the multiplier-accelerator mechanism, an increase in demand for primary products can only lead to a once-over extension in cultivation, which is bound to come to a stop as soon as the extensive margin of natural resources has been reached. This argument is attractive and plausible at first sight but will not stand up to a critical examination. It seems to be the result of an implicit assumption that international division of labour is only horizontal between different types of commodities. But once we take into account that it may also be vertical between different stages in the production of the same commodity through "re-exports," there does not seem to be any necessary reason why the secondary rounds of economic activities created by the increase in demand for manufactured products of a particular country should be localised there. If the local resources are such that the comparative costs are unfavourable, then, however long the chain reaction started by the initial increase in demand in that country, some or all of the secondary rounds of activities may leak out of the country. On the same basis, the lack of secondary rounds of activities in the backward countries may be due not as much to a lack of effective demand[17] as to a lack of resources and the ordinary operation of the

17. However, remittances abroad of earnings of the foreign companies and immigrant labour may have a deflationary effect on a backward country after the expansion process has tapered off, e.g. Burma in the decade 1930–40. But this is an argument for plugging the "drain" rather than for industrialisation.

comparative costs principle. But beyond this surface contrast between "agriculture" and "manufactures" there may be institutional rigidities arising, not from the external pattern of the international division of labour, but from the internal economic structure of the backward countries. Thus it may be possible to find an analogue of "non-competing groups" in the foreign and domestic sectors of the backward countries which contributes to a lack of secondary rounds of activities.[18] This leads us to the second argument, that the dynamic gains from specialisation in industry are likely to be greater because it has a greater "educative" effect on the people of the country than agriculture. Here it must be admitted that, in contrast to the tremendous stimulus to further economic development enjoyed by the advanced countries, international trade seems to have had very little "educative" effect on the people of the backward countries except in the development of new wants. Apart from the introduction of modern transport, it is difficult to observe any revolutionary changes in their methods of production and efficiency, both in the peasant and the non-peasant sectors. The peasants "specialise" for international trade simply by going on producing traditional crops by traditional methods or new crops which can be readily produced by traditional methods.[19] It is also fair to say that this extensive farming of land in the peasant sector was paralleled by an "extensive farming" of labour in the non-peasant sectors. But the real question is whether this unequal "educative" effect of international trade on the advanced and the backward countries is simply due to specialisation of "manufactures" and "agriculture" as such, or whether it is due to efficient manufactures contrasted with "poor"

18. E.g., "When the first railways were built they were naturally equipped with British locomotives and rolling stock. Thereafter, as a matter of course, the managers of India's railways continued to order their equipment, spare parts and miscellaneous items from Britain—not only those items which were not available in India, but also, right down to the 1920's, items that were, or could be, made in India." See D. Thorner, "Great Britain and the Development of Indian Railways," *The Journal of Economic History,* Fall, 1951, p. 398.
19. Cf. A. McPhee, *The Economic Revolution of West Africa,* pp. 39–40; J. S. Furnival, op. cit., pp 324–332; W. K. Hancock, op. cit., Vol. II, Part II, p. 225, and Chapter II, Section III, *passim.*

or, more accurately, badly developed agriculture.[20] In the light of our previous analysis it would appear that those who advocate the industrialisation of the backward countries tend to underrate the possible "educative" effects of agriculture by identifying all agriculture with the bad and inefficient agriculture which actually developed in the backward countries. Thus, inefficient methods of production and marketing and bad systems of credit and land tenure are not necessary evils of agricultural production even under the peasant system. Further, with the cheap labour policy, we cannot expect the "educative" influences to work on labour whether it is employed in the mines and plantations or in the factories. Given that policy, the people of the backward countries could not have been better off even if the nineteenth-century pattern of international division of labour had been completely reversed and the backward countries had specialised in the export of manufactures instead of primary products. Indeed, when we consider the implications of the cheap labour policy in an urban and industrial setting, it seems probable that they would have been a great deal worse off. In this connection, the frequent proposal to attract private enterprise to set up manufacturing industries by the offer of cheap labour guaranteed by the government needs to be very carefully considered. Whatever its merits may be for the over-populated countries with large surplus labour, for the "semi-empty" type of backward country we have been considering it could easily develop into a switch-over from agriculture, with the cheap labour policy, to industry, with the cheap labour policy.

V

We are now able to summarise the conclusions which have emerged from our analysis.

20. Cf. J. Viner, op. cit., p. 52. Our analysis, however, suggests that the badness of agriculture may be due not only to the initial social and economic backwardness emphasised by Professor Viner, but also to the way in which agriculture in these countries was developed under the pressure to expand production rapidly at whatever longer-run costs.

(1) The people of the "semi-empty" backward countries appear to have obtained a smaller share of the gains from international trade than can be satisfactorily accounted for in terms of the initial social and economic conditions of these countries and in terms of the relative scarcities and effectiveness of the "domestic" factors compared with the "foreign" factors of production. This seems to have been caused not only by monopolistic and monopsonistic factors in the static sense, but also by the dynamic pressures of the need to expand export production rapidly, acting on the institutional rigidities of the internal economic structure, fossilising the earnings and efficiency of the "domestic" factors at their low initial levels or sometimes depressing them even lower.

(2) This does not, however, mean that this type of backward country should react blindly against the "nineteenth century" pattern of international trade and embark on a policy of protection to foster domestic manufacturing industries. Our analysis suggests that the chief source of trouble lies with the internal pattern of economic development rather than with the external pattern of international trade. The former failed to pass on the full benefits of the international division of labour to the people of the backward countries. It also appears to be partly responsible for whatever disadvantages the backward countries may have suffered in the way of unfavourable external terms of trade and lack of dynamic economic stimulus from international trade.

(3) This would suggest that the people of the backward countries are likely to gain most from a compromise policy of external free trade combined with internal state control. In the peasant sectors, state control should take the form of a more effective use of the marketing boards already in existence. In the non-peasant sectors, state investment and partnership with private concerns may be needed to facilitate the switch-over from the cheap labour policy to a better labour policy with a greater vertical mobility of labour into skilled grades.

(4) This conclusion, of course, applies only to the particular, but not unimportant, type of backward country we have been considering

and not to the overpopulated backward countries where the case for
a protectionist policy of industrialisation may well be stronger. But
even for the former type of backward country, we have by no means
been able to cover all the ramifications of the free-trade versus protection controversy. But our analysis does suggest that those who
favour protectionism for all backward countries may be over-rating
the advantages from manufactures and under-rating the advantages
from agriculture, by identifying all manufacturing industries with
those of the industrially most advanced countries of the world and
all agriculture with the poor and badly developed agriculture of the
backward countries.

(5) How far can we keep external free trade and internal state
control in water-tight compartments without the latter reacting un-
favourably on the former? Thus those who favour "the competitive
solution" all the way have criticised the state marketing boards on
the ground that their policy of accumulating large profits tends to
reduce the long-term output of the peasant sectors. There are a
number of points involved here which should be dealt with separately: (a) It would be quite consistent with our analysis if the
marketing boards acted merely as marketing agencies turning over
the whole of the proceeds (not required for price stabilisation) to the
peasants. Even then the peasants' share of the gains from international trade would have been greatly increased. But our analysis
suggests that if it were decided that the marketing board profits
should be used for long-term economic development, improvements
in agriculture should not be starved for the sake of would-be infant
industries. (b) It may be admitted that, from the peasants' point of
view in the short run, it does not appear to matter whether the
profits go into the hands of the marketing boards, in the form of
"disguised taxation," or into the hands of the private companies.
It may be admitted even further that sometimes the peasants may
tend to suffer from the "jam yesterday, jam to-morrow" type of
promise from their government. But even so, there is a great
difference between the profits of the marketing boards on which
they have some claims and the profits of the private companies

which used to be remitted outright in the form of large export surpluses. (*c*) As we have noted above,[21] on the basis of the available evidence, it is debatable whether the peasants get less under the marketing board system than they would have got under *laissez-faire*, and whether, therefore, the marketing boards tend to reduce their long-term output. There is also the further and more general criticism that any attempt at internal state control in the backward countries in favour of the "domestic" factors of production will tend to raise the cost of production of raw materials and reduce their output below *the* optimum level. But the optimum output cannot be defined in the abstract, divorced from the pattern of income distribution. As we have seen, the free play of economic forces in the backward countries operated under conditions which diverged widely from the ideal competitive norm and the past pattern of income distribution between the "domestic" and "foreign" factors cannot be said to be determined by purely rational economic factors only. Thus even if state control, e.g. particularly in raising wages and working conditions, leads to a reduction in output, it cannot be said to be a divergence from the optimum in some unique sense. Further, those who fear that state control would lead to dearer raw materials appear to rule out the substantial possibilities of increasing productivity through a better labour and agricultural policy which may well result in cheaper raw materials in the long run.

21. See footnote 16.

5 | The "Classical Theory" of International Trade and the Underdeveloped Countries

There has recently been a considerable amount of controversy concerning the applicability of the "classical theory" of international trade to the underdeveloped countries.[1] The twists in this controversy may be set out as follows. The critics start with the intention of showing that the "nineteenth-century pattern" of international trade, whereby the underdeveloped countries export raw materials and import manufactured goods, has been unfavourable to the economic development of these countries. But instead of trying to show this directly, they concentrate their attacks on the "classical theory," which they believe to be responsible for the unfavourable pattern of trade. The orthodox economists then come to the defence of the classical theory by reiterating the principle of comparative costs which they claim to be applicable both to the developed and the underdeveloped countries. After this, the controversy shifts from

1. Of the very extensive literature on the subject, we may refer to two notable recent works, the first stating the orthodox position and the second the position of the critics: J. Viner, *International Trade and Economic Development,* Oxford, 1953, and G. Myrdal, *An International Economy,* London, 1956.

This paper has benefited from comments by Sir Donald MacDougall, Professors H. G. Johnson, R. M. Sundrum and G. M. Meier.

From *The Economic Journal,* Vol. LXVIII, June 1958, pp. 317–37. Reprinted by permission.

the primary question whether or not the nineteenth-century pattern of international trade, as a historical reality, has been unfavourable to the underdeveloped countries to the different question whether or not the theoretical model assumed in the comparative-costs analysis is applicable to these countries. Both sides then tend to conduct their argument as though the two questions were the same and to identify the "classical theory" with the comparative-costs theory.

It will be argued in this paper that this has led to the neglect of those other elements in the classical theory of international trade which are much nearer to the realities and ideologies of the nineteenth-century expansion of international trade to the underdeveloped countries. In Sections I and II we shall outline these elements and show that they are traceable to Adam Smith and to some extent to J. S. Mill. In Section III we shall show how one of Adam Smith's lines of approach can be fruitfully developed to throw a more illuminating light on the past and present patterns of the international trade of the underdeveloped countries than the conventional theory. In Section IV we shall touch upon some policy implications of our analysis and show certain weaknesses in the position both of the orthodox economists and of their critics.

The neglected elements in the classical theory of international trade may be traced to Adam Smith, particularly to the following key passage in the *Wealth of Nations*:

> Between whatever places foreign trade is carried on, they all of them derive two distinct benefits from it. It carries out that surplus part of the produce of their land and labour for which there is no demand among them, and brings back in return for it something else for which there is a demand. It gives a value to their superfluities, by exchanging them for something else, which may satisfy a part of their wants, and increase their enjoyments. By means of it, the narrowness of the home market does not hinder the division of labour in any particular branch of art or manufacture from being carried to the highest perfection. By opening a more extensive market for whatever part of the produce of their labour may exceed the home consumption, it encourages them to improve its productive powers, and to augment its annual produce to the utmost, and thereby to increase the real revenue and wealth of society [Vol. I, Cannan ed., p. 413].

There are two leading ideas here. (1) International trade overcomes the narowness of the home market and provides an outlet for the surplus product above domestic requirements. This develops into what may be called the "vent for surplus"[2] theory of international trade. Later we hope to remove some of the prejudice aroused by this "mercantilist" sounding phrase. (2) By widening the extent of the market, international trade also improves the division of labour and raises the general level of productivity within the country. This develops into what may be called the "productivity" theory. We shall be mainly concerned with the "vent for surplus" theory and the light it throws upon the growth of international trade in the underdeveloped countries in the nineteenth century. But first it is necessary to consider the "productivity" theory briefly.

The "productivity" doctrine differs from the comparative-costs doctrine in the interpretation of "specialisation" for international trade. (a) In the comparative costs theory "specialisation" merely means a movement along a static "production possibility curve" constructed on the given resources and the *given techniques* of the trading country. In contrast, the "productivity" doctrine looks upon international trade as a dynamic force which, by widening the extent of the market and the scope of the division of labour, raises the skill and dexterity of the workmen, encourages technical innovations, overcomes technical indivisibilities and generally enables the trading country to enjoy increasing returns and economic development.[3]

2. This term is borrowed from Professor J. H. Williams, who in turn quoted it from a passage in J. S. Mill's *Principles,* in which Mill was criticising this particular aspect of Smith's theory of international trade. Professor Williams is the only modern economist to sponsor this "crude" doctrine. While he is mainly concerned with the loss to a country on being deprived of the export market for its surplus product, we shall pay special attention to the gain to a hitherto isolated underdeveloped country on obtaining a "vent" for its surplus productive capacity. Cf. J. H. Williams, "The Theory of International Trade Reconsidered," *Economic Journal,* June 1929, pp. 195–209.
3. Cf. Adam Smith, *op. cit.,* Chapters II and III, Book I. This aspect of Smith's theory has been made familiar by Professor Allyn Young's article

This distinction was clearly realised by J. S. Mill, who regarded the gains in terms of comparative-costs theory as direct gains and the gains in terms of Adam Smithian increases in productivity as "indirect effects, which must be counted as benefits of a high order." Mill even went on to extend this doctrine to countries at "an early stage of industrial advancement," where international trade by introducing new wants "sometimes works a sort of industrial revolution" (*Principles,* Ashley ed., p. 581). (*b*) In the comparative-costs theory "specialisation," conceived as a reallocation of resources, is a completely reversible process. The Adam Smithian process of specialisation, however, involves adapting and reshaping the productive structure of a country to meet the export demand, and is therefore not easily reversible. This means that a country specialising for the export market is more vulnerable to changes in the terms of trade than is allowed for in the comparative-costs theory. We shall come back to this point later.

In the expansive mental climate of the late nineteenth century the "productivity" aspect of international specialisation completely dominated the "vulnerability" aspect. At a semi-popular level, and particularly in its application to the underdeveloped countries, Smith's "productivity" doctrine developed beyond a free-trade argument into an export-drive argument. It was contended that since international trade was so beneficial in raising productivity and stimulating economic development, the State should go beyond a neutral and negative policy of removing barriers to trade and embark on a positive policy of encouraging international trade and economic development. Under its influence, many colonial governments went far beyond the strict *laissez-faire* policy in their attempts to promote the export trade of the colonies.[4] Further, although these governments were

---

on "Increasing Returns and Economic Progress," *Economic Journal,* December 1928, pp. 527–42.

4. See for instance, L. C. A. Knowles, *The Economic Development of the British Overseas Empire,* London, 1928, Vol. I, pp. 119–20, 248–49 and 486–87. However, in Section IV below we shall argue that, in spite of the attention they have received, these export-drive policies were not successful enough to cause a significant "export-bias."

frequently obliged to use "unclassical" methods, such as the granting of monopolistic privileges to the chartered companies or the taxing of the indigenous people to force them to take up wage labour or grow cash crops, they nevertheless sought to justify their policy by invoking the Adam Smithian doctrine of the benefits of international division of labour. This partly explains why some critics have associated the "classical theory" with "colonialism" and why they have frequently singled out Adam Smith for attack instead of Ricardo, the founder of the official classical free-trade theory.

It is fair to say that Smith's "productivity" doctrine is instructive more in relation to the ideological than to the actual economic forces which characterised the nineteenth-century expansion of international trade to the underdeveloped countries. It is true, as we shall see later,[5] that both the total value and the physical output of the exports of these countries expanded rapidly. In many cases the rate of increase in export production was well above any possible rate of increase in population, resulting in a considerable rise in output per head. But it is still true to say that this was achieved not quite in the way envisaged by Smith, viz., a better division of labour and specialisation leading on to innovations and cumulative improvements in skills and productivity per man-hour. Rather, the increase in output per head seems to have been due: (1) to once-for-all increases in productivity accompanying the transfer of labour from the subsistence economy to the mines and plantations, and (2) what is more important, as we shall see later, to an increase in working hours and in the proportion of gainfully employed labour relatively to the semi-idle labour of the subsistence economy.

5. See footnotes 11–14 below. See also Sir Donald MacDougall's *The World Dollar Problem*, London, 1957, pp. 134–43. Sir Donald's argument that the productivity of labour in the underdeveloped countries has been rising faster than is generally assumed is mainly based on figures for productivity *per capita*. These figures are not inconsistent with our argument that on the whole the expansion of the export production has been achieved on more or less constant techniques and skills of indigenous labour, by increasing working hours and the proportion of gainfully employed labour rather than by a continuous rise in productivity per man-hour.

The transfer of labour from the subsistence economy to the mines and plantations with their much higher capital-output ratio and skilled management undoubtedly resulted in a considerable increase in productivity. But this was mostly of a once-for-all character for a number of reasons. To begin with, the indigenous labour emerging from the subsistence economy was raw and technically backward. Moreover, it was subject to high rates of turnover, and therefore not amenable to attempts to raise productivity. Unfortunately, this initial experience gave rise to or hardened the convention of "cheap labour," which regarded indigenous labour merely as an undifferentiated mass of low-grade man-power to be used with a minimum of capital outlay.[6] Thus when the local labour supply was exhausted the typical reaction was not to try to economise labour by installing more machinery and by reorganising methods of production but to seek farther afield for additional supplies of cheap labour. This is why the nineteenth-century process of international trade in the underdeveloped countries was characterised by large-scale movements of cheap labour from India and China.[7] This tendency was reinforced by the way in which the world-market demand for raw materials expanded in a series of waves. During the booms output had to be expanded as quickly as possible along existing lines, and there was no time to introduce new techniques or reorganise production; during the slumps it was difficult to raise capital for such purposes.

This failure to achieve Adam Smith's ideal of specialisation leading on to continuous improvements in skills can also be observed in the peasant export sectors. Where the export crop happened to be a traditional crop (*e.g.*, rice in South-East Asia), the expansion in export production was achieved simply by bringing more land under cultivation with the same methods of cultivation used in the subsistence economy. Even where new export crops were introduced, the essence of their success as peasant export crops was that they could

6. Cf. S. H. Frankel, *Capital Investment in Africa*, London, 1938, pp. 142–46, and W. M. Macmillan, *Europe and West Africa*, London, 1940, pp. 48–50.
7. Cf. Knowles, *op. cit.*, pp. viii and 182–201.

be produced by fairly simple methods involving no radical departure from the traditional techniques of production employed in subsistence agriculture.[8]

Thus instead of a process of economic growth based on continuous improvements in skills, more productive recombinations of factors and increasing returns, the nineteenth-century expansion of international trade in the underdeveloped countries seems to approximate to a simpler process based on constant returns and fairly rigid combinations of factors. Such a process of expansion could continue smoothly only if it could feed on *additional* supplies of factors in the required proportions.

II

Let us now turn to Smith's "vent-for-surplus" theory of international trade. It may be contrasted with the comparative-costs theory in two ways.

(*a*) The comparative-costs theory assumes that the resources of a country are given and fully employed before it enters into international trade. The function of trade is then to reallocate its given resources more efficiently between domestic and export production in the light of the new set of relative prices now open to the country. With given techniques and full employment, export production can be increased only at the cost of reducing the domestic production. In contrast, the "vent-for-surplus" theory assumes that a previously

8. Thus A. McPhee wrote about the palm-oil and ground-nut exports of West Africa: "They made little demand on the energy and thought of the natives and they effected no revolution in the society of West Africa. That was why they were so readily grafted on the old economy and grew as they did" (*The Economic Revolution in West Africa,* London, 1926, pp. 39–40). Some writers argue that there was a studied neglect of technical improvements in the peasant sector to facilitate the supply of cheap labour to other sectors. Cf., for example, W. A. Lewis, "Economic Development with Unlimited Supplies of Labour," *Manchester School,* May 1954, pp. 149–50. For a description of imperfect specialisation in economic activity in West Africa see P. T. Bauer and B. S. Yamey, "Economic Progress and Occupational Distribution," *Economic Journal,* December 1951, p. 743.

isolated country about to enter into international trade possesses a surplus productive capacity[9] of some sort or another. The function of trade here is not so much to reallocate the given resources as to provide the new effective demand for the output of the surplus resources which would have remained unused in the absence of trade. It follows that export production can be increased without necessarily reducing domestic production.

(b) The concept of a surplus productive capacity above the requirements of domestic consumption implies an inelastic domestic demand for the exportable commodity and/or a considerable degree of internal immobility and specificness of resources. In contrast, the comparative-costs theory assumes either a perfect or, at least, a much greater degree of internal mobility of factors and/or a greater degree of flexibility or elasticity both on the side of production and of consumption. Thus the resources not required for export production will not remain as a surplus productive capacity, but will be reabsorbed into domestic production, although this might take some time and entail a loss to the country.

These two points bring out clearly a peculiarity of the "vent-for-surplus" theory which may be used either as a free-trade argument or as an anti-trade argument, depending on the point of view adopted. (a) From the point of view of a previously isolated country, about to enter into trade, a surplus productive capacity suitable for the export market appears as a virtually "costless" means of acquiring imports and expanding domestic economic activity. This was how Adam Smith used it as a free-trade argument. (b) From the point of view of an established trading country faced with a fluctuating world market, a sizeable surplus productive capacity which cannot be easily switched from export to domestic production makes it "vulnerable" to external economic disturbances. This is in fact how the present-day writers on the underdeveloped countries use the same situation depicted by Smith's theory as a criticism of the nineteenth-century pattern of international trade. This concept

9. A surplus over domestic requirements and *not* a surplus of exports over imports.

of vulnerability may be distinguished from that which we have come across in discussing the "productivity" theory of trade. There, a country is considered "vulnerable" because it has adapted and reshaped its productive structure to meet the requirements of the export market through a genuine process of "specialisation." Here, the country is considered "vulnerable" simply because it happens to possess a sizeable surplus productive capacity which (even without any improvements and extensions) it cannot use for domestic production. This distinction may be blurred in border-line cases, particularly in underdeveloped countries with a large mining sector. But we hope to show that, on the whole, while the "vulnerability" of the advanced countries, such as those in Western Europe which have succeeded in building up large export trades to maintain their large populations, is of the first kind, the "vulnerability" of most of the underdeveloped countries is of the second kind.

Let us now consider the "vent-for-surplus" approach purely as a theoretical tool. There is a considerable amount of prejudice among economists against the "vent-for-surplus" theory, partly because of its technical crudeness and partly because of its mercantilist associations. This may be traced to J. S. Mill, who regarded Smith's "vent-for-surplus" doctrine as "a surviving relic of the Mercantile Theory" (*Principles,* p. 579).

The crux of the matter here is the question: why should a country isolated from international trade have a surplus productive capacity? The answer which suggests itself is that, given its random combination of natural resources, techniques of production, tastes and population, such an isolated country is bound to suffer from a certain imbalance or disproportion between its productive and consumption capacities. Thus, take the case of a country which starts with a sparse population in relation to its natural resources. This was broadly true not only of Western countries during their mercantilist period but also of the underdeveloped countries of South-East Asia, Latin America and Africa when they were opened up to international trade in the nineteenth century. Given this situation, the conventional international-trade theory (in its Ohlin version) would say that this initial disproportion between land and labour would have been equilibrated away by appropriate price adjustments: *i.e.,* rents would be low and relatively land-using commodities would have low prices, whereas wages would be high and relatively labour-using commodities would have high prices. In equilibrium there would be no surplus productive capacity (although there might be surplus land by itself) because the scarce factor, labour, would have been fully employed. Thus when this country enters into international trade it can produce the exports only by drawing labour away from domestic production. Now this result is obtained only by introducing a highly developed price mechanism and economic organisation into a country which is supposed to have had no previous economic contacts with the outside world. This procedure may be instructive while dealing with the isolated economy as a theoretical model. But it is misleading when we are dealing with genuinely isolated economies in their proper historical setting; it is misleading, in particular, when we are dealing with the underdeveloped countries, many of which were subsistence economies when they were opened to international trade. In fact, it was the growth of international trade itself which introduced or extended the money economy in these countries. Given the genuine historical setting of an isolated economy, might not its initial disproportion between its resources, techniques, tastes and population show itself in the form of surplus productive capacity?

Adam Smith himself thought that the pre-existence of a surplus productive capacity in an isolated economy was such a matter of common observation that he assumed it implicitly without elaborating upon it. But he did give some hints suggesting how the "narrowness of the home market," which causes the surplus capacity, is bound up with the underdeveloped economic organisation of an isolated country, particularly the lack of a good internal transport system and of suitable investment opportunities.[10] Further his con-

10. Adam Smith, *op. cit.,* Vol. I, pp. 21 and 383. This is similar to what Mrs. J. Robinson has described as "primitive stagnation." Cf. *The Accumulation of Capital,* London, 1956, pp. 256–58.

cept of surplus productive capacity is not merely a matter of surplus land by itself but surplus land combined with surplus labour; and the surplus labour is then linked up with his concept of "unproductive" labour. To avoid confusion, this latter should not be identified with the modern concept of "disguised unemployment" caused by an acute shortage of land in overpopulated countries. Although Smith described some cases of genuine "disguised unemployment" in the modern sense, particularly with reference to China, "unproductive" labour in his sense can arise even in thinly populated countries, provided their internal economic organisation is sufficiently under-developed. In fact, it is especially in relation to those underdevel-oped countries which started off with sparse populations in relation to their natural resources that we shall find Smith's "vent-for-surplus" approach very illuminating.

III

Let us now try to relate the "vent-for-surplus" theory to the nine-teenth-century process of expansion of international trade to the underdeveloped countries. Even from the somewhat meagre histori-cal information about these countries, two broad features stand out very clearly. First the underdeveloped countries of South-East Asia, Latin America and Africa, which were to develop into important export economies, started off with sparse populations relative to their natural resources. If North America and Australia could then be described as "empty," these countries were at least "semi-empty." Secondly, once the opening-up process had got into its stride, the export production of these countries expanded very rapidly, along a typical growth curve,[11] rising very sharply to begin with and taper-

11. For instance, the annual value of Burma's exports, taking years of high and low prices, increased at a constant proportional rate of 5 per cent per annum on the average between 1870 and 1900. Similar rates of ex-pansion can be observed for Siam and Indonesia (Cf. J. S. Furnivall, *Colonial Policy and Practice,* Cambridge, Eng., 1948, Appendix I; J. H. Boeke, *The Structure of Netherlands Indian Economy,* New York, 1942, p. 184; and J. C. Ingram, *Economic Change in Thailand since 1850,* Stanford,

ing off afterwards. By the Great Depression of the 1930s, the expansion process seems to have come to a stop in many countries; in others, which had a later start, the expansion process may still be continuing after the Second World War.

There are three reasons why the "vent-for-surplus" theory offers a more effective approach than the conventional theory to this type of expansion of international trade in the underdeveloped countries.

(1) The characteristically high rates of expansion which can be observed in the export production of many underdeveloped countries cannot really be explained in terms of the comparative-costs theory based on the assumption of given resources and given techniques. Nor can we attribute any significant part of the expansion to revolutionary changes in techniques and increases in productivity. As we have seen in Section I, peasant export production expanded by extension of cultivation using traditional methods of production, while mining and plantation sectors expanded on the basis of increasing supplies of cheap labour with a minimum of capital outlay. Thus the contributions of Western enterprise to the expansion process are mainly to be found in two spheres: the improvements of transport and communications[12] and the discoveries of new mineral resources. Both are methods of increasing the total volume of resources rather than methods of making the given volume of resources more productive. All these factors suggest an expansion process which kept itself going by drawing an increasing volume of hitherto unused or surplus resources into export production.

(2) International trade between the tropical underdeveloped countries and the advanced countries of the temperate zone has grown out of sharp differences in geography and climate resulting in absolute differences of costs. In this context, the older comparative-costs theory, which is usually formulated in terms of qualitative

1955, Appendix C). African export economies started their expansion phase after 1900, and the official trade returns of the Gold Coast, Nigeria and Uganda show similar rates of increase after that date, although the expansion process was arrested by the depression of the 1930s.
12. This is what Professor L. C. A. Knowles described as the "Unlocking of the Tropics" (*op. cit.,* pp. 138–52).

differences[13] in the resources of the trading countries, tends to stress the obvious geographical differences to the neglect of the more interesting quantitative differences in the factor endowments of countries possessing approximately the same type of climate and geography. Thus while it is true enough to say that Burma is an exporter of rice because of her climate and geography, the more interesting question is why Burma should develop into a major rice exporter while the neighbouring South India, with approximately the same type of climate and geography, should develop into a net importer of rice. Here the "vent-for-surplus" approach which directs our attention to population density as a major determinant of export capacity has an advantage over the conventional theory.[14]

(3) Granted the importance of quantitative differences in factor endowments, there still remains the question why Smith's cruder "vent-for-surplus" approach should be preferable to the modern Ohlin variant of the comparative-costs theory. The main reason is that, according to the Ohlin theory, a country about to enter into international trade is supposed already to possess a highly developed and flexible economic system which can adjust its methods of production and factor combinations to cope with a wide range of possible variations in relative factor supplies (see Section II above). But in fact the economic framework of the underdeveloped countries is a much cruder apparatus which can make only rough-and-ready adjustments. In particular, with their meagre technical and capital resources, the underdeveloped countries operate under conditions

13. Cf. J. Viner, *International Trade and Economic Development*, pp. 14–16.
14. Those who are used to handling the problem in terms of qualitative differences in factors and differential rent may ask: why not treat the surplus productive capacity as an extreme instance of "differential rent" where the transfer cost of the factors from the domestic to export production is zero? But this does not accurately portray the situation here. The transfer cost of the factors is zero, not because land which is used for the export crop is not at all usable for domestic subsistence production but because with the sparse population in the early phase there is no demand for the surplus food which could have been produced on the land used for the export crop. As we shall see, at a later stage when population pressure begins to grow, as in Java, land which has been used for export is encroached upon by subsistence production.

nearer to those of fixed technical coefficients than of variable technical coefficients. Nor can they make important adjustments through changes in the outputs of different commodities requiring different proportions of factors because of the inelastic demand both for their domestic production, mainly consisting of basic foodstuff, and for their exportable commodities, mainly consisting of industrial raw materials. Here again the cruder "vent-for-surplus" approach turns out to be more suitable.

Our argument that, in general, the "vent-for-surplus" theory provides a more effective approach than the comparative-costs theory to the international trade of the underdeveloped countries does not mean that the "vent-for-surplus" theory will provide an exact fit to all the particular patterns of development in different types of export economies. No simple theoretical approach can be expected to do this. Thus if we interpret the concept of the surplus productive capacity strictly as pre-existing surplus productive capacity arising out of the original endowments of the factors, it needs to be qualified, especially in relation to the mining and plantation sectors of the underdeveloped countries. Here the surplus productive capacity which may have existed to some extent before the country was opened to international trade is usually greatly increased by the discovery of new mineral resources and by a considerable inflow of foreign capital and immigrant labour. While immigrant labour is the surplus population of other underdeveloped countries, notably India and China, the term "surplus" in the strict sense cannot be applied to foreign capital. But, of course, the existence of suitable surplus natural resources in an underdeveloped country is a precondition of attracting foreign investment into it. Two points may be noted here. First, the complication of foreign investment is not as damaging to the surplus-productive-capacity approach as it appears at first sight, because inflow of foreign investment into the tropical and semi-tropical underdeveloped countries has been relatively small both in the nineteenth century and the inter-war period.[15]

15. Cf. R. Nurkse, "International Investment To-day in the Light of Nineteenth Century Experience," *Economic Journal,* December 1954, pp.

Second, the nineteenth-century phenomenon of international mobility of capital and labour has been largely neglected by the comparative-costs theory, which is based on the assumption of perfect mobility of factors within a country and their imperfect mobility between different countries. The surplus-productive-capacity approach at least serves to remind us that the output of mining and plantation sectors can expand without necessarily contracting domestic subsistence output.

The use of the surplus-productive-capacity approach may prove in particular to be extremely treacherous in relation to certain parts of Africa, where mines, plantations and other European enterprises have taken away from the tribal economies the so-called "surplus" land and labour, which, on a closer analysis, prove to be no surplus at all. Here the extraction of these so-called "surplus" resources, by various forcible methods in which normal economic incentives play only a part, entails not merely a reduction in the subsistence output but also much heavier social costs in the form of the disruption of the tribal societies.[16]

When we turn to the peasant export sectors, however, the application of the "vent-for-surplus" theory is fairly straightforward. Here, unlike the mining and plantation sectors, there has not been a significant inflow of foreign investment and immigrant labour. The main function of the foreign export–import firms has been to act as middlemen between the world market and the peasants, and perhaps also to stimulate the peasants' wants for the new imported consumers' goods. As we have seen, peasant export production expanded by using methods of production more or less on the same technical level as those employed in the traditional subsistence culture. Thus the main effect of the innovations, such as improvements in transport and communications[17] and the introduction of the new

---

744–58, and the United Nations Report on *International Capital Movements during the Inter-war Period.*

16. Cf. The United Nations Report on the *Enlargement of the Exchange Economy in Tropical Africa,* New York, 1954, pp. 37 and 49–51.

17. It may be noted that the expansion of some peasant export crops, notably rice in South-East Asia, depended to a much greater extent on

crops, was to bring a greater area of surplus land under cultivation rather than to raise the physical productivity per unit of land and labour. Yet peasant export production usually managed to expand as rapidly as that of the other sectors while remaining self-sufficient with respect to basic food crops. Here, then, we have a fairly close approximation to the concept of a pre-existing surplus productive capacity which can be tapped by the world-market demand with a minimum addition of external resources.

Even here, of course, there is room for differences in interpretation. For instance, there is evidence to suggest that, in the early decades of expansion, the rates of increase in peasant export production in South-East Asian and West African countries were well above the possible rates of growth in their working population.[18] Given the conditions of constant techniques, no significant inflow of immigrant foreign labour and continuing self-sufficiency with respect to the basic food crops, we are left with the question how these peasant economies managed to obtain the extra labour required to expand their export production so rapidly. A part of this labour may have been released by the decline in cottage industries and by the introduction of modern labour-saving forms of transport in place of porterage, but the gap in the explanation cannot be satisfactorily filled until we postulate that even those peasant economies which started off with abundant land relative to their population must have had initially a considerable amount of underemployed or

------

pre-existing indigenous transport facilities, such as river boats and bullock carts, than is generally realised.

18. For instance, cocoa output of the Gold Coast expanded over forty times during the twenty-five year period 1905–30. Even higher rates of expansion in cocoa production can be observed in Nigeria combined with a considerable expansion in the output of other export crops. Both have managed to remain self-sufficient with regard to basic food crops (cf. West African Institute of Economic Research, *Annual Conference*, Economic Section, Achimota, 1953, especially the chart between pp. 96 and 98; *The Native Economies of Nigeria*, ed. M. Perham, Vol. I, Part II). In Lower Burma, for the thirty-year period 1870–1900, the area under rice cultivation increased by more than three times, while the population, including immigrants from Upper Burma, doubled. (Cf. also Furnivall, *op. cit.*, pp. 84–85.)

surplus labour. This surplus labour existed, not because of a short-age of co-operating factors, but because in the subsistence econo-mies, with poor transport and little specialisation in production, each self-sufficient economic unit could not find any market outlet to dispose of its potential surplus output, and had therefore no incentive to produce more than its own requirements. Here, then, we have the archetypal form of Smith's "unproductive" labour locked up in a semi-idle state in the underdeveloped economy of a country iso-lated from outside economic contacts. In most peasant economies this surplus labour was mobilised, however, not by the spread of the money-wage system of employment, but by peasant economic units with their complement of "family" labour moving *en bloc* into the money economy and export production.

The need to postulate a surplus productive capacity to explain the rapid expansion in peasant export production is further strength-ened when we reflect on the implications of the fact that this expan-sion process is inextricably bound up with the introduction of the money economy into the subsistence sectors. To the peasant on the threshold of international trade, the question whether or not to take up export production was not merely a question of growing a different type of crop but a far-reaching decision to step into the new and unfamiliar ways of the money economy.

Thus let us consider a community of self-sufficient peasants who, with their existing techniques, have just sufficient land and labour to produce their minimum subsistence requirements, so that any export production can be achieved only by reducing the subsistence output below the minimum level. Now, according to the conven-tional economic theory, there is no reason why these peasants should not turn to export production if they have a differential advantage there, so that they could more than make up for their food deficit by purchases out of their cash income from the export crop. But, in practice, the peasants in this situation are unlikely to turn to export production so readily. Nor is this "conservatism" entirely irrational, for by taking up export production on such a slender margin of reserves, the peasants would be facing the risk of a possible food shortage for the sake of some gain in the form of imported consumers' goods which are "luxuries" to them. Moreover, this gain might be wiped off by unfavourable changes in the prices of both the export crop they would sell and the foodstuffs they would have to buy and by the market imperfections, which would be considerable at this early stage. Thus, where the margin of resources is very small above that required for the minimum subsistence output, we should expect the spread of export production to be inhibited or very slow, even if there were some genuine possibilities of gains on the comparative costs principle.[19]

In contrast, the transition from subsistence agriculture to export production is made much easier when we assume that our peasants start with some surplus resources which enable them to produce the export crop *in addition* to their subsistence production. Here the surplus resources perform two functions: first they enable the peasants to hedge their position completely and secure their subsistence minimum before entering into the risks of trading; and secondly, they enable them to look upon the imported goods they obtain from trade in the nature of a clear net gain obtainable merely for the effort of the extra labour in growing the export crop. Both of these considerations are important in giving the peasants just that extra push to facilitate their first plunge into the money economy.

Starting from this first group of peasants, we may picture the growth of export production and the money economy taking place in two ways. Firstly, the money economy may grow extensively, with improvements in transport and communications and law and order, bringing in more and more groups of peasants with their

19. Of course, this argument can be countered by assuming the differences in comparative costs to be very wide. But, so long as export production requires withdrawing some resources from subsistence production, some risks are unavoidable. Further, remembering that the middlemen also require high profit margins at this stage, the gains large enough to overcome the obstacles are likely to arise out of surplus resources rather than from the differential advantages of the given fully employed resources. The risk of crop-failure is, of course, present both in subsistence and export production.

complements of family labour into export production on the same "part-time" basis as the first group of peasants. Secondly, the money economy may grow intensively by turning the first group of peasants from "part-time" into "whole-time" producers of the export crop.[20] In the first case, surplus resources are necessary as a lubricant to push more peasants into export production at each round of the widening circle of the money economy. Even in the second case, surplus resources are necessary if the whole-time export producers buy their food requirements locally from other peasants, who must then have surplus resources to produce the food crops above their own requirements. Logically, there is no reason why the first group of peasants who are now whole-time producers of the export crop should buy their food requirements locally instead of importing them. But, as it happens, few peasant export economies have specialised in export production to such an extent as to import their basic food requirements.

The average economist's reaction to our picture of discrete blocks of surplus productive capacity being drawn into a widening circle of money economy and international trade is to say that while this "crude" analysis may be good enough for the transition phase, the conventional analysis in terms of differential advantages and continuous marginal productivity curves must come into its own once the transition phase is over. Here it is necessary to distinguish

20. In either case the expansion process may be looked upon as proceeding under conditions approximating to constant techniques and fixed combinations between land and labour once equilibrium is reached. The distinctive feature of peasant export economies is their failure to develop new and larger-scale or extensive methods of farming. It is true that in subsistence agriculture "fixed factors," such as a plough and a pair of bullocks, were frequently used below capacity, and one important effect of cash production was to increase the size of the holding to the full capacity of these "fixed factors." But this may be properly looked upon as equilibrium adjustments to make full use of surplus capacity rather than as the adoption of new and more land-using methods of production. Increasing the size of holding to make a more effective use of a pair of bullocks is different from the introduction of a tractor! Our assumption of constant techniques does not preclude the development of large-scale ownership of land as distinct from large-scale farming.

between the expansion phase and the transition phase. It is true that in most peasant export economies the expansion process is tapering off or has come to a stop, as most of the surplus land suitable for the export crop has been brought under cultivation. This, of course, brings back the problem of allocating a fixed amount of resources, as we shall see in the next section when we consider issues of economic policy. But even so, the surplus-productive-capacity approach is not entirely superseded so long as the transition from a subsistence to a fully developed money economy remains incomplete. In most underdeveloped countries of Asia and Africa[21] this transition seems not likely to be over until they cease to be underdeveloped.

The continuing relevance of the surplus-productive-capacity approach may be most clearly seen in the typical case of a peasant export economy which with its natural resources and methods of production has reached the limit of expansion in production while its population continues to grow rapidly. According to the surplus-productive-capacity approach, we should expect the export capacity of such a country to fall roughly in proportion as the domestic requirement of resources to feed a larger population increases. This common-sense result may, however, be contrasted with that obtainable from the conventional theory as formulated by Ohlin. First, it appears that the Ohlin theory puts to the forefront of the picture the *type* of export, *i.e.,* whether it is more labour-using or land-using as distinct from the total export capacity measured by the ratio of total exports to the total national output of the trading country. Secondly, in the Ohlin theory there is no reason why a thickly populated country should not also possess a high ratio of (labour-intensive) exports to its total output.

The ideal pattern of trade suggested by the Ohlin theory has a real counterpart in the thickly populated advanced countries of Europe, which for that very reason are obliged to build up a large export

21. Cf. the United Nations Report cited above on the *Enlargement of the Exchange Economy.* Even in the most developed peasant export economies the money economy has not spread to the same extent in the market for factors of production as in the market for products.

trade in manufactures or even in agriculture as in the case of Holland.
But when we turn to the thickly populated underdeveloped countries,
however, the ideal and the actual patterns of international trade
diverge widely from each other. Indeed, we may say that these
countries remain underdeveloped precisely because they have not
succeeded in building up a labour-intensive export trade to cope with
their growing population. The ratio of their export to total production could, of course, be maintained at the same level and the pressure of population met in some other way. But given the existing
conditions, even this neutral pattern may not be possible in many
underdeveloped countries. Thus, in Indonesia there is some evidence
to suggest that the volume of agricultural exports from the thickly
populated Java and Madura is declining absolutely and also relatively
to those of the Outer Islands, which are still sparsely populated.[22]
Of course, there are other causes of this decline, but population
pressure reducing the surplus productive capacity of Java seems to
be a fundamental economic factor; and the decline spreads from
peasant to plantation exports as more of the plantation lands, which
were under sugar and rubber, are encroached upon by the peasants
for subsistence production.[23] In general, given the social and economic conditions prevailing in many underdeveloped countries, it

22. Cf. J. H. Boeke, *Ontwikkelingsgang en toekomst van bevolkings-en
ondernemingslandbouw in Nederlandsch-Indie* (Leiden, 1948). p. 91. I owe
this reference to an unpublished thesis by Mr. M. Kidron.
23. The same tendency to transfer land from plantation to subsistence
agriculture may be observed in Fiji with the growing population pressure
created by the Indian immigrant labour originally introduced to work in the
sugar plantations. The outline is blurred here by the decline in the sugar
industry. The reason why this tendency does not seem to operate in the
West Indies is complex. But it may be partly attributable to the tourist
industry, which helps to pay for the food imports of some of the islands.
24. The surplus-productive-capacity approach also partly helps to explain
why underdeveloped countries, such as India, which started off with a
thick population tend to retain large and persistent pockets of subsistence
sectors in spite of their longer contacts with the world economy, while the
subsistence sectors in thinly populated countries, such as those in West
Africa, tend to disappear at a faster rate in spite of their much later start
in international trade.

seems fair to conclude that the trend in their export trade is likely to be nearer to that suggested by the surplus-productive-capacity approach than to that suggested by the theory of comparative costs.[24]

IV

This paper is mainly concerned with interpretation and analysis, but we may round off our argument by touching briefly upon some of its policy implications.

(1) We have seen that the effect of population pressure on many underdeveloped countries, given their existing social and economic organisation, is likely to reduce their export capacity by diverting natural resources from export to subsistence production. If we assume that these natural resources have a genuine differential advantage in export production, then population pressure inflicts a double loss: first, through simple diminishing returns, and secondly, by diverting resources from more to less productive use. Thus, if Java has a genuine differential advantage in growing rubber and sugar, she would obtain a greater amount of rice by maintaining her plantation estates instead of allowing them to be encroached upon by peasants for subsistence rice cultivation. The orthodox liberal economists, confronted with this situation, would, of course, strongly urge the removal of artificial obstacles to a more systematic development of the money economy and the price system. Now there are still many underdeveloped countries which are suffering acutely from the economic rigidities arising out of their traditional social structure and/or from discriminatory policies based on differences in race, religion and class. Here the removal of barriers, for instance, to the horizontal and vertical mobility of labour, freedom to own land and to enter any occupation, etc., may well prove to be a great liberating force.[25] But our analysis has suggested that it is much easier to

25. This is why the case for the "liberal" solution is strong in places such as East and Central Africa, where due both to the general backwardness of the indigenous population and the presence of a white settler population, both types of rigidity prevail (cf. *The Royal Commission Report on East Africa*).

promote the growth of the money economy in the early stage when a country is newly opened up to international trade and still has plenty of surplus land and labour rather than at a later stage, when there are no more surplus resources, particularly land, to feed the growth of the money economy. Thus in a country like Java there is a considerable amount of artificial restriction, customary or newly introduced, which the liberal economists can criticise, *e.g.,* restriction on land ownership. But given the combination of population pressure, large pockets of subsistence economy and traditional methods of production which can no longer be made more labour-intensive, it seems very doubtful whether the mere removal of artificial restrictions can do much by itself without a more vigorous policy of state interference. The truth of the matter is that in the underdeveloped countries where, for various reasons described above, the exchange economy is still an extremely crude and imperfect apparatus which can make only rough-and-ready responses to economic differentials, it may require a considerable amount of state interference to move toward the comparative-costs equilibrium. Thus given that Java has genuine differential advantages in the production of rubber and sugar, a more optimal reallocation of her resources may require, for instance, the removal of her surplus population either to the thinly populated Outer Islands or to industries within Java and a vigorous export-drive policy supplemented by bulk purchase and subsidies on the imported rice. Here we come to a fundamental dilemma which is particularly acute for the orthodox liberal economists. On a closer examination it turns out that their free-trade argument, although ostensibly based on the comparative-costs principle, is buttressed by certain broad classical presumptions against protection and state interference:[26] *e.g.,* the difficulty of selecting the right industry to protect, the virtual impossibility of withdrawing protection once given, the tendency of controls to spread promiscuously throughout the economic system strangling growth, and so on. These presump-

26. Cf. J. Viner, *International Trade and Economic Development,* Oxford, 1953, pp. 41–42. See also Sidgwick, *Principles of Political Economy,* London, 1924, Book III, Chapter V.

tions gain an added strength from the well-known administrative inefficiency and sometimes corruption of the governments of some underdeveloped countries. Thus even if we believe in the "nineteenth-century pattern" of international trade based on natural advantages, how can we be sure that the state is competent enough to select the right commodities for its export-drive policy when it is considered incompetent to select the right industry for protection?

(2) We have seen that the rapid expansion in the export production of the underdeveloped countries in the nineteenth century cannot be satisfactorily explained without postulating that these countries started off with a considerable amount of surplus productive capacity consisting both of unused natural resources and underemployed labour. This gives us a common-sense argument for free trade which is especially relevant for the underdeveloped countries in the nineteenth century: the surplus productive capacity provided these countries with a virtually "costless" means of acquiring imports which did not require a withdrawal of resources from domestic production but merely a fuller employment for their semi-idle labour. Of course, one may point to the real cost incurred by the indigenous peoples in the form of extra effort and sacrifice of the traditional leisurely life[27] and also to the various social costs not normally considered in the comparative-costs theory, such as being sometimes subject to the pressure of taxation and even compulsory labour and frequently of having to accommodate a considerable inflow of immigrant labour creating difficult social and political problems later on. One may also point to a different type of cost which arises with the wasteful exploitation of natural resources.[28]

---

27. It may be formally possible to subsume the surplus-productive-capacity approach under the opportunity-cost theory, by treating leisure instead of foregone output as the main element of cost. But this would obscure the important fact that the underdeveloped countries have been able to expand their production very rapidly, not merely because the indigenous peoples were willing to sacrifice leisure but also because there were also surplus natural resources to work upon.

28. The social cost of soil erosion can be very great, but this may be caused not merely by an expansion of export production but also by bad methods of

But for the most part it is still true to say that the indigenous peoples of the underdeveloped countries took to export production on a voluntary basis and enjoyed a clear gain by being able to satisfy their developing wants for the new imported commodities. Thus our special argument for free trade in this particular context still remains largely intact. The orthodox economists, by rigidly insisting on applying the comparative-costs theory to the underdeveloped countries in the nineteenth century, have therefore missed this simpler and more powerful argument.

(3) We have seen in Section I that the deep-rooted hostility of the critics towards the "classical theory" and the nineteenth-century pattern of international trade may be partly traced back to the time when Western colonial powers attempted to introduce export-drive policies in the tropical underdeveloped countries; and tried to justify these policies by invoking the "classical theory" of free trade and the Adam Smithian doctrine of international trade as a dynamic force generating a great upward surge in the general level of productivity of the trading countries. To the critics, this appears as a thinly disguised rationalisation of the advanced countries' desire for the markets for their manufactured products and for raw materials. Thus it has become a standard argument with the critics to say that the nineteenth-century process of international trade has introduced a large "export bias" into the economic structure of the underdeveloped countries which has increased their "vulnerability" to international economic fluctuations.

In Section II we have seen that once we leave the ideal world of the comparative costs theory in which the resources not required for the export market can be re-absorbed into domestic production, every country with a substantial export trade may be considered "vulnerable." Thus a country may be said to be vulnerable because

---

cultivation and population pressure. The problem of adequately compensating the underdeveloped countries for the exploitation of their non-replaceable mineral resources belongs to the problem of the distribution of gains from trade. Here we are merely concerned with establishing that the indigenous peoples do obtain some gains from trade.

it has built up a large ratio of export to its total production simply by making use of its pre-existing surplus productive capacity.
A fortiori, it is vulnerable when it has genuinely improved upon its
original surplus productive capacity. How does the idea of "export
bias" fit into our picture?

The term "export bias" presumably means that the resources of
the underdeveloped countries which could have been used for domestic production have been effectively diverted into export production
by deliberate policy. The implication of our surplus-productive-
capacity approach is to discount this notion of "export bias." In
the peasant export sectors, at the early stage with sparse populations
and plenty of surplus land, the real choice was not so much between
using the resources for export production or for domestic production
as between giving employment to the surplus resources in export
production or leaving them idle. In the later stage, when the population pressure begins to increase as in the case of Java, we have seen
that the bias is likely to develop against, rather than in favour of,
the export sector. Even when we turn to the mining and plantation
sectors, it is difficult to establish a significant "export bias" in the
strict sense. Here the crucial question is: how far would it have been
possible to divert the foreign capital and technical resources which
have gone into these sectors into the domestic sector? The answer
is clear. For a variety of reasons, notably the smallness of domestic
markets, few governments of the underdeveloped countries, whether
colonial or independent, have so far succeeded in attracting a significant amount of foreign investment away from the extractive export
industries to the domestic industries. In criticising the colonial
governments it should be remembered that the only choice open to
them was whether to attract a greater or a smaller amount of foreign
investment within the export sector and not whether to attract investment for the domestic or the export sector.

This is not to deny that the colonial governments had a strong
motive for promoting export production. Apart from the interests
of the mother country, the individual colonial governments themselves had a vested interest in the expansion of foreign trade because

they derived the bulk of their revenues from it.[29] In their search
for revenue they have pursued various policies designed to attract
foreign investment to the mining and plantation sectors, such as
granting favourable concessions and leases, favourable tariff rates
for rail transport, taxation policy designed to facilitate the supply of
labour, provision of various technical services, etc.[30] But on the
whole it is still true to say that the most important contribution of
the colonial governments towards the expansion of the colonial
exports is to be found, not in these export-drive policies, but in
their basic services, such as the establishment of law and order and
the introduction of modern transport, which enabled the pre-existing
surplus productive capacity of the colonies to be tapped by the
world market demand. If we wish to criticise the export-drive
policies of the colonial governments it would be more appropriate
to do so, not on the ground of "export bias" but on the ground that
they may have diverted too great a share of the gains from international trade and of the public services of the colonies to the
foreign-owned mines and plantations at the expense of indigenous
labour and peasant export producers.

It may be argued that we have given too strict an interpretation
of the "export-bias" doctrine which is merely meant to convey the
general proposition that, whatever the exact cause, the nineteenth-
century process of international trade has landed many underdeveloped countries with a large ratio of raw materials exports to their
total national products, making it desirable to reduce their "vulnerability" to international economic fluctuations. But the trouble is
that the "export bias" doctrine tends to suggest that the raw-materials
export production of the underdeveloped countries has been artificially over-expanded, not merely in relation to their domestic
sector, but absolutely. Given the strong feelings of economic nation-

29. This is true for the governments of most underdeveloped countries,
whether colonial or independent, past or present.
30. For a discussion of the question of the possible export bias through the
operation of the 100 per cent sterling exchange system of the colonies, see
A. D. Hazlewood, "Economics of Colonial Monetary Arrangements,"
Social and Economic Studies, Jamaica, December 1954.

alism and anti-colonialism in the underdeveloped countries, this can be a very mischievous doctrine strengthening the widespread belief that to go on producing raw materials for the export market is tantamount to preserving the "colonial" pattern of trade. Thus already many underdeveloped countries are giving too little encouragement to their peasant export sectors by diverting too much of their capital and technical resources to industrial-development projects, and are also crippling their mining and plantation export sectors by actual or threatened nationalisation and various restrictions and regulations. The effect is to reduce their foreign-exchange earnings so urgently needed for their economic development. Of course, no competent critic of the nineteenth-century pattern of international trade would ever suggest the drastic step of reducing exports absolutely; some would even concede the need for vigorous export drive policies.[31] But having built up a pervasive feeling of hostility and suspicion against the "nineteenth-century" or the "colonial" pattern of international trade, they are not in a position to ram home the obvious truths: (a) that, even on an optimistic estimate of the possibilities of international aid, the underdeveloped countries will have to pay for the larger part of the cost of their economic plans aiming either at a greater national self-sufficiency or at the export of manufactured goods; (b) that the necessary foreign exchange for these development plans can be earned by the underdeveloped countries at the present moment only by the export of raw materials (though not necessarily the same commodities for which they were supposed to have a differential advantage in the nineteenth century); and (c) that therefore to pursue their development plans successfully it is vitally important for them to carry out the "export-drive" policies, which in their technical properties may not be very different from those of the colonial governments in the past.[32] In trying to carry

31. Cf., for example, Gunnar Myrdal, *An International Economy,* p. 274.
32. Colonial governments have frequently defended their export-drive policies as the means of taxing foreign trade to finance services needed for internal development. But because they were colonial governments, their motives were suspect. At first sight we might imagine that the new

Infant Industry Arguments for Assistance
to Industries in the Setting of
Dynamic Trade Theory

The aim of this paper is to survey the protectionist arguments which
have been commonly put forward in relation to the economic development of the under-developed countries. I shall begin in Section
I with a brief account of the traditional "infant industry" and
kindred arguments for protection. In Sections II and III I shall
consider a number of more recent arguments for protection, first
on the cost side and next on the demand side of the question, which
claim to deal with the broader structural and dynamic problems of
economic development of the under-developed countries. In Section
IV I shall consider some of the difficulties of pursuing an effective
protectionist policy in the setting of the present-day under-developed
countries, which suggest a conflict, *at the practical level,* between
such a policy and the commonly adopted form of over-all economic
development planning involving an all-round restriction of imports.

I THE TRADITIONAL INFANT INDUSTRY ARGUMENT

The theory of comparative costs is a branch of welfare economics
and, in so far as the free trade argument is based on it, the logically
acceptable cases for protection may be regarded as the deviations

From R. F. Harrod and D. C. Hague, eds., *International Trade Theory in a
Developing World,* Macmillan and Co., Ltd., 1963, chapter 7. Reprinted
by permission of the publisher and the International Economic Association.

from the optimum due to a divergence between social and private costs. This is how free trade theorists like Professor Haberler would regard both the infant industry case and the related case of external economies and diseconomies which need not be associated with decreasing costs.

Social as well as private costs may be increasing, and the underlying situation may therefore be quite stable and still there may be a deviation between social and private costs due to external economies or diseconomies, i.e., due to certain cost-raising or cost-reducing factors which would come into play if one industry expanded and another industry contracted—factors which for some reason or other are not, or not sufficiently, allowed for in private cost calculations.[1]

Given a wide enough divergence between the two, private comparative costs may lead a country into a "wrong" pattern of international specialization, say exporting commodity *B* and importing commodity *A,* while the true social transformation ratio between the two commodities would require the opposite pattern with the given international price ratio. This can happen even if both *B* and *A* are working under conditions of increasing costs. Thus the "infant industry" argument, which further postulates that the neglected industry *A* may enjoy decreasing costs as its output expands, can therefore be regarded as a particular case (although a highly dramatic one) of the divergence between social and private costs.[2]

1. G. Haberler, " Some Problems in the Pure Theory of International Trade," *Economic Journal,* June 1950, pp. 236 *et seq.*
2. Diagrammatically, it is possible to have two variants of the "infant industry" argument. Firstly, we may depict increasing returns in industry *A* as in Figure 1, by a shift in the production possibility curve from *BA* to *BA₁* as the output of *A* is increased. This is the version adopted by Haberler (*loc. cit.* p. 239).

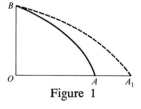

Figure 1

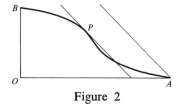

Figure 2

Having conceded the logical possibility of this divergence, the free trade theorists would, however, maintain that "as a rule the ratios of private money costs do reflect the true social real cost ratios," and that "the burden of proof is on those who maintain that the exceptions are numerous, persistent, large and, last but not least, practically recognizable and calculable."[3] They would also stress that in order to make a valid case for protecting an "infant industry" with potential decreasing costs, the following rather restrictive conditions have to be fulfilled. (a) The economies should be external to the firm: if they are internal to the firm output will be expanded automatically and there is no need of protection. (b) On the other hand, the economies should be internal to the industry. If the industry is not the true source of the economies but derives them from somewhere outside, then there is no case for protecting the particular industry in question. Professor Knight in his criticism of the Graham case expressed doubts concerning the existence of these economies which are external to the firm and internal to the industry and their compatibility with the assumption of competition.[4] Even Professor Viner, who would not go so far as to deny their existence, concluded that "the scope for the application of the argument is extremely limited."[5] Murray C. Kemp, in a recent review of the Mill-Bastable version of the "infant industry" argument making the "learning process" of new methods of produc-

---

Secondly, we may depict increasing returns in industry A on the same production possibility curve by a change in the curvature as in Figure 2. Here, if at a given international price ratio specialization takes place at point P, the country has not attained a full optimum position, because although the marginal conditions are fulfilled, what Professor Hicks described as "total conditions" are not fulfilled. Full optimum will be attained only by complete specialization at point A. This is Tinbergen's suggested version of the Graham argument (J. Tinbergen, International Economic Co-operation, Amsterdam, 1945, Appendix I).

3. Haberler, loc. cit. pp. 237–38.
4. F. H. Knight, "Some Fallacies in the Interpretation of Social Cost," Quarterly Journal of Economics, 1924.
5. J. Viner, Studies in the Theory of International Trade, London, 1937, pp. 478–79.

tion the essential cause of decreasing costs, also drew a parallel distinction between a firm learning internally from its own experience only and learning externally from the experiences of other firms and again stressed the special nature of the assumptions required to justify complete protection.[6]

If the free traders are lukewarm, the present-day protectionists are definitely cool towards the accepted version of the "infant industry" argument—but for different reasons. Their position is that all the notable protectionist writers from Hamilton, List to Manoilesco have meant their arguments to be applied to the industrially under-developed countries of their times; that, in tearing the protectionist argument from its original context and applying it to minor deviations from the static optimum on the basis of a very narrow concept of "infant industry," the orthodox economists have, not surprisingly, reduced it to the status of a theoretical curiosity; and that it is only when the protectionist argument is reconsidered in its proper setting of the present-day under-developed countries that it can be restored to its full stature having important applications to the broader structural and dynamic problems of the economic development of these countries.

II COST ASPECT OF CURRENT ARGUMENTS

We can most conveniently consider the current trend in protectionist theory in terms of two main groups of arguments for protection, both of which claim to have a much broader scope than the infant industry argument and both of which are closely related to the leading theories on the economic development of the under-developed countries.

On the cost side of the question, we have a revival of the "Manoilesco" type of argument for protection which has been stimulated by the widespread adoption of the concept of "disguised

6. M. C. Kemp, "The Mill-Bastable Infant Industry Dogma," *Journal of Political Economy*, Feb. 1960.

unemployment" among the writers on the under-developed countries. This argument accepts the basis of the static optimum analysis, but maintains that social and private costs will diverge significantly over large areas of the under-developed economies due to various market imperfections and structural rigidities, particularly those affecting the allocation of labour between rural and urban sectors.

The starting-point of the argument is the assumption that in the rural sectors of the under-developed countries there is a vast surplus of labourers whose marginal product in agriculture is zero, but who are maintained by their relatives at a subsistence level approximately equal to the average product of labour in agriculture. This labour cannot, however, be attracted to industry at this subsistence wage although this already exceeds its marginal product in agriculture. To overcome inertia and immobility, a considerable premium would have to be added to this subsistence wage before the rural surplus labour would become available to the urban industrial sector. Thus the private transfer wage of rural surplus labour to industrial employment far exceeds its true social opportunity cost which is determined by its marginal product in agriculture which is equal to zero. In formulating the argument, some writers stress the zero marginal product of the surplus labour in agriculture while others stress the observed gap between the industrial and agricultural wages which, they maintain, may be larger than can be accounted for in terms of "net advantages." In any case, the conclusion is that labour is systematically over-valued for the urban industrial sector and this should be corrected by protecting manufacturing industry.

(*a*) Professor W. A. Lewis has given a clear formulation of the first version of the argument based on the zero marginal product of labour.

We assume that two countries can produce the same things and trade with each other. *A* is the country where labour is scarce, *B* the country where unlimited supply of labour is available in the subsistence (food) sector. Using the classical framework for comparative costs, we write that one day's labour,

in *A*, produces 3 food or 3 cotton manufactures;
in *B*, produces 2 food or 1 cotton manufacture.

This, of course, gives the wrong answer to the question, "Who should specialize in which?" since we have written the average instead of the marginal products. We can assume that these coincide in *A* and also in cotton manufacture in *B*. Then we should write in marginal terms that one day's labour,

in *A*, produces 3 food or 3 cotton manufactures;
in *B*, produces 0 food or 1 cotton manufacture.

B should specialize in cotton manufacture and import food. In practice, however, wages will be 2 food in *B* and between 3 food and 6 food in *A*, at which levels it will be "cheaper" for *B* to export food and import cotton.[7]

Thus, to correct this difference between private money costs and true social marginal costs, *B* should protect its textile industry.

(*b*) There are many exponents of the second version of the argument stressing the gap between wages in agriculture and industry. In so far as this gap is explained in terms of rural surplus population,[8] this is not really very different from the first version. But it is also possible to formulate the argument on the basis of an empirically observed gap between agricultural and industrial wages which may or may not be due to rural over-population. Professor E. E. Hagen has recently put forward an interesting variant of this, which seems to be based simply on

the empirically observed fact that in any economy in which *per capita* income is rising secularly, the output of manufacturing and mining grows secularly relative to agriculture. . . . As a result of this secular trend, except in the unreal case of perfect geographic and occupational mobility of labour, wages in manufacturing industry must be higher than in agriculture. This is true even in the long run and even assuming complete absence of monopoly in all markets. . . . As a result of this wage disparity, manufacturing industry having a real comparative advantage will be undersold by imports when foreign exchanges are in

7. W. A. Lewis, "Economic Development with Unlimited Supplies of Labour," *Manchester School,* May 1954, p. 185.
8. Cf. for example G. Myrdal, *An International Economy,* London, 1956, pp. 277–78.

equilibrium. Protection which permits such industry to exist will increase real income in the economy.[9]

In appraising this "Manoilesco" type of argument, we may start with a number of qualifications which reduce its range of application. Firstly, in so far as it is based on the concept of rural surplus population, it will not be applicable to the thinly populated under-developed countries such as those in Latin America, South-east Asia and West Africa. It is necessary to point this out, partly because of the frequent assumption that surplus labour exists in *all* under-developed countries[10] and partly because these thinly populated under-developed countries, many of which are "export economies," are themselves very anxious to protect their manufacturing industries to reduce the ratio of their primary exports to national income. In these thinly populated countries, there may be a considerable degree of urban exploitation of the agricultural sector due to the widespread pattern of using the proceeds from Government Marketing Boards and taxation on primary exports to subsidize industry.[11] Secondly, even in the thickly populated under-developed countries, quantitative estimates of the extent of the "surplus" population are by no means reliable and may be frequently subject to considerable exaggeration,[12] and the observed gap between agricultural and urban wages may be in part due to rational considerations and "net advantages"[13] which have not been fully taken into account.

Next, let us accept that there is a genuine over-valuation of labour for the manufacturing sector due to surplus population, or to Professor Hagen's growth mechanism or to any other cause. How-

9. E. E. Hagen, "An Economic Justification for Protection." *Quarterly Journal of Economics*, 1958, pp. 497–98.

10. E.g. Myrdal, *op. cit*. p. 278.

11. See Viner's trenchant remarks on the urban exploitation of the rural sectors in such countries, *International Trade and Economic Development,* Oxford, 1953, p. 51.

12. Cf. Doreen Warriner, *Land Reform and Economic Development,* Cairo, 1955, pp. 25–26.

13. Viner, *op. cit*. pp. 47–49.

ever, this by itself does not provide a conclusive argument for protection. Labour is merely one of the factors of production and in particular it is widely recognized that rates of interest are much higher and capital is more "over-valued" in the rural sectors of the under-developed countries than in the urban industrial sectors. Thus the question whether manufacturing costs as a whole are over-valued relatively to agricultural costs will depend on the relative capital-labour ratios in the two sectors and the relative sizes of the wage and the interest gaps. The effects in the opposite direction of the higher rate of interest in the rural sector and the higher capital-labour ratio in the urban industrial sector (not to speak of other advantages such as better transport and public utility services) may more than counterbalance the handicap which the latter may suffer due to "over-valued" labour. In so far as the champions of the under-developed countries recognize these opposite effects, their remedy would seem to be to recommend both protection for the industrial sector and cheaper loans for the rural sector, thus having the best of both worlds, but adding to the pressure of inflation and rising prices which these countries are already suffering.[14]

Finally, we may question how far the complex historical and dynamic factors which enter into the movement of labour from the subsistence agricultural sector to the urban industrial sector can be satisfactorily analysed in terms of a rather simplified static analysis. First, it is not realistic at all to speak of the two types of labour in the two sectors as though they were a homogeneous factor, when complex changes involving the way of life, attitudes, rhythm of work, etc., have to take place before an agricultural worker from the traditional rural society can become even an unskilled worker in an urban industrial sector.[15] Next we may refer to the only large-scale

14. It is sometimes alleged that, even in the urban industrial sectors, it is only the *foreign* entrepreneurs who enjoy cheap credit facilities from the banks, while indigenous entrepreneurs have to pay higher rates of interest. Whatever the truth of this allegation, it does not affect the point that even an indigenous industrial entrepreneur is likely to be able to borrow at a lower rate of interest than the indigenous peasant.

15. This is not to deny the possibility or desirability of training rural labour

historical experience which the tropical under-developed countries had of transferring labour from subsistence agriculture to wage employment—viz. to the plantations and mines in the export sectors. Here, leaving aside the complication of the introduction of cheap immigrant labour from abroad, the existence of an indigenous subsistence agricultural sector seems to have worked, at least in the transition stage, for the *lowering* of the wage in the mines and plantations. The migrant labourers who still had a foothold in the rural society and were therefore willing to accept low money wages which they regarded merely as a subsidiary source of income; the freezing of "customary" wage rates at the initial level; and the persistence of the "cheap labour" policy are familiar experiences of these under-developed countries.[16] Here no one has suggested that the mines and plantations should be subsidized because labour was "over-valued," although the mine and plantation owners in fact complained that the raw labour was "dear" even at the low wage. On the contrary, many writers on the under-developed countries, including the leading exponents of the protectionist argument,[17] have complained that the colonial powers have been able to maintain low wages in the mines and plantations by neglecting and impoverishing the subsistence agricultural sector. Yet within the framework of the static optimum analysis, the essential situation governing the structure of money wages and productivities in the under-developed countries is exactly the same whether we are thinking of the transfer of agricultural labour from the subsistence sector to the manufacturing sector or to the mines and plantations. In terms of the static analysis we are indifferent whether labour is employed in peasant agriculture, or in mines or plantations or in urban manufacturing industry, provided the static social pro-

---

for industrial employment. In fact the creation of a trained labour force is the most important type of external economy to be claimed by manufacturing industries. But this gets us back to the "infant industry" argument proper and we do not need a separate "Manoilesco" argument to stress this point.

16. For a fuller treatment of this point see Chapter 4 above, pp. 102–8.
17. Cf. Lewis, *loc. cit.* pp. 149–50.

ductivities are equated to wages in these occupations. Thus the divergence between social and private marginal costs due to the "over-valuation" of labour in wage employment would apply both to manufacturing industry and to mines and planations:[18] and in both cases it may be corrected either by protecting (or subsidizing) the sectors in which labour is employed on a money wage basis or by subsidizing various policies to raise the productivity of labour in the non-wage subsistence agricultural sector so that it is no longer "over-valued" in the money wage sector. Therefore, in order to argue that this wage-productivity gap between the subsistence agricultural sector and the urban industrial sector should be corrected only by subsidising or protecting the latter, we need to go beyond the static optimum analysis and postulate that the manufacturing sector is more desirable than agriculture on some other grounds, e.g. its broader dynamic effects in stimulating economic development.

III DEMAND ASPECTS OF CURRENT ARGUMENTS

We may now turn to the second group of protectionist arguments which are concerned with the demand aspects of the question and with the enlargement of the domestic markets of the under-developed countries. Many of these arguments are amorphous and are concerned only indirectly or implicitly with protection. But it is worth trying to piece them together as they exert a pervasive influence on current protectionist thinking in relation to the under-developed countries. The starting-point of these arguments is stated in general terms by Professor Myrdal as follows:

One of the difficulties of industrial development in under-developed countries, and one of the great hindrances to giving real momentum to a development policy, is that internal demand must be built up simultaneously with supply. The unlikelihood or, anyhow, the exasperating slowness of any self-engendered process of "natural growth" offers a

18. Professor Hagen explicitly includes mines under the heading of "industry," *loc. cit.* p. 490.

main explanation why sustained stagnation becomes a sort of natural equilibrium and why policy interventions are called for. Indeed the entire idea of a policy of economic development is to break away from this low-level equilibrium. Now import restrictions afford a means of by-passing altogether the process of "natural growth" and creating at once the necessary demand for a particular domestic industry. They create a sizeable internal demand for a specific commodity, without the necessity of waiting for the slow and difficult growth of the entire economy.[19]

For the further development of this idea of imports as the creator of potential domestic markets, we may turn to Professor Hirschman.

But imports still provide the safest, most incontrovertible proof that the market is there. Moreover, they condition the consumer to the product, breaking down his initial resistance. Imports thus reconnoitre and map out the country's demand; they reduce uncertainty and reduce selling costs at the same time, thereby bringing perceptibly closer the point at which domestic production can be economically started.[20]

Professor Hirschman uses a somewhat different frame of reference from Professor Myrdal. He starts, not from a "low-level equilibrium," but from a situation where there is already some autonomous growth of income and exports and is interested in protection only in so far as it enlarges the size of the domestic market for a particular import, thereby inducing further investment in the setting-up of an import-substitute industry. Professor Hirschman's argument may be best summarized in terms of his input-output model with fixed coefficients which is "dis-aggregated" for imports so that the total direct and indirect imports at a given income level are clearly shown as $M_1, M_2 \ldots M_k$. As income automatically expands the M's will expand so that sooner or later the domestic market for one of the exports, say M_1, crosses its threshold T_1 which is determined by the minimum economic size of domestic production for it and so on along the line. Now under ideal conditions, as soon as the demand for the particular import crosses the

19. G. Myrdal, *An International Economy*, p. 276.
20. A. O. Hirschman, *The Strategy of Economic Development*, New Haven, 1958, p. 121.

threshold of its domestic production is will cease to be imported, as private entrepreneurs will now find it worth their while to set up the import-substitute industry. But in the realistic conditions of the under-developed countries, this induced-investment mechanism is not likely to work smoothly. Further, at any given moment of time we may not find any import which has actually crossed the threshold but only those which are approaching it and are expected to cross it in the near future. In a slow-moving economy, Professor Hirschman is willing to consider protection to help those industries which are on or near the threshold, provided protection is given to one industry at a time.

The first difficulty in this argument is the concept of the "threshold" to be determined by the minimum economic size of production. This involves assumptions made to give a preponderant weight to technical factors, viz. (1) that it is possible to determine the minimum economic size of a new industry (which is in fact a single factory) by studying the conditions governing it in other countries where the general economic conditions, relative factor supplies, etc., may be quite different; and (2) that once this minimum size is attained, the domestic producer of the import-substitute commodity can compete with foreign producers whose scale of production is likely to be much larger. At first sight, this amounts to a denial of the comparative costs doctrine that the cost of producing a given product is likely to differ in different countries due to differences in factor endowments or factor productivities. But it is not too implausible when we remember that in many under-developed countries, setting up new industries frequently means importing from a common source not only all the equipment, but also foreign managers and many of the semi-finished materials and parts. Thus the concept of a "threshold" may have a greater degree of validity than an economist is normally inclined to believe; at least, for the range of light consumers' goods industries which are likely to be set up in the under-developed countries. As for the second question, whether a fairly small-sized domestic industry is likely to be able to compete with its large-scale foreign competitors, there is some support for the view that the cost curves in manufacturing industries, at least in the U.S., are shaped like either a very flat U (‿‿‿‿) or a J on its side (‿‿‿‿).[21] Here again the argument comes out much better than at first sight.

The second difficulty is somewhat more serious from the point of view of many writers on the under-developed countries. They would say that Hirschman's model works on the assumption that there is already some autonomous expansion in incomes and exports whereas the real problem facing the under-developed countries is the "low-level equilibrium" with small domestic markets, and low incomes, combined with a world demand for their primary exports which (with a few exceptions like petroleum) is *not* autonomously expanding. Here Professor Nurkse in particular reiterated the view that while in the nineteenth century the industrial centres of the world transmitted their economic growth to the periphery of the under-developed countries by a vigorous expansion in demand for primary products, this is no longer true at present, and that this relative decline in world trade in primary products may be attributed to various factors, mainly on the demand side, such as the special position of the United States as the world's dominant economy, the low income elasticity of demand for primary exports, the shift in the industrial centres from light to heavy engineering and to chemical industries with a lower raw material content, the invention of synthetic substitutes for raw materials, etc.[22]

It is to meet this problem of trying to find a substitute for the nineteenth-century dynamic mechanism of growth through an expansion in primary exports that Professor Nurkse put forward his version of the doctrine of "balanced growth."

21. Joe S. Bain, *Industrial Organization,* New York, 1968, pp. 153–55.
22. R. Nurkse, "Some International Aspects of Economic Development," *American Economic Review,* May 1952; and "The Conflict between 'Balanced Growth' and International Specialisation," published by Istanbul and Ankara Universities (to be referred to hereafter as the "Istanbul Lecture"); and "The Trade of Poor Countries and the International Economics of Growth," a lecture given at the Institut de Science Économique Appliqué, Paris, 1958.

Now domestic markets are limited because of mass poverty due to low productivity. Private investment in any single industry considered by itself is discouraged by the smallness of the existing market . . . the solution seems to be a balanced pattern of investment in a number of different industries so that people working more productively with more capital and improved techniques become each other's customers. In the absence of vigorous upward shifts in the world demand for exports of primary products, a low-income country through a process of diversified growth can seek to bring upward shifts in domestic demand schedules by means of increased productivity and therefore increased real purchasing power. In this way, a pattern of mutually supporting investments in different lines of production can enlarge the size of the market and help fill the vacuum in the domestic economy.[23]

This doctrine of "balanced growth" designed for the "closed" economy has somewhat equivocal implications for the protectionist argument. In the version expounded particularly by Professor Nurkse and Professor Lewis, agriculture is explicitly included as one of the "industries"; and the export sector, the domestic agricultural sector and the domestic manufacturing sector are to be expanded in balanced proportions according to the relative expansion in demand expected in each sector.[24] Stated in this way, the "balanced-growth" doctrine can be used as a criticism of those pro-trade economists who mistake the special dynamic or growth-transmitting aspect of the nineteenth-century international trade for the general static gains from international specialization and continue to urge the under-developed countries to concentrate on their export of primary products in the face of a passive or declining world demand for these products. On the other hand, the same doctrine can also be used as a criticism of one-sided concentration on industrialization: for, in order to create the demand for domestic manufactures, domestic agriculture should also be expanded in a balanced proportion. But this only deals with the allocation of resources on the production side. What about the imports and the possible inflation and balance

23. R. Nurkse, Istanbul Lecture, pp. 8–10.
24. R. Nurkse, *ibid*. pp. 12 and 16; W. A. Lewis, *Theory of Economic Growth*, London, 1955, pp. 277–83.

of payments pressure of a "balanced-growth" programme? Here
Professor Nurkse reluctantly admitted that "while it is not to be
denied that import restriction can help a policy of domestic balanced
investment," it should be used very sparingly because of its tendency
to encourage costly and inefficient production of import substitutes.
"Import restrictions imposed in spite of such unfavourable effects
can be justified only on the grounds of future benefits, which is the
infant industry argument for protection.[25] Professor Lewis also
prefers to use either the "infant industry" argument or the "disguised unemployment" argument rather than the "balanced-growth"
argument for protection, but has a keener appreciation of the possibility that a balanced-growth programme might lead to inflationary
pressure on balance of payments requiring import controls to econo-
mize foreign exchange rather than to protect domestic industry.[26]

But there is, however, a narrower and incidentally older version
of the "balanced-growth" doctrine which is meant to be regarded
as a method of industrialization to be applied *inside* the manufacturing sector only.[27] This version is favoured by those who
believe that the under-developed countries are currently starting
from a position not of balance, but of extreme imbalance amounting
to a "structural disequilibrium" which has to be corrected by a
concentrated effort to expand the manufacturing sector before we
can proceed along the path of inter-sectoral balanced growth. Some
of them would argue that this "structural disequilibrium" exists not
only in over-populated countries with rural "disguised unemployment" but also in thinly populated "export economies," as the result
of the "export-bias" of the nineteenth-century pattern of international trade and investment.

The export-bias argument may be summarized as follows. The
expanding world market for primary products contrasted with the
very small domestic markets for manufactures in the under-devel-

25. R. Nurkse, Istanbul Lecture, pp. 17–18.
26. W. A. Lewis, *op. cit.* pp. 348–49; pp. 282–83; pp. 387–88.
27. Cf. P. N. Rosenstein-Rodan, "Problems of Industrialisation of E. and S.E.
Europe," *Economic Journal*, 1943.

oped countries first attracted foreign capital and enterprise into their export sectors, entirely by-passing their domestic sectors. But this very process aggravated the initial disparity in the productivity of resources between the two sectors and further served to divert, not only foreign, but also indigenous, capital and enterprise from the domestic to the export sector. As the result of this cumulative bias in development, the export economies now have a high rate of export to national income and a "dualistic economic structure" with the highly specialized and technically advanced export sector existing side by side with the backward domestic sector. This means that they not only suffer from a high degree of instability through their fluctuating and frequently deteriorating terms of trade but also are unable to shift resources easily from the export to the domestic sectors to adjust to the changing terms of trade.[28] Thus in order to correct this cumulative export-bias, it may be necessary to protect, not one or two industries, but a fairly large group of industries which would form a sort of "infant" manufacturing sector.

It may be noted that although this argument uses the disparity in the sizes of the domestic and the export markets of the under-developed countries to trigger off the process of cumulative bias, the essential mechanism which is supposed to cause the bias is the "wrong" allocation of the flow of resources over a period of time between the export and the domestic sectors. Thus this "export bias" thesis turns out to be a species of the familiar argument based on the divergence between social and private products. At first sight, therefore, it seems that the purely demand type of protectionist argument has not been strengthened by the shift from the broader inter-sectoral version of "balanced growth" to the narrower version of the doctrine confining it within the manufacturing sector. We do not seem to have progressed beyond the propositions conceded by Professor Nurkse: viz. (1) that the taking over of ready-made

28. The most articulate exponent of this argument is H. W. Singer, "The Distribution of Gains between Investing and Borrowing Countries," *American Economic Review,* Papers and Proceedings, May 1950, pp. 473 *et seq.* Dr. Singer, however, is rather silent on the protection issue.

markets for imports by domestic import-substitute industries will
undoubtedly help a "balanced-growth," programme (of either, version); (2) that, nevertheless, we cannot entirely rely on the balanced-
growth principle (in its narrower version) to show convincingly that
instead of protecting one industry at a time it is better to protect a
group of industries simultaneously because of the external economies
and complementarities arising only from the demand side; and (3)
that therefore, in order to justify the protection of a group of industries, we shall have to fall back on the "infant industry" argument
to show that there are substantial external economies on the cost
side likely to accrue to the group as a whole.

But on further examination, the demand side of the protectionist
argument has in fact made some progress. This can be seen by
having a closer look at the type of industries which balanced-growth
theorists choose to set up simultaneously as a group. They would
advocate that the group should be selected on a horizontal basis to
consist of light consumers' goods industries for two reasons. (1)
Firstly, these industries most readily create a market for each others'
products and lighten the burden of the sacrifice required by the industrialization process. (2) Secondly, the under-developed countries
can still enjoy the advantages of international division of labour by
producing, and even exporting, the simpler manufactured goods
and importing heavy capital goods which require more complicated
and capital-intensive methods of manufacture.[29] But given the
horizontal grouping of light consumers' goods industries, we can
say two things about the type of external economies on the cost side
which they are likely to generate for each other. Firstly, the types
of economies (though not necessarily their quantitative magnitude)
are much the same as those recognized by the traditional "infant
industry" argument such as the creation of a growing pool of skilled
industrial labour, the overcoming of the "indivisibilities" in the pro-

29. On this basis, Professor Myrdal has emphasized that protection adopted
by the under-developed countries will not reduce the world volume of trade,
but merely shift the pattern of the advanced countries' exports from light
consumers' goods to heavy capital goods.

vision of various "social overhead" facilities such as power, transport, etc. Secondly, and what is more important for our argument,
these external economies are not likely to be specific but may be
generated without glaring quantitative differences by almost any
type of light industries. Thus in trying to select a sub-set of industries for protection, we shall have to put a greater weight on the
demand factors, and select that group which contains those commodities with the highest income elasticities and cross elasticities
(or complementarities) of demand.

But for a more radical development of the demand approach to
industrialization, we shall have to go to critics of the balanced-
growth approach such as Professor Marcus Fleming and Professor
Hirschman. Profesor Marcus Fleming in his critique of the balanced-
growth doctrine has argued that in any realistic situation where the
supplies of labour, capital and other resources are not perfectly
elastic, the simultaneous setting-up of a group of light consumers'
goods industries is likely to result in the external diseconomies for
each other through their competition for the limited supplies of
resources and that these diseconomies are likely to outweigh the
external economies which such a horizontally selected group of
industries is likely to generate for itself. He suggests that more
substantial economies might be obtained by a *vertical group* of
industries at different stages of production, each of which is the
other's supplier or customer.[30] This concept of vertical linkages
between different industries has been systematically developed by
Professor Hirschman and used as the basis of his unbalanced-growth
approach to economic development.[31] Professor Hirschman argues
that the balanced-growth approach is unsatisfactory not only because
of the inelastic supply of certain factors, notably entrepreneurs required to run a whole flock of new industries, but also because its
concept of the nature of economic development is basically wrong.

30. J. M. Fleming, "External Economies and the Doctrine of Balanced
Growth," *Economic Journal*, June 1955.
31. A. O. Hirschman, *Strategy of Economic Development,* especially Chapter
3, etc.

Economic development, according to him, is not a once-over shift from "low-level equilibrium" to a "balanced growth" equilibrium and then coming to a stop at this plateau of a higher level of income. Rather it should be a continuous process, generated and sustained by a chain of disequilibria and it should be the aim of economic development policy to try to prolong and keep alive this disequilibrium process by a series of autonomous investments injected into strategic places in the economic structure which will lead to the maximum amount of imbalances inducing further investments. An autonomous investment in a given industry can induce further investments through the pressure of excess demand on the industries which are its suppliers. It can also induce investment through the pressure of excess supply on the industries who are its customers. Ideally, we should start with an autonomous investment in an industry which is capable of generating induced investments in both directions on its suppliers and on its customers; but if that is not available we should start by generating the pressure of *excess demand* which is to be regarded as a more powerful and reliable force.[32]

Applying this approach to international trade, Professor Hirschman points out that the typical light consumers' goods industries of the under-developed countries are what may be described as the "finishing-touches" industries, importing not only machinery, but also materials which are semi-processed or frequently very nearly completely processed. Thus the domestic net value added consists mainly of the wages of the workers engaged in giving the "finishing touches" to the imported materials so that a large proportion of the expansion in the demand for the product of these "domestic" industries leaks out in the form of further imports of materials and machinery from abroad. In many under-developed countries the normal process of economic development in fact consists in industrialization working its way backward from the "finishing-touches" stage to the domestic production of intermediate, and

32. Hirschman, *ibid*. pp. 116–17.

finally to that of basic industrial materials. But this process of introducing industry by small successive bits of domestic value-added may be too slow to pay off and the under-developed country may try to bite off a somewhat larger piece of value-added by jumping a few stages backwards from the "finishing-touches" stage to some intermediate stage which may also open out a wider network of linkage effects with other industries.

In so far as Professor Hirschman's approach can be used in support of the protectionist case, it is notable on two counts. Firstly, if we accept the Fleming-Hirschman view that the *vertical* transmission of external economies between different stages of industries is likely to be more powerful than the horizontal transmission of external economies between a group of light consumers' goods industries, we are led to consider a protectionist policy "in depth" as contrasted with a protectionist policy "in breadth" suggested by the balanced-growth approach. A policy of protection "in depth" cannot be dismissed particularly for a large under-developed country like India with a population pressure requiring heroic methods of economic development. Secondly, and more generally, Professor Hirschman's approach has the merit of putting forward, explicitly and at a formal level, a basic proposition which has been implied in very general terms in most protectionist arguments: viz. that manufacturing industry is to be preferred to agriculture, not because it is supposed to be more "productive," not because there are "divergences" from the optimum and deviations from the balanced-growth path, but simply because it is likely to be a more powerful generator of induced investment through the vertical linkage effects.[33] Now, one may challenge Professor Hirschman's generalizations at the empirical level of pointing out various exceptions: for instance, why should not an improved method of agriculture using fertilizers and machinery generate as much induced investment, say in the chemical and engineering industries, as any manufacturing industry? But logically, it is a notable step to strike out boldly to the position

33. Hirschman, *Strategy of Economic Development,* pp. 109–10.

that manufacturing industry is to be preferred to agriculture because of its dynamic (but not conclusively demonstrable) effects in stimulating economic development. This is perhaps as far as we can usefully go at the present stage of development of economic analysis.[34] Looking back, we can now appreciate the difference between Professor Hirschman's approach and many of the other arguments on protection which fail to live up to their claim to be based on "dynamic" considerations of economic growth because, at some stage or other, they fall back on the extended applications of concepts such as the deviation from the optimum or the balanced-growth equilibrium which essentially belong to the framework of static analysis.

IV PROTECTION VERSUS OVER-ALL BALANCED-GROWTH
DEVELOPMENT PLANNING

Let us now turn to the practical difficulties of pursuing an effective protectionist policy in the setting of the present-day underdeveloped countries. The orthodox economists considered the question of protection in a situation where free trade conditions prevailed in the other parts of the economy and where the balance of payments is in equilibrium. In contrast, in the present-day under-developed countries we start from a situation which is already rife with all types of control on international trade, particularly with direct quantitative restrictions of imports. Typically, these quantitative restrictions have been imposed on an *ad hoc* basis and allowed to spread over the whole range of imports to ease foreign exchange difficulties. These foreign exchange difficulties in their turn arise from the inflationary pressure exerted by investment pro-

34. Beyond this we get into the broader sociological generalizations concerning the "educative" effects of manufacturing industry and its superiority in providing "the growing points for increased technical knowledge, urban education, the dynamism and resilience that goes with urban civilization," etc. Cf. H. W. Singer, "The Distribution of Gains between Investing and Borrowing Countries," *American Economic Review,* Papers and Proceedings, May 1950, pp. 476–77.

grammes for economic development. The characteristic results are not only a rising general price level and an all-round premium on all imported goods, but also distorted price differentials between different types of imports haphazardly reflecting short run and speculative factors.

There are a number of difficulties in trying to pursue an effective protectionist policy in such a setting. (1) Firstly, however broadly we may choose to define the area for protection, a protectionist policy remains essentially a method of selective encouragement of a given sector of the economy by conferring on it a sectional price increase. Thus in order to make protection effective, the price-differential in the protected sector must be maintained in sharp relief for some time and not allowed to be neutralized by random price rises in the non-protected sectors. It is difficult to fulfil this condition when the inflationary pressure is continually threatening to boil over with a further round of import restrictions. (2) Secondly, in order to protect a given sector effectively, it is necessary to be able to import the non-protected items freely and easily. This is fairly obvious where these non-protected items happen to be machinery and materials needed by the protected industries. But this requirement stands even when the non-protected items are other consumer goods, because an unintended rise in their prices might weaken the stimulus to the protected industries and might also possibly draw away the scarce resources from them. Thus, for instance, the restrictions on imported luxuries frequently lead to the setting-up of import substitute industries for these luxuries where non-luxury goods with a wider domestic market might have been a more suitable candidate for protection. But again this liberalization of the import of the non-protected items is not possible where a large balance of payments deficit cannot be met except by an all-round restriction of imports. (3) Thirdly, even assuming the existence of "disguised unemployment," the protected sector cannot expand without attracting the scarce capital and entrepreneurial resources from the rest of the economy. But, given inflation and a general shortage of imported goods, capital and enterprise tend to be attracted into trading and speculation in these scarce imports, particularly so when, due to the inefficiency or corruption in import controls, large monopoly profits can be made in these activities.[35]

Some under-developed countries have attempted to meet these difficulties by imbedding permanent tariffs on some selected industries amongst the quantitative controls over all imports. The idea here is to try to induce the more far-sighted entrepreneurs into the selected industries by offering a permanent tariff shelter as distinct from the quantitative controls which are supposed to be temporary. The success of such a policy depends on how far the balance of payments pressure and the general premium on imports can be kept under reasonable control. During an export boom which expands the foreign exchange receipts of the under-developed countries, such a policy can claim a double advantage. Firstly, the protected industries will enjoy an increase in price differential because the prices of the non-protected imports will be lowered as the authorities feel able to relax the temporary restrictions on them. Secondly, the increase in foreign exchange earnings will ease the supply of investible funds for the protected industries. Unfortunately, given the passive trend in the world demand for primary products, what tends to happen more frequently is that due to severity of the quantitative restrictions, the rise in the prices of the "non-protected" imports soon outstrips the height of the fixed tariff in the "protected" industries, so that quantitative restrictions have to be clamped down on the latter also on top of formal tariffs. Since these restrictions look like being continued indefinitely, it becomes somewhat academic to draw a distinction between "per-

35. In many under-developed countries such as in South-east Asia, where the export-import trade has been in the hands of foreigners, the governments use import control and licensing as a weapon to replace the foreign merchants by indigenous merchants. Thus the scarce import licences are not auctioned to the highest hidders for fear that they would go into the hands of the more efficient foreign merchants, but are rationed out somewhat haphazardly to a privileged class of indigenous merchants who frequently make their monopoly profits not so much by selling the imports as by selling the import licences.

manent" and "temporary" shelter against foreign competition. Even if things do not reach such a pass, it is still rather doubtful whether the somewhat reduced price differential which can be offered even by a high permanent tariff imbedded amongst quantitative restrictions is sufficient to overcome the difficulties we have listed.[36]

Now the basic and continuing cause of inflation and balance of payments difficulties in the under-developed countries must be attributed directly or indirectly to their economic development plans along "balanced-growth" lines requiring an all-out drive for a high percentage ratio of aggregate investment to national income. Theoretically, of course, the balance of payments difficulties can be kept under reasonable control by stricter fiscal and monetary policy. But in practice, in many under-developed countries, investment programmes for economic development tend to outstrip the amount of savings which can be mobilized with the existing administrative machinery so that recurring foreign exchange crises seem unavoidable. We are then faced with an important practical question: How far is an effective protectionist policy compatible with the type of over-all economic development planning attempted in most under-developed countries?

To a large extent this is really a conflict between the "balanced-growth" and the "unbalanced-growth" approach to economic development in another form. If we believe that economic development

36. It may be asked whether all-round quantitative restrictions on imports even if they do not give special encouragement to any particular branch of industry might nevertheless encourage resources to move generally from export production to domestic import-substitute industries. If what is desired is a uniform height of protection in all imports, it would be more satisfactory to impose an *ad valorem* tax on all imports or adopt multiple foreign exchange rates, or simply devalue. The imposition of all-round quantitative restrictions, although it has the same general effect, tends to be accompanied by considerable short-run fluctuations between the relative prices of different imports and thus increases the risks to an entrepreneur contemplating the setting up of an import-substitute industry. But however broadly we define the "infant" manufacturing sector, an effective protectionist policy would have to be more selective than a uniform *ad valorem* tax on all imports.

can be achieved only by a critical minimum amount of investment to break away from the "low-level equilibrium" and to push ahead simultaneously on all fronts, then we should be prepared to accept a considerable amount of inflationary pressure and quantitative restrictions of imports. This should be regarded as a necessary consequence of the "big push" when the indivisible critical minimum amount of investment required happens to exceed total savings, including the savings potential from the use of disguised unemployment. Here our main hope is that the inflation will be "self-destroying" when the forced investment dramatically expands the national output, and the "infant economy" as a whole gets over the hump. If we seriously believe in this approach to economic development, then we should be prepared to give up pursuing a serious protectionist policy rather than forgo the quantitative restrictions on imports which offer the most important and flexible instrument of control over the foreign exchange accounts of the developing economy. If, on the other hand, we believe that economic development can be more effectively pursued by concentrating on certain strategic sectors instead of trying to push ahead on all fronts, a protectionist policy would appear to be the most promising instrument of such an approach. If inflationary pressure and quantitative restrictions on imports interfere with an effective pursuit of a protectionist policy, then we should be prepared to cut down the attempted rate of over-all investment and pursue a fairly conservative monetary policy. We should then be in a position to liberalize the imports in non-protected sectors and confine trade restrictions and tariffs to certain selected sectors, thus giving them a maximum stimulus. Behind this conflict between the balanced- and the unbalanced-growth approach there is also the important further conflict between the reliance on the market mechanism implied by the protectionist policy, and its replacement by direct controls implied by the over-all type of planning.

The existence of this conflict at the practical level between an effective protectionist policy and the over-all economic development planning of the type favoured by many under-developed countries has been obscured by writers who are firmly attached to both types of policies and try to compromise between their conflicting pulls. But there is no doubt that this conflict is more important and more immediate in the setting of the present-day under-developed countries than the traditional conflict between protection and free trade.

To round off our argument, let us conclude with a very brief comment on the traditional free-trade-protection issue. Starting from the typical situation of the under-developed countries in which all types of controls, including quantitative controls, have been allowed to spread promiscuously over all international transactions, it is difficult to imagine wiping the slate clean and returning to the free traders' basic point of reference, viz. the ideal free trade equilibrium. Further, if we are concerned not only with static allocative efficiency but with promoting economic development, it is difficult not to share Professor Nurkse's doubts whether the advantages of international specialization by itself (whatever its static gains) are sufficient to provide a powerful enough dynamic mechanism in the existing passive condition of world demand for primary products. Thus we are led to view with some leniency the traditional evils of protection emphasized by the orthodox economists. Firstly the difficulties of selecting singly the right industry to protect are reduced when we are prepared to experiment with a fairly large group among which we may have a greater chance of picking some winners. The free traders may reply that the chance of picking the losers will also be increased and thus the wastage from misallocation of resources will be correspondingly greater. But if we use as our point of reference the existing situation in the under-developed countries, such wastages already exist so that the net cost of a protectionist policy is small. It may therefore be worth the gamble when the winners may bring us a very considerable dynamic impetus for the further development of the economy. Next, the evils of the tariff-sheltered monopolies are not too frightening when we start from a situation where pure monopoly profits are already reaped in merchandise trading in imports and where the continuance of the haphazard and indiscriminate import controls perpetuates

these large trading profits. From a dynamic point of view, a monopolistic class of manufacturers may be preferable to a monopolistic
class of traders, particularly for its more favourable effect on the
rate of investment. While profits in trading are likely to trickle only
slowly into manufacturing industry, profits made inside the manufacturing sector are likely to be more easily reinvested. This process
may perhaps also encourage a new and vigorous class of entrepreneurs with an entirely different outlook from the traditional
mentality of the traders. There finally remains the difficulty of ever
removing the tariffs when these have outgrown their use. This evil
cannot be avoided and our only consolation is that a protectionist
policy is merely replacing the "temporary" quantitative controls on
imports which are, in practice, equally likely to be permanent.

7 | International Trade and the Developing Countries

There has been a spate of discussion on the future of international economic relations between the developed and the underdeveloped countries, following the first United Nations Conference on Trade and Development.[1] In this paper, we shall consider some of the broader theoretical issues arising out of these discussions. Since these issues are deeply rooted in the traditional free trade versus protection controversy, they can be most clearly brought out by reformulating the old controversy in the new setting.

In the current context, the free trade view is represented by those who hold that the underdeveloped countries can make a more effective use of their external economic opportunities, both trade and aid, by reducing their existing network of controls over international trade and investment and by allowing the outside world market forces to transform their internal economic structure according to their potential comparative advantage. Some would go on to maintain that the more promising path of economic development

1. For a very useful survey of these discussions, see Harry G. Johnson, *Economic Policies Toward Less Developed Countries,* Brookings Institution, 1967.

From Paul A. Samuelson, ed., *International Economic Relations,* Proceedings of the Third Congress of the International Economic Association, Macmillan and Co., Ltd., 1969, pp. 15–35. Reprinted by permission of Macmillan and Co., Ltd. and the International Economic Association.

for many underdeveloped countries is to pursue an "outward-look-ing" and "export-led" policy of economic growth. The protectionist view is represented by those who hold that the comparative costs theory is too "static" for the "dynamic" problems of promoting economic development and that the underdeveloped countries should continue with their policy of "import-substitution" and domestic industrialization, insulating their "infant" industries and "infant" economies against the pressure of world market forces. Some would go on to maintain that in so far as the underdeveloped countries cannot earn sufficient foreign exchange through exports to meet the import requirements of their domestic industrialization policies, their "foreign exchange gap" should be filled by international aid.

We begin, in Section I of this paper, by showing that the broad historical and sociological hypotheses underlying current discussions on the "dynamic" effects of trade policy on the economic develop-ment of the underdeveloped countries can be traced to the older free trade versus protection controversy. In Section II, we shall extend the theory of comparative costs to the problem of a developing country choosing between the "indirect" method of trade and the "direct" method of domestic production in converting its available savings into economic development. We shall then use this framework to expose the "fallacy of misplaced concreteness" in some of the cur-rent thinking on import-substitution and the "foreign exchange re-quirements" of the underdeveloped countries. In Section III, we shall contrast the infant industry argument with the current attempts to extend it to justify the protection of the "infant" manufacturing sector as a whole either in the form of a "horizontal" group of import-substituting consumers' goods industries or in the form of a "vertical" group of industries linked to each other through input-output relationships. We conclude, in section IV, by showing that further attempts to extend the infant industry argument from the "infant" manufacturing sector to the "infant economy" lead us beyond the theory of international trade to the theory of interna-tional aid, but that the concept of international aid suggested by the notion of the "infant economy" does not correspond to the current

UNCTAD concept of aid as the means of filling the "foreign exchange gap" of the underdeveloped countries calculated on the basis of fixed technical coefficients and constant returns to scale.

I

The theory of comparative costs, as a branch of the static theory of allocation of resources, is neutral between foreign trade and domestic production. In order to maximise the direct gains from trade, resources should be allocated impartially between the export sector and the domestic sector according to the existing comparative advantage. In contrast, current discussions of the trade policies for the underdeveloped countries centre on the clash between pro-trade and anti-trade attitudes towards economic development. The introduction of the new terms, viz., "outward-looking" versus "inward-looking" policies, and "export-led" versus "import-substitution" policies are symptomatic of the attempts to stretch or break out of the neutral conventional framework of the comparative costs theory. When we examine the ideas behind the new terminology, we find that they are made up of broad historical and sociological hypotheses concerning the "indirect" or "dynamic" effects of trade policy on economic development which are deeply rooted in the older nineteenth century debates on free trade and protection.

What is currently described as the "outward-looking" approach is essentially an elaboration of the well known classical belief concerning the "educative effect" of an open economy. The advocates of this approach stress the advantages which the underdeveloped countries can obtain by keeping their economies open and receptive to new ideas, new wants, new techniques of production and methods of economic organization from abroad. According to them, the existing network of controls over international trade and investment in the underdeveloped countries, not only imposes direct losses of consumers' satisfaction, but also entails the more important "indirect" losses by isolating them from the stimulating contact with the world economy. They would therefore advocate not only freer trade but also a freer admission of foreign private enterprises into the underdeveloped countries as a powerful means of spreading modern technology and economic organisation to these countries.[2]

On the protectionist side, this is countered by the well known hypothesis concerning the "educative effect" of manufacturing industry originally put forward by Friedrich List. As a modern exponent of this view puts it, manufacturing industries "provide the growing points for increased technical knowledge, urban education, and the dynamism and resilience that goes with urban civilization, as well as the direct Marshallian external economies."[3] Clearly, there is no easy way of adjudicating between the rival hypotheses concerning the "educative effect" of the open economy and the "educative effect" of manufacturing industry. Without venturing into sociology, we may however legitimately question whether the "industrialization" of the underdeveloped countries in the sense relevant for their economic development can be defined so narrowly in terms of manufacturing industry only, without taking into account the other essential ingredients: viz., the growth of modern forms of economic institutions and organization, the building up of social overhead capital and above all, the "industrialization" of agriculture through the application of modern science and technology and capital investment. As we shall see, the "fallacy of misplaced concreteness" in some of the contemporary protectionist arguments springs from this narrow concept of industrialization.

In addition to the "educative effect" argument, there are two

2. For the classical origins of the various pro-trade arguments discussed in this section, see above, Chapter 5; for current expositions of the "outward-looking" approach, see D. B. Keesing, "Outward-looking Policies and Economic Development," *Economic Journal*, June 1967 and below, Chapter 12. See also W. W. Lockwood, *The Economic Development of Japan*, Princeton University Press, 1954, Ch. 6, for a case study of "Trade as a Highway of Learning."

3. H. W. Singer, *International Development: Growth and Change*, McGraw-Hill, New York 1964, pp. 164–65; also Friedrich List, *The National System of Political Economy*, S. S. Lloyd's translation, London, Longrmans, 1922, pp. 108, 113 and 161.

further pro-trade arguments and both of these can be traced back to Adam Smith.

First, there is Adam Smith's argument that foreign trade, by enabling a country to overcome the narrowness of its home market and widening its scope for division of labour, will raise the productivity of its resources through the growth of specialised skills and the introduction of specialised techniques and capital equipment in the export sector. The gains from such specialization are "dynamic" in the sense that they represent an outward shift in the production possibility curve of the country in the direction of export production. These gains are distinct from the direct "static" gains from trade obtained by moving along the same production possibility curve. It is then argued that the benefits from the increased productivity in the export sector will spread to the rest of the economy in varying degrees, resulting in an "export-led" economic growth.

The "export-led" theory gains an added significance from the fact that many of the underdeveloped countries are very small countries. For instance, out of the 90 underdeveloped countries usually listed, 72 have less than 15 million population and 51 have less than 5 million population.[4] Given the very small domestic markets, which in many cases may be too small even for the simpler types of manufactured consumers' goods, there would seem little choice for the smaller underdeveloped countries except to seek economic development through the expansion of exports. The limitations of a policy of "inward-looking industrialization" for the underdeveloped countries with small domestic markets is freely admitted by protectionist writers, notably Prebisch who first introduced this term into current discussions.[5] But, instead of drawing the traditional free trade conclusion, the remedy sought by Prebisch is to form regional economic groups with wider protected markets.

Here we have an interesting situation in which the economies of large scale production have been invoked in favour of two different

4. Cf. J. Pincus, *Trade, Aid and Development,* McGraw-Hill, 1967 p. 66.
5. R. Prebisch, *Towards a New Trade Policy for Development,* United Nations, New York, 1964, pp. 20–22.

types of policy: in favour of a greater freedom of trade and international specialization and in favour of creating larger sheltered markets for the manufacturing industries of the underdeveloped countries. There is however a crucial difference in the way in which the argument for obtaining the economies of large scale production has been used by the two sides. For the free trade minded economists, the size of the market available to a country's export industry is a share of the international market which can be increased only by that industry's own capacity to lower costs and improve its competitive power. Thus the country's capacity to improve efficiency and reduce costs in its export production is a prior condition for taking advantage of the scope for the economies of large scale production offered by international trade. In contrast, for the protectionist-minded economists, the creation of a larger sheltered "home" market, either within a country or within a regional group, is a prior condition for taking advantage of the economies of large scale production offered by the technological indivisibilities of modern industry. Thus while the free traders stress the importance of international competition required to stimulate the country's capacity to improve the efficiency of its export industry, the protectionists tend to stress, not the country's own capacity to lower costs through competition, but the enlargement in the size of the surrounding sheltered market to be obtained through negotiation. Now, while the importance of technical indivisibilities is generally recognised in the sphere of social overhead capital, much empirical research remains to be done to find out how important the economies of large scale production really are for the types of manufacturing industry which are set up in the underdeveloped countries. In particular, we may ask how far the enlargement of a protected "home" market is, by itself, sufficient to ensure an industry's capacity to lower its costs. This point is crucial to our distinction between the economies of scale argument and the "infant industry" argument for protection in Section III.

Finally, there is the pro-trade argument derived from Adam Smith's "vent for surplus" theory of international trade. There is a considerable amount of historical evidence to show that the export expansion of peasant products, particularly from the Southeast Asian and West African countries, has taken place, not so much through the reallocation of the given and fully employed resources from the domestic to the export sector, but through the spread of the exchange economy drawing the hitherto underutilised land and labour of the subsistence sector into export production. Thus, the function of international trade in these countries, is not so much to reallocate given resources, but to provide a market outlet for the surplus productive capacity of the subsistence sector which would have remained underutilised in the absence of international trade. The striking feature of the "vent for surplus" mechanism of export expansion is that it can take place without a necessary reduction in output for the domestic sector and without any noticeable change in the techniques of peasant production.[6]

Applied to the present context, those who favour this type of pro-trade argument would put their case as follows. (1) Many under-developed countries still have a substantial proportion of their resources in the subsistence sector and a considerable number of them in Africa, Southeast Asia and Latin America do not as yet suffer from heavy population pressure on their available land. Thus, there is a *prima facie* case, to be verified by detailed factual studies, for believing that there still remains a considerable scope for export expansion making use of the underutilised resources of the subsistence sector in these countries.[7] (2) In so far as this is true, the more promising line of development policy for these countries is to encourage the growth of the exchange economy by improving transport and communications and marketing facilities for the peasant producers and by permitting free imports of cheap manufactured consumers' goods which are required as "incentive goods" to en-

6. For a detailed exposition of the "vent for surplus" theory, see above, Chapter 5.
7. For an account of export expansion in Southeast Asia and Africa in the post-war decades, see below, Chapter 12; and Walter Chudson, "Comparative Costs and Economic Development: The African Case," *American Economic Review,* (Papers and Proceedings), May 1964.

courage peasant production of export crops. (3) Whatever the
external terms of trade of an underdeveloped country, the setting up
of domestic manufacturing industries under heavy protection worsens
the internal terms of trade between agriculture and manufactures
for the peasant producers and discourages their further entry into
the exchange economy. Thus apart from "static" consumers' losses,
the setting up of high cost domestic manufacturing industries under
heavy protection causes a "dynamic" loss by retarding the growth
of the exchange economy.

Protectionist writers like Prebisch would counter this argument by
maintaining that, whatever the potential supply of resources for
export production, international trade can no longer provide the
"engine of growth" as it has done in the past because of a long-
run tendency for the prices of primary products to deteriorate relative to the prices of manufactured goods. Much has been written
challenging both the empirical and the theoretical basis of this thesis.[8]
Here we need merely add that gloomy forecasts about the declining
trend in the world demand for primary products in the aggregate,
whether true or not, do not offer much guidance to an individual
underdeveloped country which must assess the demand conditions
for its particular export products, actual and potential. Thus in
global terms, during the period 1955–63, the value of total exports
from Africa increased by 42 per cent while those from Latin
America and Asia increased by 22 per cent and 10 per cent respectively. But both in Latin America and Asia, there are individual
countries such as Peru, Mexico, Thailand, Malaya and the Philippines
which have enjoyed rapid rates of growth in the postwar period
through the expansion of primary exports (other than petroleum).
Further, when we look closer into the causes of slow export expansion in other Latin American or Asian countries, we frequently find
that internal domestic factors, such as political instability, inflation

8. Eg. H. G. Johnson, *Economic Policies Towards Less Developed Countries,*
Appendix A; R. E. Lipsey, *Price and Quantity Trends in the Foreign Trade
of the United States,* Princeton University Press, 1963; and M. June Flanders,
"Prebisch on Protectionism: An Evaluation," *Economic Journal,* June 1964.

and overvalued currencies and excessive hostility towards foreign-
owned mines and plantations, play a more important part than the
demand factors in slowing down the expansion in exports on the
supply side. Thus slow recorded rates of export expansion do not
necessarily mean that the "export-led" strategy of economic development will be ineffective because of unfavourable world demand conditions. Frequently, they merely suggest a failure to take full advantage of the available trade opportunities.[9]

We may conclude this section by examining a deep-seated source
of distrust of primary exports. This is the belief that expansion of
primary exports, even if it leads to fast rates of economic growth
during certain periods, is not sustainable and that sooner or later,
the pressure of population on land and diminishing returns will put
a stop to this type of economic expansion. This again harks back to
the classical distinction between agriculture which is subject to
diminishing returns and manufactures subject to increasing returns.

There are two important points to be cleared up here. (1) The
distinction between "export-led" policy and "import-substitution"
policy is not the same as that between agriculture and manufacture.
The real point of difference is that while the "export-led" policy
favours the "specialization" of resources in selected lines of production, whether primary production or manufacturing, for the export market, the "import-substitution" policy favours the "diversification" of resources to match the pattern of domestic demand for
manufactured consumers' goods. Successful "export-led" growth
can be achieved either through the expansion of primary exports or
through the expansion of manufactured exports as shown by Hong

9. For details of recent export trends from the underdeveloped countries, see
J. Pincus, *Aid, Trade and Development,* Ch. 7. For case studies of slow
growing Latin American countries, see C. F. Diaz-Alejandro, "An Interpretation of Argentine Economic Growth since 1930," Parts I and II, *Journal
of Development Studies,* Oct. 1966 and Jan. 1967; and M. Mamalakis and
Clarke Reynolds, *Essays on Chilean Economy,* Irwin, 1965. On the importance of domestic factors in the unsatisfactory export performance of the
underdeveloped countries, see A. I. Macbean, *Export Instability and Economic
Development,* Allen and Unwin, 1966, and my paper, below, Chapter 12.

Kong and Puerto Rico. Conversely, as we shall hope to show, successful "import-substitution" need not be confined to manufacturing industry; it can equally take place in agriculture and in raw materials production for the domestic market. (2) The identification of diminishing returns with agriculture is based on the assumption of given techniques and resources which rules out the possibility of improving or augmenting them through investment and research. On the other hand, the experience of the developed countries suggests that technical progress and increasing productivity can occur as frequently in primary production as in manufacturing industry, depending on the amount of investment and research which has been devoted to each. Thus, instead of relying on broad generalisations about the growth prospects of agriculture and manufacturing, we need to study the economic circumstances of each underdeveloped country in detail in order to make a more reliable assessment of the relative productivity of investment in primary production and in manufacturing industry both for the export and the domestic markets. This is merely another way of saying that we should consider the comparative advantage of investment in alternative uses.

To conclude: our survey has brought out some plausible hypotheses supporting a pro-trade view of economic development which deserve to be followed up in the light of the detailed economic circumstances of each underdeveloped country. Ultimately however we have to fall back on the theory of comparative costs in assessing the relative merits of the "export-led" and the "import-substitution" policies of economic development.

II

It is frequently said that the comparative costs theory is too "static" to deal with the "dynamic" problems of economic development. But the principle of allocation of resources according to comparative costs can be readily extended to the problem of a developing country trying to use a given amount of its investible resources to promote economic development measured in terms of a "final output." Basically, the problem has two stages: first, how to convert domestic savings into "capital goods"; and second, how to use these "capital goods" to obtain the largest amount of "final output." At each stage, there is the problem of choice between using the "direct" method of domestic production and the "indirect" method of international trade according to comparative costs. The domestic savings can be converted into capital goods by producing them at home; alternatively, they may be imported. Assuming no aid, the foreign exchange necessary to pay for them can be acquired either by cutting down other imports or by cutting down domestic expenditure and shifting the resources thus released into export production. Having obtained the "capital goods," the "final output" can be acquired either by producing it directly at home or indirectly, by using the capital goods to produce exports which can be exchanged for the "final output."[10] Depending on our philosophy of economic development, the "final output" to be maximised may be defined in two ways. It may be defined as the output of consumers' goods to be made available during a plan period, subject to leaving a certain minimum target amount of "terminal" capital equipment at the end of the plan period. Or, the "final output" to be maximised may be defined as the "terminal" amount of capital equipment available at the end of the plan period, subject to a minimum amount of consumption goods to be made available during the plan.

There can be little disagreement between the free traders and the protectionists about this general formulation. What they really disagree about is the potential comparative advantage of using the indirect method of trade with that of direct home production at each of these two stages. The present-day protectionists are only too willing to emphasise the comparative advantage of trade in the first stage, i.e. in converting domestic savings into capital goods.

10. I owe this formulation to J. R. Hicks, *Essays in World Economics,* Oxford University Press, 1960, Ch. 8; See also his *Capital and Growth,* Oxford University Press, 1965, pp. 206–7 on the alternative approaches to maximising the "final output" of a plan.

In fact, it is their chief theme in current discussions that the developing countries have been held back in their economic growth because of shortage of foreign exchange to pay for the imports of capital goods and other inputs technically necessary for their import-substitution industries. But when they come to the second stage, i.e. in converting capital goods into "final output" which they identify with manufactured consumers' goods, they reverse their position. Invoking various arguments, particularly the economies of scale and the infant industry arguments, they maintain that the long-run potential comparative advantage will lie with the direct method of import-substitution. The free-traders, on the other hand, stress the potential gains to be obtained by using the capital goods indirectly to produce exports in which the country has a comparative advantage and thus acquiring through trade a larger amount of "final output" than can be obtained through direct import substitution.

We shall consider the economies of scale argument and the various extensions of the infant industry argument in the next section. Before we do so, it is necessary to point out that the current protectionist thinking based on a distinction between "capital goods" and "consumers' goods" according to the physical, as distinct from the economic properties of these goods, is very liable to the "fallacy of misplaced concreteness."

The notion that "capital goods" essentially consists in pieces of machinery and durable capital equipment which are to be regarded as "missing components" for economic development follows from identifying "industrialization" with the growth of manufacturing industry in the narrow sense. But in the underdeveloped countries, with inadequate economic infra-structure and rapidly growing populations, one would expect the share of total investment required for agriculture and social overhead capital to be much larger than that required for durable producers' equipment in the manufacturing sector. Once we go on to consider the requirements of investment in agriculture and social overhead capital, there does not seem to be any strong reason for thinking that the potential comparative advantages of the underdeveloped countries will always lie at the consumers' goods end rather than at the capital-goods end of import-substitution.

Peasant agriculture in the underdeveloped countries typically requires simpler forms of capital equipment than the manufacturing sector and indeed, a large part of agricultural investment made by peasants in improving their land may require no cash outlay at all, let alone foreign exchange. Similarly, a large part of investment in social overhead capital, such as transport and communications and irrigation, takes the form of building and construction work requiring such materials as cement, bricks and tiles, where domestic production has a strong locational advantage. Investment in social overhead capital may require some imported machinery; but like agriculture, it also requires large inputs of labour directed towards the production of future output and workers engaged in these types of investment activity have to be maintained during the period before their work yields consumable output. Thus for a large part of investment in agriculture and social overhead capital, the classical concept of capital as "wage fund" seems to be more relevant than the modern concept of capital as durable capital equipment. This significantly alters our views about what should be the "normal" pattern of import substitution available to the underdeveloped countries, according to their potential comparative advantage.[11]

Now a number of underdeveloped countries are having to import their food and raw material requirements because of the backwardness of their agriculture combined with population pressure on land (as in India) or even without any great population density (as in some of the Latin American countries). For these countries, an

11. See W. W. Lockwood, *The Economic Development of Japan,* Ch. 5, for an illustration of what he describes as "the general truth that the real capital assets required in various forms of economic growth must be largely produced at home" (p. 243). Writing about the experiences of the advanced countries over long periods, Kuznets notes that the share of producers' equipment in total capital formation was as low as a fifth in earlier years rising to well over a third in recent years. S. Kuznets, *Modern Economic Growth: Rate, Structure and Spread,* Yale University Press, 1966, p. 257 and Table 5.6.

increase in domestic agricultural production can offer a considerable scope for "import-substitution," either by cutting down their foreign exchange expenditure on primary imports or by absorbing purchasing power which at present seeks outlet in other imports. For countries already suffering from population pressure, "import-substituting" investment would have to be mainly directed towards raising agricultural productivity. For the less densely populated countries, "import-substitution" may be promoted also by investment in transport and communications and improvements in marketing facilities in agriculture. Where the expansion of agricultural production has been held back because local manufacturing industries cannot supply the peasants with consumers' goods on attractive terms, then even a liberalisation in the imports of these "incentive" consumers' goods may indirectly promote "import-substitution."

This type of intangible and indirect economic effect is obscured by the current practice of equating the imports of finished consumers' goods with consumption and the imports of capital goods and other inputs with investment. As we have suggested, in certain circumstances, cheap incentive consumers' goods have as much right to be considered as "inputs" into agriculture as the technical inputs. Conversely, the fact that an underdeveloped country is importing only capital goods and technical inputs and no finished consumers' goods from abroad does not mean that there is no further scope for cutting down "inessential" imports. In many underdeveloped countries where domestic industries catering to luxury consumption by the urban classes have been encouraged to grow through a combination of ineffective taxation and a desire to possess "sophisticated" manufacturing industries, it does not require much penetration to see that a considerable proportion of imported capital goods and "essential" inputs merely serve to satisfy luxury consumption inside the country.

The crux of the matter is that unless the import-substituting industries in the underdeveloped countries are assumed to be desired for their own sake as show pieces and not as the means of economic development, we cannot simply take them as *given* and confine ourselves to calculating the "import requirements" which follow purely as a technical consequence of their continued operation. We are bound to ask the "economic" question whether the foreign exchange required to pay for their technically necessary inputs cannot be used more advantageously in other ways of import-substitution or in export production. The fundamental economic problem of choice is most clearly defined when we start from a *given* amount of foreign exchange available, both from domestic savings and from aid and consider the comparative advantage of using the indirect method of trade and the direct method of home production in converting this limited supply of foreign exchange into economic development measured in terms of some "final output." The economic problem is obscured when we start, as is the current fashion, from a certain target of growth for the underdeveloped countries and estimate the foreign exchange requirement for that rate of growth from fixed technical coefficients of foreign inputs to total output. The motive for adopting this procedure is, of course, to calculate the "gap" between the projected foreign exchange requirements and the projected foreign exchange receipts from exports, on the assumption or the pious hope that a perfectly elastic supply of foreign aid will be forthcoming to fill this gap. Whatever the "bargaining value" of this assumption in negotiations for international aid, it seriously distracts the underdeveloped countries from the real issues of development policy facing them. For instance, the central problem facing the import-substitution industries is how to improve their efficiency and lower their costs. The reason for their high costs is not to be found in the foreign exchange component of their costs but in the domestic component. The constant emphasis on the foreign exchange requirements of these industries distracts attention from the vital domestic component of their costs which can make or mar their future development.

III

According to Friedrich List, an underdeveloped country at an earlier stage of development characterised by a backward agriculture should not protect its industries. On the contrary, it should pursue free trade, both for the material gains and for the educational gains from contact with the more advanced countries. It is only after a country has attained a certain level of general economic development, including a thoroughly developed agriculture, that it should start giving protection to the "main branches" of its manufacturing industry which would promote "the increase of the mental and material capital, of the technical abilities and spirit of enterprise of the nation." (List, *op. cit.* pp. 144–45).

The neo-classical economists detached the infant industry argument from the notion of the stages of economic development but accepted the beneficial "educative effect" of learning by doing. They therefore accepted the case for offering temporary protection to an industry during the initial period of high costs on the understanding that the infant industry would eventually be able to compete on equal terms with the established foreign producers both in the domestic and in the export markets. The neo-classical economists would look upon the lowering of costs to be achieved by the infant industry through learning and experience as "irreversible" by a subsequent shrinkage in its market. Thus it can be formally distinguished from the lowering in costs through the economies of large scale production (but with the same level of skill and experience) which is "reversible" by a shrinkage in the size of the market. The neo-classical economists also emphasised that protection is essentially a selective method of granting a differential price or cost advantage to a particular industry or group of industries relative to the other domestic industries. They would say that to try to give protection to all industries is to give special protection to none and that a general encouragement to domestic production should be more appropriately given by a devaluation or deflation rather than by tariffs and subsidies.

In current discussions, the neo-classical interpretation of the infant industry argument has been questioned both from the free trade and from the protectionist standpoints.

From the free trade side, it has been argued that the mere fact that an industry incurs losses during the initial stages to be followed by profits later is not in itself a sufficient ground for giving it protection. If the future profits were high enough to more than compensate the initial losses, private enterprise would not be deterred from investing in this industry provided that there is an efficient capital market to advance loans to tide over the losses during the initial period. In order to justify government intervention to encourage an industry, the industry must not only yield a beneficial educative effect but it must also be shown that this beneficial effect is not appropriable by the private investor: that is to say, the social returns exceed the private returns from investment. Further, even if there is a genuine excess of social over private returns from investment in a given industry, this is a case for encouraging it by a subsidy and not by a tariff protection. A "domestic distortion" should be cured by applying a subsidy at the source of the distortion, i.e. within the domestic economy. To try to cure it by a tariff is not only to adopt an indirect and less theoretically reliable remedy; it is also to introduce a new unnecessary distortion in foreign trade causing additional losses to the consumers.[12]

From the protectionist side, it has been argued that the neoclassical economists have emasculated the infant industry doctrine by taking it out of List's original context of promoting economic development and by applying it too narrowly to a single industry on its own instead of applying it to the whole of the "infant" manufacturing sector of an underdeveloped country as List had intended. But the attempt to extend the infant industry argument from an individual industry to the manufacturing sector as a whole seems to be based on a vague analogy, rather than on a genuine extension of the infant industry concept. As we shall now show, even if we accept the infant industry argument in its broader neo-classical

12. Cf. H. G. Johnson, "Optimal Trade Intervention in the Presence of Domestic Distortions" in *Trade, Growth and the Balance of Payments,* Essays in Honor of Gottfried Haberler, Chicago, 1965; also J. Bhagwati and V. K. Ramaswami, "Domestic Distortions, Tariffs and the Theory of Optimum Subsidy," *Journal of Political Economy,* Feb. 1963.

sense, it cannot be used as a convenient umbrella to cover the underdeveloped countries' current practice of protecting their "infant" manufacturing sector as a whole.

The manufacturing sector in most underdeveloped countries typically consists of a collection of industries producing import-substituting consumers' goods. The proposal to protect the manufacturing sector as a whole therefore amounts to selecting the industries for protection according to their capacity to satisfy the existing pattern of domestic demand for manufactured consumers' goods. On the other hand, the infant industry argument, however broadly interpreted, is concerned with an industry's capacity to lower its costs in the future through the process of learning-by-doing. *Prima facie*, we would not, therefore, expect a group of import-substituting industries selected to match the pattern of domestic demand to be the same as a group of genuine infant industries selected on their prospects of lowering costs in the future.

The issues have however been clouded by mixing up an industry's prospects of lowering its costs and improving its efficiency through the infant industry process of learning with its prospects of lowering its costs through the economies of large scale production expected from the enlargement in the size of the domestic market. Thus the most commonly adopted justification for the underdeveloped countries' policy of protecting, in one way or another, all their existing consumers' goods industries may be stated as follows: (1) it is only by simultaneously setting up and protecting a large group of consumers' goods industries on the "balanced growth" principle that the *total* size of the domestic market can be expanded sufficiently to allow each of these industries to attain an optimum scale of production; (2) the optimum output for each industry is determined by the technically efficient minimum unit of production and since these technically required minimum units of production are much smaller in the consumers' goods industries than in the capital goods industries, a protectionist policy to encourage import-substitution should start with the former.

In the light of our analysis in Section I, it is not difficult to see how the concept of lowering costs by overcoming the indivisibilities differs from the infant industry concept of lowering costs through learning. In the import-substitution approach, the emphasis is on the enlargement of the domestic market; as the overall size of the domestic market increases, each industry obtains a proportionate share of this protected market according to the given income elasticity of demand for its product. Thus an industry's capacity to lower its costs by moving towards its optimum scale of output does not depend on its special capacity to improve efficiency, but is assumed to follow automatically from the enlargement in the overall size of the protected domestic market. In contrast, in the infant industry approach, the emphasis is on an industry's own capacity to improve its efficiency and lower costs through learning and experience; as its costs and price are reduced, it obtains a larger share of the given market through the substitution effect according to the price elasticity of demand for its product. The size of the domestic market and the economies of large scale production can of course help an infant industry to lower its costs, but they do not enter into the infant industry concept as essential ingredients. Whatever the size of the domestic market, a genuine infant industry is ultimately supposed to be able to lower its costs sufficiently to withstand international competition or even to break out into the export market.

The contrast between the infant industry and the import-substitution arguments can be carried further. The import-substitution argument is based on the principle of promoting economic growth through the "diversification" of resources to cater for the domestic market. On the other hand, if we accept the proposition that a developing country is likely to have different aptitudes and capacities to improve its efficiency through learning in different lines of industry, the infant industry argument is ultimately based on the principle of promoting economic growth through the "specialization" of resources. In this respect, it differs from the free trade theory only in that it allows the protected industry a period of learning and acquiring experience before it is ready to specialise along the lines of its potential comparative advantage as indicated by the development of its skills. Thus the chief objection that can be raised against the import-substitution theory from the standpoint of the infant industry argument is that the mere enlargement in the overall size of the protected domestic market and the potential economies of large scale production do not ensure that an individual industry will be able to lower its costs without an improvement in its own capacity to specialise, enabling it to take advantage of these opportunities.

If the import-substitution industries of the underdeveloped countries were genuine infant industries they would not only be able to dispense with protection but would also ease the balance of payments situation on attaining maturity: the lower costs of the domestically manufactured consumers' goods would switch demand away from imports and agricultural products. Few countries which have embarked on an import substitution policy have been able to reduce protection or ease their balance of payments problems. But without a detailed study of the individual economic circumstances, it is not easy to assess how far the balance of payments difficulties of the underdeveloped countries are due to the wrong choice of industries for protection and how far they have been aggravated by the macro-economic factors, such as inflation, budget deficits, over-valued rates of exchange, excessively high level of urban wages, etc. What is however fairly clear is that, given the present-day situation in many underdeveloped countries where the process of import-substitution has been slowed down by "foreign exchange shortage," the infant-industry approach would suggest a very different line of policy from that proposed by the exponents of the import-substitution approach, notably Prebisch.

Given the arbitrary short-run fluctuations in the prices of importable goods which characterise the underdeveloped countries suffering from continual foreign exchange crises, it is extremely difficult to offer proper protection in the form of effective differential price or cost advantage to the selected infant industries.[13] Thus the

13. For an elaboration of this argument, see above, Chapter 6.

infant industry approach would suggest a tighter fiscal and monetary discipline to reduce inflationary pressures leading to the intensification of import controls combined with a narrowing in the
range of industries to be protected, these being selected solely on
their prospective ability to reduce costs in the future. In contrast,
the exponents of the import-substitution approach like Prebisch
would advocate the maintenance of the present tempo of import-
substitution combined with the extension of import-substitution
from consumers' goods industries to capital goods industries, through
the formation of regional economic groups, such as LAFTA.

In the light of our previous analysis, the proposal to form regional
economic groups may be treated as a simple extension of the size-
of-the-market and the economies-of-scale argument for import-substitution, involving no new conceptual developments. But now, it
opens itself to two further difficulties. (1) The first, which was
already latent in our previous analysis, arises in connection with
the concept of the overall size of the protected home market. This
concept has to be treated with caution even when it is applied to a
single underdeveloped country where the coherence of its internal
market economy is undermined by various factors, such as poor
internal transport and communications or the importance of subsistence production. When the concept of the overall size of the
protected home market is applied to a collection of underdeveloped
countries, such as LAFTA, these difficulties are multiplied. It then
becomes increasingly unreliable to gauge the overall size of the
protected regional market from such indicators as the aggregate
area, population or income of the region as a whole. (2) The second
difficulty arises from the extension of import-substitution from
consumers' goods to capital goods, on the assumption that both are
to be sheltered from outside competition. In the case of a single
underdeveloped country, carrying on import-substitution of consumers' goods on the basis of capital goods imported at competitive
world market prices, the only reason for the high costs of the protected consumers' goods industries is their own inefficiency. Now,
the consumers' goods industries within the proposed regional group

would have to buy the capital goods from the less efficient producers within the group and would therefore be faced with two sources of high costs: from their own inefficiency in using the capital goods and from the higher cost of the regionally produced capital goods. Thus "technical complementarities" which figure so prominently in development theories, turn out, in the context of protection, to be a mechanism by which the high cost of production at one stage of production is transmitted to another within the protected group.

The doctrine that manufacturing industry in the underdeveloped countries should be protected because it can generate secondary rounds of economic activities through technical complementarities and "forward" and "backward-linkages" with agriculture on the "unbalanced growth" principle is as widely accepted as the doctrine that manufacturing industry should be protected because it can generate economies of scale through the enlargement of the domestic market on the "balanced growth" principle. We may briefly examine it to find out whether it offers an alternative basis for the extension of the infant industry argument for the protection of a "vertical" group of industries linked through input-output relationships as distinct from a "horizontal" group of consumers' goods industries linked by the pattern of domestic market demand for their products.

The case of the "forward-linkage" where the output of manufacturing supplies the input for agriculture, e.g. the fertiliser industry, is exactly parallel to the relationship between the capital goods industries and the consumers' goods industries within a regional economic group. In the light of our previous discussion, it is now easy to see that the fertiliser industry can help agriculture only if it can supply fertiliser at a lower price than imported fertiliser, in which case it will require no protection. Granting a subsidy to the fertiliser industry so that it can sell its product at the same price as the imported fertiliser may help the fertiliser industry if it turns out to be a genuine infant industry; but it cannot help agriculture. Putting a tariff on imported fertiliser to help the domestic fertiliser industry can only harm agriculture.

The case of the "backward-linkage" where manufacturing industry requires the output of agriculture as its input, e.g. a textile industry setting up demand for locally grown cotton, is similar to the type of import-substitution which we have discussed in Section II, with the difference that we were then concerned with import-substitution in agriculture according to potential comparative costs to be attained through capital investment. We are now concerned, not merely with the question whether import-substitution in agriculture should be encouraged by a subsidy but whether the protection of manufacturing industry can be defended on the ground that it promotes agricultural expansion.

The underdeveloped countries can provide many instances where the setting up and protection of manufacturing industry has stimulated the expansion of local agricultural production.[14] But on closer examination, it appears that manufacturing industry is able to generate these secondary rounds of agricultural expansion only because of the special condition which is explicitly recognised in the "vent for surplus" argument for free trade: viz. there exists uncultivated land and untapped capacity for agricultural production. Thus the real question is, under what conditions the protected local manufacturing industry will offer a more advantageous "vent for surplus" for local agriculture than export expansion, and how far there is a case for *joint* protection of manufacturing and raw material production on grounds of technical complementarity.

Let us return to our illustration of a textile factory and the encouragement of local cotton production. Suppose that the underdeveloped country in question genuinely has unused land and labour suitable for cotton growing so that it can eventually become competitive in the world cotton market. Then following the principle that a "domestic distortion" should be cured at its source, it would be cheaper and more reliable to encourage cotton production for export by a subsidy or by improving transport and marketing facilities instead of indirectly encouraging it by setting up a textile

14. Cf. A. O. Hirschman, *The Strategy of Economic Development,* New Haven, 1958.

factory which may or may not be a genuine infant industry. Suppose that the textile factory is also a genuine infant industry, in the sense it will eventually be able to withstand international competition in cloth production while paying world market price for raw cotton. Then the case for encouraging cotton production and a textile industry is really a case for encouraging two infant industries separately and does not gain any strength from their technical complementarity. The case for joint protection arises only *if* the local cotton is not quite competitive in the world market but has its *fob* price lower than the *cif* price of the imported cotton, and *if* the textile industry will not be competitive without the locational advantage of being able to use locally produced cotton at a lower price than imported cotton. How far this sort of case for protection is likely to be quantitatively important in the underdeveloped countries is a subject for further empirical research.

IV

While invoking the spirit of List, modern protectionist writers have ignored his injunction that an underdeveloped country with a backward agriculture should not adopt protection. In List's original argument, since manufacturing industry was to be protected only after agriculture had been fully developed, there could only be one "infant" sector, viz. the manufacturing sector. Modern writers have attempted to extend the analogy and frequently speak of the need to give "protection" to the "infant economies" of the underdeveloped countries. Presumably this means that the underdeveloped countries have an "infant" manufacturing sector combined with an "infant" agricultural sector both of which should be protected and encouraged by the granting of trade preferences by the advanced countries.

This last extension of the "infant industry" argument takes us beyond the theory of protection to the theory of international aid. For as far as trade theory is concerned, the co-existence of a backward agricultural sector with a backward manufacturing sector does not dispense with the necessity of assessing the comparative advantage of allocating resources between the two sectors and of judging which is likely to be the more promising "infant" sector. Thus, if it is desired to "protect" and encourage the "infant economy" as a whole, the resources required to do so must come from outside the "infant economy" in the form of international aid. This is merely another way of saying that trade preferences to the underdeveloped countries may be regarded as being equivalent to a devaluation on their part plus a transfer of aid to compensate for the change in the terms of trade.[15]

But the concept of the "infant economy" also implies a certain theory of international aid and this does not correspond to the UNCTAD concept of aid required to fill the foreign exchange gap of the underdeveloped countries resulting from their attempts to maintain the tempo of their import substitution. For one thing, this concept of aid is mainly concerned with the expansion of the manufacturing sector and virtually ignores the needs of the infant agricultural sector. Further, the hypothesis of the "infant economy" requires some convincing explanation of how it would be able to improve its general level of productivity and stand on its own feet after a well defined period of infancy. In particular, we would require a more convincing mechanism for generating increasing returns relative to the scale of total output than is offered by the balanced growth theory which relies on the economies to be obtained by overcoming technical indivisibilities in each producing unit in the manufacturing sector. Here again, the current fashion of calculating the foreign exchange requirements of the underdeveloped countries in relation to a target rate of growth, assuming fixed technical coefficients of foreign inputs to domestic output and constant returns to scale does not square with the "infant economy" interpretation of the underdeveloped countries.

The concept of international aid which corresponds closely to the "infant economy" view of the underdeveloped countries is to be found in the older notion of aid as "pre-investment" first put forward

15. Cf. H. G. Johnson, *Economic Policies Toward Less Developed Countries,* pp. 182–83.

in the UN Report on *Measures for Economic Development of the Underdeveloped Countries,* 1951, para. 269. Here, the argument is that the underdeveloped countries need a large amount of "pre-investment" in social overhead capital and in health and education before they can absorb a substantial amount of loan capital on commercial terms and that the basic task of international aid is to finance this "pre-investment."

The analogy between the "infant economy" and an underdeveloped country passing through an initial phase of building up its social overhead capital is obvious; the possibilities of reaping economies of scale by overcoming technical indivisibilities in public utilities, notably transport and communications, and power are also well known. There are further points which strengthen the "infant industry" analogy. First, investment in social overhead capital tends to have much longer gestation and infancy periods and there is a greater need to build capacity ahead of demand than in the case of investment in ordinary manufacturing industry. This suggests that the case of supplementing the normal working of the capital market with aid is stronger for investment in social overhead capital than in ordinary "direct investment." Further, public utilities typically have the widest network of input-output relationships with the rest of the economy and are therefore in a strategic position to be able to transmit their internal economies as external economies to the other sectors, both agriculture and manufacturing. Finally, it is worth remembering that, unlike the products of the import-substitution industries, the output of social overhead capital, such as "electric power, irrigation and inland transport services cannot be imported."[16]

The case for improving the productivity and efficiency of the underdeveloped countries through "pre-investment" in education and research is also widely accepted. Here however, we should put in a note of warning. Much in the way that "industrialization" tends to be identified too narrowly with manufacturing industry, "educational progress" tends to be identified too narrowly with the expan-

16. R. Nurkse, *Equilibrium and Growth in the World Economy,* Harvard University Press, 1962, Ch. 10, p. 270.

sion of formal educational facilities. The tendency to treat the "steel mill" and the "university" as the twin symbols of industrialization and educational progress tends to distract attention from the fact that education, in the sense relevant for promoting economic development, must take into account the broader effect of the whole economic environment on the economic competence of the people of the underdeveloped countries. Typically, in the current setting, most underdeveloped countries trying to promote domestic industrialization using a network of import controls in an atmosphere of economic nationalism tend to neglect the less tangible and less dramatic effect of the "outward-looking" economic policies on the economic education of their people.

The governments of the underdeveloped countries usually prefer to absorb modern techniques and organizational methods by recruiting foreign technical experts on short-run contracts in the public sector rather than by permitting foreign private enterprise to operate in their countries on a long-term basis. Even where foreign private enterprises are permitted, the preference is against enterprises in primary export production and for manufacturing industry catering for the domestic market. Frequently, foreign manufacturing companies may be induced by tax concessions and tariff protection to open branch factories. It is arguable whether such "tariff factories" have a greater educational effect on the people of the underdeveloped countries than the competitive foreign enterprises in primary export production. The net result is however to enlist foreign private enterprise for domestic industrialization rather than for export expansion with less favourable effects on the balance of payments. Furthermore, given the network of quantitative import controls, the indigenous entrepreneurs find it more profitable to divert their energy and ingenuity from the task of raising productivity and efficiency to the task of procuring the necessary import licences, by hook or by crook, and exploiting the loopholes in the government regulations. Such perverse "educative effects" of the current trade policies of the underdeveloped countries are not likely to be cured by expanding investment in formal educational facilities or by a technical aid programme from outside.

What is really required is a reconsideration of the educative effect of international trade policies in the broader sense suggested by the "outward-looking" approach to economic development. Given their emergent nationalism, the underdeveloped countries are unwilling or unable to adopt the full "outward-looking" policy of freer commodity trade combined with freer admission of foreign private enterprises. But it may be wondered whether, instead of their current policies of protection and selective admittance of foreign manufacturing industry, they might not find a more promising "second-best" policy in combining restrictions on all foreign enterprises with free trade.[17] Then at least the indigenous entrepreneurs of the underdeveloped countries would be subject fully to the "educative" pressures of the world market forces to transform the internal economic structure of their countries according to their potential comparative advantage. As in the pure theory of international trade, so also in the policital economy of educative effect, movements of commodities may be a substitute for movements of factors of production.

17. Japan, during the Meiji period, approximated to this policy of restricting or discouraging private foreign enterprise while pursuing other aspects of the "outward-looking" policy, viz. free trade, recruitment of foreign technicians and sending a large number of students abroad. It was only after 1900 that the suspicion of foreign business enterprise was relaxed. Cf. W. W. Lockwood, *The Economic Development of Japan,* pp. 321–23.

III | Education and Development

8 | Education and Economic Development

In recent years, economists working on the problems of development of the underdeveloped countries have turned their attention towards education for a number of reasons.

1. The experience of the advanced countries has suggested that the rate of economic growth they have enjoyed cannot be satisfactorily explained purely in terms of quantitatively measurable increases in material capital and in the size of the working population. This has led to the hypothesis that a substantial "residual" of economic growth must be accounted for in terms of a rise in the productivity of the resources due to technical innovations and other qualitative improvements in the methods of production and organization. These "residual" factors of economic growth are thought to be related directly or indirectly to better education.

2. The experience of the underdeveloped countries also seems to point in the same direction. In the early 1950's, it was fashionable to look upon material capital as the chief "missing component" of economic development, and much was made of the idea of mobilizing the underemployed *unskilled* labour to build roads, irrigation works, etc. It is now increasingly realized that a massive injection of capital into an underdeveloped country will not necessarily start a successful

From *Social and Economic Studies,* Vol. 14, No. 1, March 1965, pp. 8–20. Reprinted by permission.

development process unless that country already possesses a suitable institutional and productive framework and the necessary skills to "absorb" capital and use it in a productive manner. Thus, now, the emphasis has shifted from investment in material capital to "investment in human capital" and from the mobilization of the brawn-power to the brain-power of the people of the underdeveloped countries.

3. Then there are the urgent practical problems of trying to launch large-scale economic development programmes without a sufficient number of people with the necessary training and skills to carry out these programmes. If the private sector of many underdeveloped countries is supposed to be short of entrepreneurs, the public sector of these countries seems to be equally short of administrators to carry out these entrepreneurial and managerial functions. There is also the notorious shortage of technicians and specialists of all types.

These considerations have combined to create a powerful current of opinion which maintains that education is the chief missing component of economic development in the underdeveloped countries, and that "investment in human capital" will yield very high and quantitatively measurable rates of return.[1] Obviously this emphasis on the need to mobilize the brain-power rather than the brawn-power of the people of the underdeveloped countries is a great advance on previous approaches. Yet there are signs that it might be carried too far and in isolation from other factors affecting the total economic setting of the underdeveloped countries. The aim of this paper is to point out the limitations of some of the pro-educational arguments. In Section I we shall consider the dangers of transposing arguments showing the high productivity of education from the advanced countries to the different setting of the underdeveloped countries. In Section II, we shall distinguish between the passive and active roles of the educational system in the development process and use this to show some of the limitations of the popular arguments for tech-

1. For a compendium of pro-educational arguments and their bibliography see T. W. Schultz, *The Economic Value of Education,* Columbia University Press, London and New York, 1963.

nical education and universal primary education. In the concluding Section III, we shall question the general presumption that the spread of education, by itself, will necessarily break down social "rigidities" and resistance.

I

There are a number of weaknesses in the general argument that because a substantial "residual" part of economic growth of the advanced countries is attributable to a "built in" stream of technical innovations, the underdeveloped countries should try to achieve this desirable state of steady technical progress through "crash programmes" in education. First, there is no necessary relation between an increase in educational expenditure and a country's capacity to improve the quality of her scientific and technical research. It depends not merely on the aggregate amount of educational expenditure but on how that expenditure is used and on a horde of other factors. Second, there is no necessary relation between the ability to carry out original scientific research leading to technical inventions and the practical capacity to apply these to solve economic problems which is the strict meaning of the term "innovation" as the economists understand it. For instance, the United Kingdom in recent decades seems to have been frequently in the forefront of scientific ideas and technical inventions but seems to lag behind other countries in the commercial exploitation of the new technical knowledge on a mass production basis. (Interestingly enough the remedy currently popular in England for this is the "crash programmes" in education.) Third, in the underdeveloped countries, the successful adoption of new knowledge for economic development frequently requires, not merely technical innovations, but also social and organizational innovations affecting the fabric of the social and economic framework. Here, the problem of new ideas and innovations merges into the problem of appropriate adaptation as contrasted with mechanical adoption of outside social, political and technological ideas in the underdeveloped countries. Even in our present state of ignorance, we can be pretty certain that the capacity to make correct judgments of the *relevance* of the ideas and knowledge from the advanced countries for their own conditions is likely to be one of the most important aims of education in the underdeveloped countries, whether we are thinking of the so-called "technical know-how" or of the social sciences.

The weakness of attempting a short-cut to technical progress through an expansion of the educational programme is even more obvious when put in terms of a particular and specific type of education. For instance, it is sometimes argued that since an increase in expenditure in agricultural education and research in the United States has resulted in dramatic increases in agricultural productivity, a similar increase in agricultural productivity in the underdeveloped countries will necessarily follow from expanding agricultural education, by opening more agricultural schools and colleges, by giving an agricultural bias to the curricula in rural schools and above all by expanding the agricultural extension services. In what follows, it should be emphasized that we are not arguing against the need to improve agricultural education in the underdeveloped countries. Our aim is merely to illustrate some of the limitations of an argument based on an illegitimate isolation of poor educational facilities from a complex of causes which have combined to depress agricultural productivity in the underdeveloped countries and the dangers of mechanically transferring conclusions from one country to another. In the United States, we start from a situation where the following conditions hold:

(a) The existing scientific agricultural knowledge is relevant to and in fact grows out of American agricultural conditions: thus there is a directly applicable body of technical knowledge available to be spread among American farmers.

(b) Both the demand conditions, i.e. salary, working conditions, etc. and the supply conditions, i.e. the general supply of educated people, are suitable for the creation of competent agricultural extension officers in a sufficient number.

(c) Agriculture is highly developed both in technical production and in economic organization, including land tenure, credit, marketing and transport facilities, etc. so that the farmers have the incentives to adopt new methods.

Unfortunately, these conditions do not normally obtain in the underdeveloped countries. In particular, while the new agricultural knowledge in the United States is tailored to the needs of the American farmers, the same cannot be said of the "modern" agricultural methods when applied to the tropical peasant agriculture in the underdeveloped countries. Too little systematic study and research has been done and too much half-baked advice has been given to the peasants. For instance, peasants have been urged to use fertilizers in conditions where the extra returns will not cover the extra costs; they have been urged to plant the whole of their land with an improved variety of crop where this will result in labour shortage at harvest time in a locality where the traditional pattern of crop-sowing is designed to stagger labour requirements for harvest; they have been urged to adopt soil conservation methods which, although having beneficial effects in the very long-run, has the immediate effect of reducing output or increasing labour input without complementary policies to relieve the immediate burden; and so on. This sort of happening is so commonplace that in many underdeveloped countries one begins to have serious doubts whether, without a great deal of further study and research, the agricultural experts, both foreign and indigenous, are currently in a position to teach the peasants genuinely better methods than their existing methods which have been evolved by trial and error over a long period to suit local conditions.

Where the new agricultural knowledge is relevant and profitable, it should not be too difficult to spread it among the peasants through a large number of fairly low-grade agricultural extension officers. Indeed, if we are to go by the history of peasant export production in Southeast Asia or West Africa, peasants were not slow to adopt new crops and new methods, when they were profitable, without assistance from agricultural departments. But where the problem is one of trying to build up a body of new knowledge and new methods appropriate to local conditions, then the agricultural extension officers have to be more highly qualified for they must select and feed back the significant problems and information to the research centres. Here, apart from the well-known difficulty of getting a sufficient number of such highly qualified people to go and work in rural areas, there is also the problem of the social and cultural gap between the agricultural extension officers and the peasants. This gap is many times larger than that between the U.S. agricultural officers and the U.S. farmers and may create serious problems in the communication of ideas both ways.

Thus when we observe that peasants in the underdeveloped countries are reluctant to adopt new farming methods, the reason may not be their "conservatism" and resistance to social change. It may simply be that the new methods are inappropriate to the local conditions or that the economic setting, including the land tenure, credit and marketing arrangements, etc. does not offer them adequate incentives to adopt the new methods. We shall return to this point later. For the moment, we conclude that the attempt to show the high economic value of education by transposing arguments applicable to the advanced countries to the different setting of the underdeveloped countries is not convincing, either at a general level or as applied to a particular type of education, such as agricultural education.

II

One of the fundamental weaknesses of current writings on education and the economic development of the underdeveloped countries is the failure to distinguish and follow up the implications of two very different views of the role of the educational system. On the one hand, we may look upon the educational system as playing a passive role, trying to supply the different types of skilled manpower which will be required by a *given* pattern and rate of economic growth. On the other hand, we may look upon the educational system as playing an active role, trying to transform the existing economic structure to accelerate the rate of economic growth. We should not underrate the first role of the educational system in our preoccupation with the "dynamic" and "transformation" aspects of education. In many newly independent countries of Asia and Africa, it is the primary function of the educational system to fill up the obvious gaps in skilled manpower, in the general administration and in the various technical services, both in the public and the private sectors, left after the departure of the expatriate personnel. Even in Latin America, this passive function of the educational system is not negligible. For example, the United Nations have produced a number of reports on "Analyses and Projections of Economic Development" for Colombia, Brazil and Peru. These reports attempt to make projections of statistical series in different sectors of economic activity with a view to providing the governments of these countries with background data and bases required to draw up over-all programmes of development. These reports are mainly concerned with financial and material capital. But if we had further information, it would be possible to estimate the manpower requirements of different types from these projections. Now economic projections, even along the existing trends, are notably subject to errors, and skilled manpower projections are especially liable to mistakes. But leaving aside the practical problems of accurate forecasting and the equally difficult problem of organizing the educational output to meet the projected requirements of manpower, conceptually at least, the function of the educational system in its passive role is clear: it is to produce a sufficient number of specific types of round pegs to fit into the round holes which will emerge in a given framework of economic activity in the different sectors, if the projections turn out to be correct.

The situation is quite different when we turn to the second view of the educational system whose function is actively to transform the existing pattern of economic development and accelerate the rate of growth. Here the function is to produce square pegs which will not fit into the round holes but will serve to tear down the existing economic patterns into new patterns. Thus we are no longer concerned with the manpower requirements if the existing trends in the export of primary products continue. Nor are we even concerned with the manpower requirements of the import-substituting manufacturing industries so long as these industries are taking over the *given* technical know-how of the advanced countries so that the skilled manpower requirements are predictable along standard lines. The educational system in its active role is concerned with two main problems which raise a horde of conceptual difficulties. First, it is concerned with technical innovations and transformation of the productive structure. This includes raising the productivity in agriculture by evolving new techniques which are genuinely superior to the existing techniques in local conditions. This also includes genuine adaptation and improvements of the western industrial technical know-how to suit local economic conditions. But as we have said, fundamental technical innovations in the underdeveloped countries are not likely to be successful without corresponding social innovations affecting the complex of the social fabric governing economic relations. For instance, many writers fear that in some Latin American countries economic development cannot be sustained unless the underlying social and political tensions which threaten political stability can be eased. Thus the second task of the educational system in its active role will be to produce men who can undertake these social and political innovations. Now it is difficult enough to specify in concrete terms the educational system which might tend to encourage technical innovations in the strictly economic and material sense. It becomes well nigh impossible to specify the norm of an educational system which will promote social innovations and political stability.

However, even if it is difficult to formulate a positive educational norm for economic development, our analysis may be used for a critical assessment of some of the popularly advocated educational norms. Consider first the view that the underdeveloped countries should make a big switch from the general "liberal" type of university education to technical and vocational education of a more specialized type. This is an extreme form of looking upon education as the chief "missing component" of economic development and is based on the assumption that it is possible to estimate how many people with what type of specific training and qualification will be required to sustain a given pattern of economic development. This approach is strongest when we are dealing with newly independent countries where there are obvious gaps in manpower and definite vacancies for specialist technicians of various types. We can also see that the very high economic value claimed for education derives partly from the vital necessity for certain types of technicians at certain stages of development. These technicians are rather like vital bits of machinery, say like sparking plugs: without them the car won't go. But the limitation of this view, apart from the practical difficulties of making accurate forecasts, is that, because technicians are by definition highly specialized and adapted to a particular type of work, it is difficult to absorb an excess supply of these types of people once the obvious gaps have been filled. Even when we are working on a given pattern of economic development it is probably necessary to have a reserve pool of more versatile people with broader education who can be trained further for a wide range of jobs to allow for mistakes in forecasting and unforeseen requirements. But once we have provided for the present and expected vacancies in specific types of technical work, it is not helpful to talk of more technical and vocational education without any clear idea of what type of specific training is required and where these newly trained people are to be fitted in. Here we have passed beyond the stage of supplying some "missing component" such as the sparking plugs in a car to the problem of redesigning the engine.

Thus, the case for more technical education is stronger the more optimistic we are about the continuance of a predictable pattern of economic development given by autonomous and exogenous forces: the educational system can then usefully continue to play the passive role of supplying specific types of skills which can be forecast within a given framework. For instance, if the world demand for an under-developed country's export is showing a steady expansion and if there is also a considerable scope for setting up import-substituting manufacturing industries on the basis of the given technical know-how from the advanced countries, then it is reasonable to look upon the role of the educational system as trying to prevent the predictable bottle-necks in specific types of skills. But if we are pessimistic about the continuance of the existing pattern of export expansion and if the scope for setting up import-substituting industries is limited, then the expansion of technical education along existing lines will not help and may even result in the future unemployment of people with the wrong sort of technical training. We shall then have to face the more difficult task of making the educational system play an active role in producing people who can innovate and branch out into new lines of economic activities in the place of the existing activities which have ceased to grow.

It is frequently said that while the underdeveloped countries need more technically trained people, students tend to go into liberal arts courses, such as law and literature. For instance, the World Bank Mission Report to Venezuela (p. 350) complained of the fact that between 1957 and 1960, too many students were enrolling for Law and Economics beyond the needs of the country, while too few students were enrolling for Agronomy and Veterinary courses. The first thing to clear up in this sort of situation is whether the need for agronomists and veterinary officers is present in the form of purely statistical estimates or whether there are unfilled vacancies with salaries and prospects as attractive as in jobs open to Law and Economics graduates. This elementary point, that is, to make the "need" for certain types of skill and training into economically effective demand by offering attractive remuneration, is apt to be forgotten by some writers bent on urging the building of more agricultural and veterinary schools and colleges. Such "investment in human capital" will not work unless there is the prospect that students from these institutions will get jobs at least as attractive as alternative opportunities open to them. Then there is the well-known reluctance of educated people in the underdeveloped countries to go and work in remoter areas as teachers, agricultural officers, etc. Part of this reluctance is the result of the centralization of the administration where prospects of promotion are brightest in the capital cities, and people in the remoter rural areas become "forgotten men" suffering a form of banishment. But beyond this also there may be genuine "sociological resistances" to taking up certain types of jobs and working in rural areas. Two points may be made in passing about these "sociological resistances." Economists are used to explaining these resistances in "rational" terms such as monetary rewards, conditions and prospects of work, etc. This rough and ready interpretation of human behaviour awaits refinements by sociologists with reference to concrete situations. The second point is that in so far as the "sociological resistances" exist they are not confined to uneducated peasants. One of the most damaging forms of "resistance" may be found in the reluctance of educated people from towns to work in the villages.

Let us now turn to the second popularly advocated educational norm for the underdeveloped countries, viz. 100 per cent primary education for all children of school age. Now, in so far as this is regarded as a desirable social and political end in itself which should be provided at all cost, it does not admit further argument. It is not for anyone to gainsay the deeply felt desire of the underdeveloped countries to provide their citizens with primary education as a basic right. But in so far as it is claimed that the spread of primary education among all children is a powerful means of promoting economic development it can be subject to critical analysis.

To begin with, it still seems doubtful whether the growth-promoting effects of widespread primary education can be measured with any certainty or accuracy. In the past, many Western countries, notably the United Kingdom, seem to have been able to launch an industrial revolution without universal primary education. The modern developments of mass media of communication such as the radio and television also seem to undermine the importance of conventional primary education as a means of communicating ideas. Yet very high and quantitatively stated claims have been made for primary education. For instance, in one study on Venezuela it has been claimed that the incremental rate of return on investment was between 82 and 130 per cent per annum during 1957–58. These figures seem to be obtained by comparing the excess in earnings of a primary school graduate over an illiterate urban or rural worker and using these as returns on the cost of six years primary education accumulated at the rate of 10 per cent.[2] Now a strong case can probably be made for expanding primary education in Venezuela if we expect her very high rate of economic expansion in the past to continue in the future. But a considerable amount of reserve must be attached to *the method* of calculating the return on primary education which seems to be based on a short-run partial analysis. The excess earnings of a primary school graduate over an illiterate worker reflects the scarcity of primary school graduates in *the present economic conditions* when these graduates are directly put to work instead of continuing with their education. Now if the present Venezuelan rate of economic expansion (determined by her petroleum industry) declines, it does not seem plausible that the mere presence of a large number of primary school graduates can do very much to help the country along new lines of economic development. What seems more likely is that the country's capacity to absorb them would decline, creating unemployment among them and reducing their excess earnings over illiterate workers to zero. Conversely, the fact that a primary school graduate can earn no more than an illiterate worker does not show that the rate of return on investment in primary education is zero. It all depends on how far the primary school graduate can be given further education and whether this further stage of education will help to transform the economy and maintain the high rate of economic expansion. Thus the economic value of primary education may be large or small according to circumstances and it should be assessed in the total economic situation of a country over a long period. This is not likely to be an exact quantitative measurement in isolation from our expectations of the future pattern of Venezuelan economic growth.

If the returns of 100 per cent primary education cannot be mea-

2. C. S. Shoup *et al.*, *The Fiscal System of Venezuela*, 1959, quoted in T. W. Schultz, *The Economic Value of Education*, p. 61.

sured with certainty or accuracy, what about the costs of such a programme? Here we should distinguish the short-run financial and material costs from the longer-run human costs. Apart from the capital costs of buildings and equipment, one of the things which makes education expensive in the underdeveloped countries is the relatively high salary of teachers. For instance, Sir Arthur Lewis has calculated that while the average American primary school teacher get less than 1½ times the *per capita* income of U.S.A., the primary school teacher gets 3 times the *per capita* income in Jamaica, 5 times in Ghana and 7 times in Nigeria.[3] Information is not available about the relative salary levels of primary school teachers in the Latin American countries, but projections for the number of school teachers, say in the World Bank Mission Report on Venezuela, seem to be based on the doubtful assumption that the same quality of teachers will continue to be available in increasing quantities at the same salary level even when they are required to work in the remoter regions of the country.

Even if we assume that, unlike the underdeveloped countries in Asia and Africa, the Latin American countries are rich enough and can raise sufficient taxes to meet the financial costs of universal primary education, one should take into account the more serious longer-term human costs of the programme. Here one of the weaknesses of the "investment in human capital" approach is that too much attention has been given to the material and financial inputs in the educational system and too little to the human inputs of teachers in the system. In a fundamental sense, one can say that a country's capacity to invest in human capital is limited by the most important of its scarce resources, viz., the quality and quantity of its existing supply of qualified people. If a larger proportion of this is to be used in "direct" production, i.e. in administration, business, army, medicine, engineering, etc., a smaller proportion will be available for the "indirect" use of trained people for teaching so as to produce a greater supply of trained people in future. But even when

3. W. Arthur Lewis, "Education and Economic Development," *Social and Economic Studies,* June 1961, p. 116.

we have demarcated a certain proportion of trained people for "indirect" use, there are choices between what sectors of the educational system, e.g. whether primary or secondary or university education, should be given priority (admitting the obvious complementary relations between different types of teachers). Advocates of crash programmes in universal primary education tend to obscure these difficult problems of choice in relation to the given scarce human resources.

Judging from the experiences of many Asian countries, the attempt to expand the primary school system beyond the existing teaching capacity has the following well known consequences. Because of limited numbers of teachers and overcrowded classrooms, the standard of primary education goes down sharply. But these countries have less capacity to offer jobs and apprentice training to primary school graduates than the advanced or fast-growing countries. Thus the "bulge" in the badly taught primary school graduates is transmitted directly to the secondary schools and the universities, creating overcrowding all along the educational ladder and resulting in very high rates of failure in examinations. If the economy is expanding and if there is still a large number of unfilled vacancies for secondary school and university graduates, this process can go on merrily for some time. But the rates of expansion in school and university graduates tend to expand faster than even a fairly fast rate of expansion in national income, and frequently the rate of expansion in national income itself is tapering-off, say, because of a levelling-off of export expansion. It is at this juncture that the serious human costs of expanding the primary school system reveal themselves.

Firstly, when people talk about "the thirst for education" in the underdeveloped countries they underplay the brutal fact that the driving force behind this is not just a disinterested desire for knowledge, but a desire among the students to get better jobs. The aim is to get a "middle-class standard of life" with a good suburban house and a car, a standard hitherto enjoyed by a favoured minority. Now it is patently impossible for an ever-growing number of graduates to enjoy a standard of living which is five to ten times the *per*

capita income of their countries, unless the national income is growing at a very fast rate indeed. On the other hand, given the low
academic standards which follow the expansion in the number of
students, the new graduates are too poorly qualified to improve the
standards of administration and introduce the new methods of
organization and production which alone can increase productivity
and incomes. Hence we have the forces piling up for an "explosion"
following the disappointment of the "revolution of rising expectations." Increasing rates of failures in the examinations are frustrating
enough and in many underdeveloped countries the pressure to lower
the standards of passing is in itself a burning political issue. But it
is the last straw when those who have passed the examination find
that there are no jobs for them, particularly in the towns where they
want to continue to live.

Secondly, perhaps the heaviest cost of indiscriminate expansion
of schools and colleges is that some really gifted children who have
the potentiality of attaining the high standards required to give
dynamic leadership to economic development are deprived of the
education they deserve by being crowded out or lost among their
less gifted fellows. This wastage results in a paradoxical situation
frequently found in Asian countries where there is a genuine shortage of top-level people amidst an army of unemployed and unemployable graduates. This may also explain why the number of
students from the underdeveloped countries who are qualified to
pursue research and graduate work in the advanced countries is
frequently insufficient to fill the scholarships offered by various
agencies and organizations, while a vast number of gifted students
who could potentially benefit from study abroad are locked up and
left to waste their brains in the overcrowded educational institutions
in their own countries.

III

The trend of our analysis has been to throw doubts on the general
presumption that providing more educational facilities will neces-

sarily help to break down "rigidities" and "resistances" to social transformation and economic development. We have suggested that when peasants in the underdeveloped countries are reluctant to adopt new agricultural methods, it may not always be due to their lack of education and conservatism. It may simply be that these new methods are inappropriate and unprofitable in their economic and social setting so that it is quite rational from their point of view not to adopt these "improved" methods. Similarly, when it is argued that unskilled labour in the underdeveloped countries tends to work shorter hours when higher hourly rates are offered (i.e. the supply curve of labour is "backward-bending"), this may not always be due to deep-seated social attitudes to work and leisure, but may be partly due to various factors, such as that the demand is short-run and seasonal, a flat-rate increase in wages has been offered instead of an overtime or bonus system which discriminates in favour of extra work, or that the goods which the worker wishes to buy with his earnings are not easily available or too expensive (due to inflation) etc.

Conversely, there is no reason to be confident that education by itself will break down rigidities and promote a greater degree of social mobility and flexibility favourable to economic growth. On the contrary, we have touched upon the possibility that education itself may tend to create new rigidities of its own. Such for instance is the tendency in many underdeveloped countries of a person with some education not to "soil his hands" in any form of manual work: it has been suggested that the labour-shortage for sugar-cane cutting in some of the West Indian islands may be due to the spread of primary education among the younger people. The most important form of rigidity created by education is, however, the tendency of all educated young people from the countryside to flock to the towns and the extreme reluctance of the urban educated classes in the underdeveloped countries to work in rural districts.

In our present uncertain knowledge of the mechanics of rapid economic development, it is possible to take two different attitudes to this tendency. We may regard economic development starting at "growing points" in the towns and creating "leading sectors" which will gradually pull the "lagging" agricultural sector in its wake. In this case we may regard the concentration of educated people in towns as a part of the dynamic process which, although creating many social difficulties, may strengthen the role of towns as "growing points." On the other hand, like many writers on Latin American economies, we may regard this as a very unjust and harmful form of "dualistic" economic development which impoverishes the countryside of capable people, thereby creating an obstacle to an increase in agricultural productivity which will ultimately prove to be a fatal bottleneck to economic growth.

Whichever of these two views we adopt, there is much work remaining to be done about the social forces and resistances which contribute to the unequal distribution of educated manpower between the towns and the countryside. For instance, it will be interesting to study systematically whether the educated young people from rural areas leave for towns because their education is not geared to agriculture or whether they go to school because they want to leave their villages for a town life. If the latter hypothesis is true, giving an agricultural bias to the curricula of rural schools will not stop the drift of their graduates to town. Similarly, it will be interesting to make a systematic study of the social forces which make many university graduates put up with underemployment in towns rather than take up jobs in rural districts. We may then have a clearer idea of the resistant factors which remain after the more familiar economic factors, including living and working conditions, pay and prospects, etc. have been allowed for. Some countries use compulsory direction of young graduates, particularly medical graduates, to rural areas; for instance in Burma and in some Indian States, this is a condition of entry to the medical courses. It will be interesting to find out what extra sociological sanctions or rewards must be added to make such a compulsory scheme effective.

To conclude: although the view that education is the chief missing component is more plausible than the older view that material capital is the chief missing component of economic development, it is in danger of being carried too far. It is no doubt true but not very helpful to say that if the people of the underdeveloped countries were better "educated" they could achieve greater political stability, carry out social and technological innovations and thus generally promote the rapid economic development of their countries. But before the actual education which can be offered with the given human and material resources in the given setting of an underdeveloped country can be transformed into this ideal education, there are many conceptual and practical problems to be solved. When we make a serious study of these problems, it seems unlikely that any single factor such as more primary education, technical education, agricultural education, university education, etc. will prove to be the magic key to all of them.

9 | The Universities of Southeast Asia and Economic Development

The differences in origin, stage of development and organisation between the different Southeast Asian universities should not be minimised. Nevertheless, it is true to say that a large and growing area of common interests and common problems is shared by these universities, because fundamentally the pressures for expansion and transformation facing them are similar and derive from the common social, political and economic forces which are operating at large on all the emergent countries of the region. The aim of this appraisal is to analyse the common pressures operating on the universities of Southeast Asia and to suggest tentatively some of the problems which may be studied further on a comparative basis with a view to strengthening the contributions of these universities to the social and economic development of the region.

In colonial days, the universities of Southeast Asia were frequently criticised for producing too few graduates and giving too much weight to liberal education at the expense of professional and technical education. The nationalist critics attributed the fewness of the graduates to the neglect of higher education by the colonial powers or their policy of creating a small and loyal Westernised élite cut off from the mass of the people. The fewness of graduates was defended

From *Pacific Affairs*, Summer 1962, pp. 116–27. Reprinted by permission.

on the ground that strict standards of entry to the university offered the only method of introducing and maintaining the high academic standards of the universities of the mother countries in the colonies. Similarly, while the critics attributed the emphasis on liberal education to a desire to have a convenient supply of civil servants and clerks for the colonial administration, the defenders attributed it to an idealistic ambition to make the local universities "as good as Oxford." Recently, however, some of the Western educators who have traditionally been on the side of the defenders have themselves begun to question the appropriateness or the relevance of the Western European models of universities for the special needs of the new countries seeking rapid economic development. It is now increasingly asked whether the academic standards suitable for the Western countries might not be relaxed in the developing countries to enable them to obtain a larger stream of trained people which they urgently need; and whether the universities in the under-developed countries should not overcome their repugnance at being "mere factories" producing the trained manpower of various types required for economic development without insisting too much on the traditional distinction between the "university" and the "non-university" subjects.

These doubts and questionings have been widespread in Southeast Asian university circles in the postwar years. But before they had time to think of these fundamental problems and systematically work out an alternative concept of a new type of university adapted to the special needs of their countries, they were caught up by fast-moving events. Most of them had barely completed the physical task of reconstruction after the war when they found themselves swamped with a growing tide of students, swollen three- or four-fold within a decade, with thousands more knocking at their doors. From then on, changes in the university structure have taken place willy-nilly, consisting of improvisations to meet day-to-day pressures. Only a few exceptions, such as the University of Malaya, still seem perhaps to be in a position to plan their expansion in an orderly manner.

The conventional explanation and justification for this tremendous expansion in the number of university students is that it is in response to the greatly expanded need for trained people of all types required to replace the "expatriates" both in the government service and in private industry. This is, however, a somewhat over-simplified picture of the real situation and obscures many of the important issues.

First, it is necessary to draw a careful distinction between the "demand" and the "need" for trained people. The effective demand for university graduates is concretely expressed by the number of unfilled vacancies or by the higher salaries offered to them. But the "need" for trained people in the under-developed countries merely represents our diagnosis of the situation and may or may not be backed up by organised "effective demand" for them. Thus, among the Southeast Asian countries, Malaya still has a genuinely unsatisfied demand for university graduates in the form of obvious gaps and unfilled vacancies. But when we turn to the other countries which have rapidly expanded their universities in the last decade, the situation is less clear-cut. Here, everyone will agree that these countries still have a great "need" for trained people in the sense that their economic development can be accelerated if their administrative, managerial, technical, and professional people are more efficient and better trained, and if expanding demand can be created for them. But, after the first phase of filling up the vacancies left by the expatriates, many of these countries are in fact finding that, with their existing slow rates of economic growth, they can create employment only for a dwindling number of new university graduates and that there may even be a considerable amount of graduate unemployment or underemployment. Thus, while all Southeast Asian countries "need" trained people, only a few of them, such as the Philippines (which has the greatest rate of economic growth in the region) and Malaya have a really effective and expanding demand for them at the moment. One of the major issues is how to translate the need for trained people into effective demand.

Second, the factors affecting the expansion in the number of students on the demand side should be distinguished from those operating on the supply side. Earlier on, the demand factors may have been influential by inducing a larger number of students with the requisite qualifications to enter the universities. But it is clear that the currently *continuing expansion* in numbers in all the Southeast Asian universities is due to the forces on the supply side. The most important factor here is, of course, the very great expansion of primary and secondary school education which these countries carried out immediately after independence. Now, the under-developed economies if these countries offer much fewer opportunities than do the more advanced economies for employment, apprenticeship, and technical training to those coming out of the secondary schools, and, in the absence of these alternative outlets, the expansion of the schools directly resulted in heavy pressure on the universities. Thus, instead of being a response to the vaguely defined "need" for trained people, the explosion of student population in the Southeast Asian universities is due to an over-supply of secondary school products aggravated by a lack of demand for them at the lower and middle grades of employment.

Third, it is necessary to distinguish education as a socially desirable public service or "consumers' good" from education as an "investment in human capital" or "producers' good" required for economic development. When the Southeast Asian countries expanded their schools, they acted on the generous principle that education is the fundamental right of all citizens and that it was socially desirable to extend education for its own sake as a "consumers' good." No one will wish to question this noble ideal and the right of countries to try to fulfil their deeply held social values. What is questionable, however, is the confusion between education regarded as a "consumers' good" and as a "producers' good" and the comforting doctrine that the extension of education in the former sense will automatically lead to an increase in investment in human capital in the latter sense and will therefore promote development. This turns out to be a dangerously misleading notion for, with the limited resources available for educational purposes (particularly the limited supply of people who have the necessary talent and training to be university teachers), a Southeast Asian country cannot avoid the basic choice of using them *either* for consumption purposes *or* for investment purposes. It is my contention that, in those Southeast Asian countries which have expanded their universities rapidly in the last decade, the extension of education as a "consumers' good" has used up so much of the available limited resources that it has seriously interfered with the training of people to the minimum standards required for economic development, and that this is one very important factor retarding the rate of economic growth in these countries.

This can be illustrated by a brief sketch of the typical patterns of educational expansion in Burma, Indonesia and Viet-Nam. Burma expanded her schools without an adequate supply of competent school teachers; that is to say, she was unwilling or unable to spare her more competent people from other uses in her rapidly expanding state sector and yet tried to pursue her social ideal of providing free education, not only at primary and secondary level but even, until recently, at university level. The result was a huge army of adolescents passing through the secondary schools who were so badly taught that they found it extremely difficult to bridge the widening gap between their schools and the university. Yet, lacking other alternatives, they all wished to enter the university. Thus, out of about 100,000 who sat for the matriculation examination in 1959 only 3 per cent passed, resulting in a renewed agitation for lowering the entrance standards to the university. But these standards were already very low, as can be seen from the fact that even those who were admitted into the university had great difficulty in following the course there. Until the university examination system was changed into the "American system" (1962), only about 30 per cent of students passed their annual examinations at the university all along the line from their first to their fourth and final year for a pass degree. At any given time, therefore, Rangoon University was crowded, not only by fresh entry but by old stocks of students who failed repeatedly in the same examination and could not be made to give up their place until they had failed three times in the same examination ("the 3 F rule"). Indonesia and Viet-Nam expanded their schools more efficiently. But their university systems on the eve of expansion were more rudimentary than in Burma, so that the overcrowding at the university seems to be even more severe, and they also have very limited power for restricting entry and discarding students who prove incapable of following the courses.

The result is that university education in non-professional courses in all these countries has degenerated into giving lectures to huge overcrowded classes with hundreds of students, lectures being frequently given at "dictation speed" so that students can get complete lecture notes which they learn by heart to be reproduced in the examinations. The overworked professors can do little else and, owing to shortages of text books and to students' difficulties in understanding them, few students read anything beyond their lecture notes. There is very little outside reading for general education, and the meagrely stocked libraries are used merely as places where students can memorise their lecture notes. The professional courses, such as medicine and engineering, still try to impose a restrictive selection on their numbers, but this seems to be a losing battle and their standards also have suffered in varying degrees from the pressure on limited laboratory facilities.

When the overcrowding of the limited facilities of the universities has proceeded to this extent, it begins to interfere with economic development in two ways. First, whatever views we hold about the usefulness of academic education for economic development, it is possible at least to say negatively that no country is likely to achieve the difficult task of accelerating economic development unless the *general run* of people in charge of its affairs attains a certain minimum standard of training and competence. This minimum is clearly recognisable in the specialist technical and professional fields, and that is why there is more resistance to the lowering of standards in the professional courses. (But here the large number of students spending their time working for admission to the degree courses means that there is a smaller number at the middle and lower levels of training, at the diploma and technical schools level.) In the general arts and science courses, however, the minimum standards are more flexible and less clearly defined and the dangers of not achieving them are not well recognized. Accordingly, the general arts and science courses, treated as convenient receptacles for all the rejects from the professional courses, have been permitted to over-expand to such an extent that they often no longer provide a minimum level of general education. Yet it has increasingly come to be realised that economic development depends not only on specialist technicians but also on having a sufficient number of competently trained people in administrative and managerial jobs; many would in fact say that, whether economic development is to be promoted by state or by private enterprise, they are the more important people. Thus the failure of Southeast Asian universities to maintain a minimum standard of general education and intellectual discipline for those going on to general administrative and managerial jobs may have a wider and more pervasive unfavourable effect on their economic development than is generally realised.

Second, if economic development requires a large number of people trained at a certain minimum level (which may be well below the average standards in Western universities), it also requires some highly trained people who should provide the leadership and the "growing points" of the economy. This means that the Southeast Asian universities should be able to produce a number of people who can be sent abroad for further studies both in academic and in technical subjects, and their number should be at least equal to the available number of scholarships offered both by their national governments and by foreign universities and other agencies. Here the high cost of overcrowding the universities shows up very clearly, for in many subjects it seems that the total available supply of scholarships abroad exceeds the total available number of graduates with the necessary qualifications to benefit from them. Of course, a few exceptionally able students emerge almost in spite of their training, but a large number of promising students who might have achieved the required standards for study abroad have been robbed of the type of education they deserve by the crowds of less able students who should not have been admitted into the universities in the first place. Thus, after a high percentage of failures among their scholars abroad, the educational authorities of Burma have been obliged to enforce certain minimum qualifications for selection of scholars to be sent abroad and, since doing so, they have found increasing difficulty in filling the modest total of fifty government scholarships annually, so that some of these scholarships have to be left unused. Yet there is no shortage of natural ability among the Burmese university students. With more selective training, they could have successfully filled two or three times the number of scholarships available. Thus, ironically enough, the continual demand in Burma to appoint more university teachers to relieve overcrowding cannot be met because overcrowding itself has reduced the potential stream of university teachers to be trained abroad.

This is perhaps symptomatic of the self-defeating tendency of the broader social and economic pressures working at large in the Southeast Asian countries. Whatever the idealism behind the governments' educational expansion policies, it is fair to say that the main motive of the parents who send their children to the schools and of the students who crowd into the universities is to obtain well-paid (preferably official) jobs after graduation. The image that inspires them is still that of the educated élite of prewar days, enjoying a middle-class standard of living many times higher than the per capita national incomes of their countries.

In the first phase after independence, where the jobs vacated by the foreigners have to be filled and when there is a redistribution of the available jobs between the expatriates and the nationals, these expectations can be realised to some extent. When all these jobs have been filled, it becomes evident that no country can go on providing a larger and larger proportion of its population with many times its present per capita income unless there is a rapid expansion in its total national income. But the overcrowding of the universities, by lowering the standards of efficiency and competence of its educated class, may reduce the possibility of such a rapid expansion in national income—rapid enough to absorb the expanding stream of graduates from the universities.

The final irony of this situation, where both the schools and universities have been overcrowded without any regard to a rational use of the limited number of competent teachers and other limited financial and material resources available for education, is that the governments' cherished policy of giving equal educational opportunities to the children of the rich and poor may be defeated. Thus, where the schools have been expanded indiscriminately with an inadequate supply of competent teachers or suitable buildings and equipment, the education they can provide is of a very poor quality. The children of the more well-to-do do not suffer because they can afford to go to the better private schools which charge high fees. The ones who really suffer are the gifted children of poor parents whose potentialities cannot be developed in the poorly run state schools. This tends to set up a continuing handicap even for those who do manage to reach the universities, because there students from the better schools enjoy a differential advantage which is again reinforced in some cases by private tuition to supplement the poor quality of university instruction. Thus, while it is desirable to have a broad-based primary education to throw a wider net over potential talent throughout the country, this will be largely negated unless a fairly ruthless policy of selection is followed so that a sharply tapering stream of students is passed through the secondary schools to the universities. This would mean a smaller but better taught secondary school system, where the gifted children would be given a larger number of scholarships while the less gifted children would be weeded out, at least from the government schools. But such a rigorously selective policy seems unacceptable, partly by reason of the prevailing ideals of extending school education to everyone, and partly because of the pressure of parents in search of middle class jobs for their children.

Thus the Southeast Asian countries need to choose between the concept of "equal educational opportunities" for the gifted children of rich and poor parents alike and the concept of "equal educational opportunities" for both the gifted and the less gifted children. Admittedly, given the first choice, the methods of selection would be somewhat imperfect and there would be some wastage. But, while

the first policy tends to mobilise human talent for economic development while narrowing the gap between rich and poor, the second
policy, even when backed by genuine idealism, will tend to defeat
itself by over-straining the available educational facilities and distorting their allocation between education as "consumers' good" and
as "producers' good."

The aim of this analysis is not to question the right of Southeast
Asian countries to try to fulfil their deeply held social values but
rather to examine the implications of such attempts in the setting of
the limited human and material resources of their universities and
their economic systems. These countries may continue along existing
paths but they should have a clear understanding of the full implications of their present educational expansion policies for their
economic development and their social and political stability.

Similarly, the countries will have other social values which they
may wish to fulfil even when these conflict with the efficient working of their educational systems for economic development in the
narrower material sense. For instance, many of them are "plural
societies" in the sense that they have large immigrant minorities,
not to speak of their own indigenous minorities. In view of this,
they will wish their educational system to function to some extent
as an instrument of social integration. This problem is not important for most Western European universities, but in the United
States, which has had a large inflow of immigrants, a considerable
part of the educational system is designed to make "good Ameri-
cans" out of the children of different origins and background. The
cost of doing this appears to be somewhat lower standards at the
undergraduate level in the American universities compared with
Western European universities. This is compensated for by having
much larger graduate schools. Faced with similar problems, some
of the Southeast Asian universities, apart from those in the Philippines, have shown an interest in switching toward the American
model. A serious drawback of the American model, however, is that
it lengthens the period of university education by about two years,
which a rich country like the United States can well afford but

which would be a heavy burden for poorer countries. But, given the already overexpanded conditions of the Southeast Asian universities, some of the American methods of dealing with large numbers may be relevant.

Another non-economic aim which many Southeast Asian countries have pursued is to give increasing emphasis to the use of their national language as a medium of instruction, not only in their schools but also in their universities. The costs of such a policy are obvious, not only in terms of human and material resources required for the translation of textbooks and so on, but also in terms of increasing the barriers of international exchange of students and teachers between these countries and the industrially advanced Western countries.

These are some of the social values which the Southeast Asian countries may legitimately wish to pursue even at some cost to the most efficient functioning of their higher educational system for economic development. Allowing for these non-economic objectives, one may now conclude this short appraisal by sketching very briefly some broad sets of problems which require further study and research on a comparative and cooperative basis strictly from the point of view of promoting economic development.

Before we can enter into the finer problems of trained manpower budgeting, it is necessary to find practical methods of easing the "traffic jam" which prevails in most Southeast Asian universities. The Philippines' method of having a large number of private universities on a commercial basis should be seriously explored. Under this system, there would be a division of labour between the state universities, which would restrict their teaching mainly to the "honours" and post-graduate type of student, while retaining examining powers over the private universities, which would cater for the bulk of the pass degree students. The commercially run universities, having their standards controlled either by the state universities or by professional bodies for various technical and vocational courses, could effectively ease the situation.

The idea of commercially run universities is disconcerting to many orthodox people, who nevertheless accept commercially run private schools, but so long as there is pent-up demand for university education, there is no reason why it should not be supplied. Further, commercially run universities, catering for students in mass at middle or lower levels of training would not compete for the same type of teaching resources as the state universities, which require a hard core of highly qualified full-time teachers. Both Indonesia, which cannot cope with the staffing of its provincial universities, and Burma, where there is a growth of tutorial colleges for the matriculation and university examinations, are moving in this direction.

Only after this "traffic jam" has been eased can one go to the longer-run problem of keeping the total supply of trained people and the total demand, or the absorptive capacity, for them at the highest possible level. As was said, these two forces interact with each other, for unless the quality of the people supplied achieves certain minimum standards of training and competence, they cannot play their part in helping economic development, and thus the absorptive capacity of the economy for trained people is slowed down. What is needed, therefore, is to mobilise the available talent in the country by a broad-based educational pyramid which tapers off sharply at high levels thus enabling the abler students to get the best education which the existing educational facilities of the country, properly used, can provide. This however requires a careful allocation of the educational resources, particularly the limited supply of competent teachers in the schools and universities, between consumption purposes of providing education as a purely social service and production purposes of training people so that they can contribute to further economic development. There is also the further choice of using a limited stream of able people directly in various non-academic fields or absorbing them back into the schools and universities for the purpose of extending and improving educational facilities. It should be noted that using some of the limited supply of able people for educational purposes withdraws them from work which would directly increase output, and thus represents true "investment in human capital" at the cost of sacrificing the direct use of these scarce human resources.

There are two problems here: first, the problem of matching demand and supply vertically for different grades and levels of training; and second, that of matching demand and supply horizontally for different types of people at approximately the same level of training. The overcrowding of the technical and professional degree courses at the universities, combined with a relative shortage of technicians at the middle and lower levels which is observable in most Southeast Asian countries except the Philippines, represents the first type of problem. This vertical maladjustment cannot be cured, however, simply by opening more technical schools and institutes. In order to solve the problem we must consider not only the supply side but also the demand side, particularly the salary differentials existing between the different grades of people. Apart from the glamour of university degrees, the overcrowding of the universities seems to indicate that the salaries at the middle and lower grades of technical skills are too low relative to those of the university graduates, particularly in the government-controlled sectors of the economy. Similarly, the demand factors and the salary differentials seem to be the more important factors in the horizontal allocation of people to different types of training at the same level.

In prewar Southeast Asia there may have been a shortage of graduates in technical fields relative to arts graduates but in the postwar years, under the influence of changing demands, a larger and larger proportion of university students are trying to get into the medical and engineering faculties. In some countries, such as Burma, this tendency has gone so far as to create a relative surplus of engineering graduates combined with a relative shortage of technicians at middle and lower grades, and also a relative shortage of better students going into the general arts and science courses. If an efficient corps of administrators and managers is important for economic development, this may involve a wrong distribution of talent and here it is difficult to apply salary differentials. While an efficient civil servant in an important position is worth more than two or three times his salary, there are the less efficient people in the same grade who do not earn their salary. A similar wrong distribution of talent may be taking place between the pure science courses and the technical and professional courses which have robbed the former of the best students. There are many fields in which the so-called Western know-how cannot be applied to Southeast Asia and fundamental research has to be undertaken to innovate and adapt scientific knowledge to local needs. Here, pure scientists may prove to be more flexible and adaptable than the specialist technologist. There is a further reason why more of the better students should be attracted into the general arts and science courses. It is extremely difficult to predict the future manpower requirements of different types with any accuracy, so that it is prudent to have a pool of more versatile and adaptable people who can be diverted into different jobs by further training in accordance with changing needs instead of having too many highly trained specialists who cannot be switched round so easily. Yet a further consideration is that it is from the general arts and science graduates that most of the higher teaching posts in schools and posts in the universities must be staffed. Finally, most Southeast Asian countries suffer from a geographical maldistribution of talent; all the available trained people crowd into capital cities and big towns away from the country districts which often need them most.

Most Southeast Asian countries have economic development plans. These generally consist of plans to invest capital in different sectors of the economy and they may be co-ordinated with varying degrees of success with the annual budget and foreign exchange availabilities. But rarely have the manpower implications of these plans been worked out. The problem here is not merely that many of the investment plans will be retarded owing to shortage of trained technicians, but also to know what extra demands and extra supplies of different types of trained men these plans create and whether they can be matched in the ways we have described above. Furthermore, too much attention is paid to the aggregate expenditure on education, both on capital and current accounts, without a further attempt to analyse how much of these eductional expenditures really promotes economic development in the ways we have analysed and how far these educational expenditures fit into the rest of the economic development plans. While a detailed budgeting of trained manpower is likely to be very difficult (certainly more difficult than the foreign exchange components which are rarely worked out accurately), some estimates should be made to match demand and supply in broad terms, with generous allowances for errors by creating pools of more versatile personnel in various broad sectors and grades. When this is done, we shall also begin to see how far the various sectors of the educational system should be strengthened and in what order of priority.

10 | The Brain Drain from the Underdeveloped Countries: A Less Alarmist View

As popularly used, the term "brain drain" denotes the migration of scientists, academics, doctors, engineers, and others with university training from one country to another. In discussing the brain drain from the underdeveloped countries to the advanced countries, we may use the term fairly broadly and include two further items under it: first, the students sent from the underdeveloped countries to the advanced countries who have stayed on more or less permanently in the latter countries; and second, the migration of "middle level" skilled people, notably nurses from the underdeveloped to the advanced countries.

Although some attempts have been made to assess the magnitude of the brain drain from the underdeveloped countries into the United States,[1] it is fair to say we have no reliable statistical information about the total numbers involved in the brain drain from the underdeveloped countries to the advanced countries as a whole. All we can do is to try to piece together a general picture from the sketchy and impressionistic information available on the subject.

1. *The Brain Drain into the United States of Scientists, Engineers, and Physicians,* A Staff Study of the Committee of Government Operations, U.S. Government Printing Office, Washington, 1967.

From Walter Adams, ed., *The Brain Drain,* The Macmillan Company, 1968, pp. 233–46. Reprinted by permission

(a) The brain drain from the underdeveloped countries to the advanced countries involving the largest number of people seems to be in the medical field. A fairly large number of Indian and Pakistani doctors have migrated into Britain to replace the British doctors who have migrated abroad and some 6000 graduates of Latin American medical schools were estimated to be resident in the United States in 1966.[2] There is also an equally noticeable migration of nurses from the underdeveloped countries to some of the advanced countries. For instance, a large proportion of the nursing staff in British hospitals is from the underdeveloped countries, notably the West Indies.

(b) The expansion of universities and government-financed research programmes, particularly in the United States and Britain, has attracted a number of scientists and university teachers from the underdeveloped countries. The numbers involved appear to be much smaller than in the case of doctors. It may also be noted that, in the field of economics and other social studies, the various bodies of the United Nations have probably attracted a larger number of people from the underdeveloped countries than the universities and the research institutes of the advanced countries.

(c) A certain proportion of students sent from the underdeveloped countries to study in the advanced countries tend to settle in the latter countries for long periods. This is true not only of foreign students in the United States, and British Commonwealth students in Britain; the same tendency can be observed for students from ex-French colonies to settle down in France. This type of brain drain is difficult to quantify, because students tend to stay on in the countries of their further education for a somewhat elastic period. Some may return home only to return a few years later either for a higher degree or to seek employment. Others who have seemingly taken permanent jobs in the advanced countries may decide to return home in mid-career. It may also be noted that those who stay

2. *Migration of Health Personnel, Scientists, and Engineers from Latin America,* Pan American Health Organization, Scientific Publication No. 142, Washington, September 1966, p. 26.

on the longest in the advanced countries are not necessarily the ablest students; many of them are "professional students" who are probably unemployable both in the underdeveloped and the advanced countries.

(*d*) In addition to the migration of nurses, there is a considerable amount of migration of people at the "middle level" of skills such as school teachers, mechanics, technicians, foremen, etc. from some of the underdeveloped countries to some of the advanced countries. In most underdeveloped countries, the salary scales for middle grade personnel tend to be excessively low relative to those of top grades and university graduates and this encourages migration at this level of skills. Further, there are political and ethnical factors, such as in the case of the considerable migration from various Asian countries of people of Eurasian origin at the middle level of skills to Australia and Britain. The migration of Asians (mainly Indians) at the middle level of skills from East and Central Africa is another illustration of this type.

Now, the subject of brain drain raises at least three distinct sets of issues.

(*a*) First, in so far as people educated at public expense in one country migrate to another country, it imposes financial losses on the losing country which may be measured either in terms of the costs of educating these people or, if we like, in terms of their potential earnings. These losses may be compensated either by the migrants themselves or by the government of the receiving country. In relation to the brain drain from the underdeveloped countries to the advanced countries, this question of compensation may be treated under the wider subject of international aid.

(*b*) Second, whether the migrants are educated at public expense or not, the migration of skilled people, particularly doctors, from one country to another involves wider problems of gains and losses in economic and social welfare. From the welfare point of view, the migration of doctors from the underdeveloped countries, where the ratio of doctors to the total population is so low, to the advanced countries where the doctors are relatively more numerous, is the most disconcerting aspect of the brain drain, whatever its effect or lack of effect on the economic development of the under-developed countries.

(*c*) Thirdly, like all discussions about the underdeveloped countries, the subject of the brain drain from the underdeveloped countries raises the question whether it is likely to have a significant effect, actual or potential, on their rate of economic development.

Current interest in the brain drain from the underdeveloped countries seems to be mainly concerned with the third issue. Using the type of argument familiar in other contexts of development economics, there is a tendency to argue that the widening gap in the incomes of the underdeveloped and the advanced countries, reflecting itself in a corresponding gap in the salary levels of the skilled occupations, will tend to exert a *general* economic pull, attracting the best brains from the former to the latter and thus set up a dynamic cumulatively disequalising process or a "vicious circle" which aggravates the economic gap between the two types of country.

In this paper we shall accordingly concern ourselves mainly with the third or the developmental aspect of the brain drain from the underdeveloped to the advanced countries. We shall argue that, whatever our views on the welfare aspects of the brain drain, its effect on the retardation of the economic development of the under-developed countries is less alarming than it appears at first sight. We shall try to show that the brain drain from the underdeveloped to the advanced countries, in so far as it is due to purely economic (as distinct from political and sociological) causes, it attributable not so much to the general economic pull generated by the disparity in the income and the salary levels as to fairly specific and particular causes of disequilibrium in the demand and supply of certain categories of skilled persons, both in the advanced countries and in some of the underdeveloped countries. We shall conclude that the brain drain may be regarded as a symptom rather than as an important cause of the slow rate of economic growth in the losing countries. In particular, we shall conclude that it is a symptom of a tendency to a serious disequilibrium between the typical pattern of expansion of higher education in these underdeveloped countries and their limited capacity to "absorb" the expanding number of graduates who turn out to be too highly specialised or too highly trained (in the formal academic sense) for their requirements.

Before we enter into the economic causes of the brain drain from the underdeveloped countries, it should be emphasized that a very considerable part of this drain is due to non-economic or political and sociological causes. For instance a very large part of the brain drain from Asia to the United States seems to be made up of Chinese political refugees. Similarly, it is possible to trace the close relationship between the time profile of the brain drain from some of the Latin American countries into the United States and the course of political upheavals in these countries.[3] Finally, the sociological and cultural pull of the "mother country" is perhaps as important as purely economic considerations in inducing students to stay on more or less permanetly in the countries in which they have further education. For instance, the students who have stayed on in Britain are not only from the poorer underdeveloped countries of Asia and Africa but also from the richer countries like Australia, New Zealand, and Canada who are themselves seeking immigrants from Britain.

Let us now turn to the economic aspects of the brain drain, particularly with reference to the migration of doctors, and to a lesser extent the migration of scientists and academics, from the underdeveloped countries to the United States and Britain. The popular view of the subject focuses attention on the large salary differentials which exist in these occupations between the advanced and the underdeveloped countries and fears for a continuous brain drain from the latter countries so long as these economic differentials persist, which they are likely to do for an indefinite period into the future. But it is worth reminding ourselves that the effective economic pull is exerted, not just simply

3. Cf. The Pan American Health Organization, Scientific Publication No. 142, cited above, pp. 42–43.

by the higher salaries in the advanced countries but by the existence of numerous unfilled vacancies in these countries in spite of the higher salaries. That is to say, there are specific factors causing a disequilibrium between the demand and the supply of doctors and academics in the United States and Britain. The readily identifiable factors are: the restrictive attitude of the American Medical Association towards the expansion of medical schools in the United States; the expansion of demand for medical services combined with an under-payment of doctors in the British National Health Service; and the tempo at which the universities of the United States and Britain expand which creates acute staffing problems in the new universities. If this is accepted, we may conclude that the brain drain from the underdeveloped countries, instead of being a continuous and cumulative process generated by the widening gap in incomes and salary levels, can be more directly explained in terms of specific causes of disequilibrium in the market for doctors and academics in the United States and Britain. Thus it may be expected to slacken off when the disequilibrium is corrected.

It is of course possible to argue that, by virtue of their greater economic dynamism, the advanced countries, particularly the United States, will always be generating successive waves of expansion in demand for new types of skill and that this will create one disequilibrium after another, and set up a more or less continuous pressure of demand on the brains from the underdevleoped countries. Even if we accept the theory of successive waves of expansion of demand for new types of skill, this model has a serious gap as a theory of continuous brain drain from the underdeveloped countries; it does not explain why the supply of locally skilled people in the United States and Britain should always be more inelastic or irresponsive to a given expansion in demand in the *better paid occupations* than the supply of skilled people from the underdeveloped countries.[4]

4. There is a fairly obvious reason why the supply of local people from the advanced countries be inelastic for the lower-paid menial occupations and why cheap unskilled labour from the underdeveloped countries may be

So far we have been concerned with the disequilibrium in the skiled labour market of the advanced countries which exerts the economic "pull." Let us now turn to the typical pattern of educational expansion and skilled manpower requirements of the underdeveloped countries, which at a latter stage of their educational expansion, can supply the "push" elements in the brain drain from these countries.

Broadly speaking, the educational expansion and the skilled manpower situation in the underdeveloped countries tends to go through two contrasting stages. In the earlier phase, a newly independent underdeveloped country with a rudimentary system of higher education suffers from an acute shortage of skilled manpower, created by the obvious need to fill vacancies and gaps left behind by the departing colonial administrators and other expatriates. It is during this phase that the notion of skilled manpower as a "missing component" to economic development takes root. The brain drain during this stage will obviously be serious. But this is also a period of easy job redistribution from the expatriates to the nationals and one would not expect much drain for economic reasons during this period. Many African countries still seem to be in this earlier phase of educational expansion and easy job redistribution. In so far as one can judge from the sketchy information available, their share of the brain drain appears to be small compared with that of the Asian and the Latin American countries, and may be attributed mainly to political and sociological factors rather than to economic reasons.

But judging from the experience of many Asian countries, an underdeveloped country can pass from this earlier phase of shortage of university graduates in the relatively short time of one or two decades. Although starting from a modest base, the typical rate of expansion in the number of university graduates soon reaches the

---

imported to fill up vacancies at the bottom end of the occupational pyramid in an advanced country with a high level of employment. But this suggests that the supply of local labour from the advanced countries will be more elastic for the better-paid skilled occupations, rather than the reverse.

order of 10 per cent to 20 per cent per annum. Since even a fast growing underdeveloped country cannot achieve a rate of growth in national income of more than 5 per cent to 6 per cent per annum, sooner or later, after the initial phase of job redistribution, an underdeveloped country inevitably faces the problem of not being able to create a sufficient number of jobs for its swelling number of new university graduates. There are powerful economic and political forces tending to expand the university system of the underdeveloped countries in this way.[5] First, the economic conditions in the underdeveloped countries offer few outlets for the training and employment of the products of the primary and the secondary schools. Thus the government's "crash programmes" to expand primary schools invariably leads, after a time-lag, to a corresponding flood of students seeking admission into the universities, since they have few alternatives. Second, in many underdeveloped countries, there is still the illusion that a university degree will bring its holder the "middle class" standard of living associated with the educated elite in the past. Thus the demand for expansion of the universities is basically the demand of a growing section of the community to try to obtain a level of income several times higher than the per capita income of the country as a whole. The driving force behind educational expansion in the underdeveloped countries is very similar to that behind inflation in these countries. As with inflation, few governments of the underdeveloped countries are politically strong enough to check educational expansion once it has got under way.

Now the expansion of the universities in the underdeveloped countries producing large numbers of ordinary arts and science graduates is not by itself likely to cause any brain drain (except among some of the university teachers whose case will be discussed separately). This is so because schools and universities are usually expanded under conditions of acute shortage of qualified teachers and overcrowding. The net result is to bury the more talented students among thousands of their less able fel-

5. For a fuller account of this tendency, see above, Chapter 9.

lows and to lower general academic standards. Thus, if the new graduates cannot be absorbed in their home countries, they are also unemployable in graduate occupations abroad and the net effect of a growing army of educated unemployed is solely to aggravate political tensions within the underdeveloped countries.

But where the university expansion is combined with the fashionable belief that it is the specialised technical and professional training, as distinct from a general arts or science degree, which promotes economic development and where the most able students are creamed off into the engineering and medical schools or are sent abroad for highly specialised technical training, then favourable conditions for brain drain are created. This can be illustrated by the following two categories of potential or actual brain drain.

(a) First, there is a growing number of students sent to the advanced countries to take advanced training in branches of technical study which are too specialised to be of any use to their countries. The aerodynamicists from Asian countries which have no aircraft industry have now become a standing joke.[6] Such types of people are obviously liable to take part in the brain drain. The real lesson to learn from this is not so much to bewail the loss of people who are too highly specialised to be usable but to select the more relevant courses of study for the students sent abroad. For many countries, students pursuing more general courses in physical sciences are likely to be more useful than specialists in particular branches of applied technology which inevitably tend to be adapted to the needs of the advanced countries rather than to those of underdeveloped countries.

(b) Next we have the potential brain drain, from among the locally trained engineers. Given the prevalent belief that engineers are somehow more important for economic development than other types of skill, many Asian countries have expanded their engineering colleges rapidly. As a consequence, there is now a considerable surplus of engineering graduates in these countries. In India, they

6. G. Myrdal noted this tendency as early as 1956. See his *International Economy*, p. 187.

simply remain unemployed and in Burma (round about 1961) the government was obliged to make a special (and not very successful) effort to absorb the surplus engineering graduates into administrative posts. So far, however, the actual brain drain of engineers from Asian countries has been much less than of the doctors, perhaps for two reasons. First, given the less restrictive conditions of entry into the engineering profession, one may deduce that the "pull" of excess demand from the advanced countries is likely to be weaker for the engineers compared with the doctors. Second, professional affiliations between the advanced and the underdeveloped countries also seem to be weaker for engineers than for doctors, so that an engineer trained in Asia is less likely to obtain a professional appointment in the United States or Britain without further training in these countries.

Somewhat more complex "pull" and "push" factors are involved in the case of the brain drain of doctors and academics.

The numbers of students in medical colleges in Asia and Latin America have been expanding steadily, but there is less likelihood of a surplus of doctors than a surplus of engineers for three reasons. First, the scope for setting up a private practice is greater for doctors than for engineers; so there can be no obvious unemployment among doctors comparable to that of engineers. Second, most people would probably accept the welfare judgment that the underdeveloped countries, particularly their rural areas, "need" many more doctors than these countries are currently able to produce. Third, the doctors have obvious contributions to make to economic development, particularly in such fields as public health, nutrition, and birth control. But against this we must place the well-known tendency of the doctors in underdeveloped countries to congregate in the bigger cities and towns to practise personal curative medicine rather than to work in the rural areas or in the field of public preventive medicine. The reason is also well known: apart from the better conditions of living in town, a successful private practice can yield an income many times more than the salary which the government can offer in public service. Some countries, such as Burma, try to correct this internal brain drain of doctors by making young doctors serve compulsorily in rural areas for a certain number of years as a condition of their admission to medical colleges. But even such compulsory measures have not been successful in combating the tendency of doctors to congregate in towns, and the question of how far compulsory measures should be used to disperse doctors to the rural areas raises the difficult problem of balancing the freedom of the doctors with the welfare of their patients. This must be viewed against the background that in many underdeveloped countries the state is the chief employer of skilled labour and many of those who have chosen medicine have done this deliberately to retain a certain measure of professional freedom. The pressure of excess demand from the advanced countries is most likely to affect the doctors in private practices in the bigger towns in the underdeveloped countries. In so far as this is true, the welfare effects are less catastrophic than if the doctors were being taken away from the rural areas and the development effect is probably negligible. Depending on the actual numbers of doctors who have migrated, for which we do not have firm figures, one can only conclude that the welfare effect of the brain drain of doctors from the underdeveloped countries is likely to be larger than its effect on economic development in a narrower sense.

Finally, we have the migration of academics from the underdeveloped countries to the United States, Britain, and in the case of social studies, to the various bodies of the United Nations. The numbers who have moved to the universities in the two countries are relatively small but have attracted great attention because some of the more distinguished academics tend to be regarded rather as "cultural monuments" in their home countries. There are three main factors which have stimulated this category of brain drain. First, as we have already noted, there is the "pull" generated by the acute staffing difficulties of the newer institutions in the United States and Britain, combined with the very low academic salaries in many underdeveloped countries. In some of these countries, academic salaries, for equivalent qualifications, are much lower than in the civil service. In other countries, notably in Latin America where the universities are run on the "continental" model, only part-time academic appointments are available, and given the conditions of inflation, academics are obliged to take outside non-academic work. Second, the post-war period has seen a great expansion in international academic contacts, through the expanding number of students sent to study in the advanced countries and in the number of academics from the underdeveloped countries who visit the universities in advanced countries on exchange basis, not to speak of the academics from the advanced countries who are on visit to the underdeveloped countries. These increasing contacts facilitate the brain drain of the academics from the underdeveloped countries who wish to leave for various reasons. Third, there are the "push" factors which may be very important in a considerable part of the academic brain drain. The first of these arises from the very rapid expansion of the universities in the underdeveloped countries which reduces university teaching in many of these countries to giving lectures at "dictation speed" to enormous classes of students who reproduce them by heart in the examinations. Next, there is the tendency of the governments in some of the underdeveloped countries to interfere with the detailed running of the universities, particularly to insist on easy standards of admission into the universities on political grounds. Finally, there is the growing political unrest among university students in most underdeveloped countries, resulting in frequent student strikes and sporadic mob violence which make normal academic life impossible. It is difficult to assess the effect of the migration of academics from the underdeveloped countries on their economic development. On the whole, it is likely to be small and uncertain, for the following reasons. First, given the unfavourable conditions of work in their home countries, the productivity of the brain drain academics is likely to be much higher in the advanced countries; this therefore exaggerates the loss to their home countries. Second, this academic productivity (or lack of it) may be in subjects which have little direct relevance to economic development. Third, even where it has relevance, the important thing from the point of view of promoting economic development is not the results of pure academic research, which the underdeveloped countries can in any case obtain from abroad, but in the practical application and utilization of these results. Even distinguished academics are not usually noted for their entrepreneurial and practical qualities.

We can now summarise our conclusions.

(a) So far it is difficult to substantiate the fear that the brain drain from the underdeveloped countries is likely to have a serious effect in retarding their economic development. In so far as the brain drain is due to economic factors, it may be attributed not so much to the general economic pull of the widening gap in salary levels, but to fairly specific and identifiable causes of disequilibrium in the demand and supply for particular types of skill. These causes are more amenable to correction by appropriate economic and educational policies, both by the advanced countries and by the underdeveloped countries. While the total number involved in the brain drain is not known, its incidence seems to be limited so far to people who are wrongly trained and too highly specialised for the requirements of the underdeveloped countries, and to doctors and academics, whose actual contributions to the promotion of economic development are likely to be small and uncertain.

(b) The welfare effect of the brain drain of the doctors from the underdeveloped countries is probably more important than its developmental effect. The most efficacious way of preventing this undesirable redistribution of welfare from the underdeveloped countries to the advanced countries is for the latter countries to train a sufficient number of doctors for their own requirements and pay them sufficiently so that they do not migrate abroad and have to be replaced by doctors from the underdeveloped countries.

(c) For the underdeveloped countries, the most important lesson to be learned from the brain drain, actual or potential, is that it is a symptom of a disequilibrium between the typical pattern of expansion of their educational system and their capacity to absorb the graduates produced by it. In particular, they should beware of the distortion in their educational expansion produced by the belief that economic development can be accelerated simply by producing more technically trained people, like so many "missing components" in a jig-saw puzzle. The "missing component" approach, plausible enough in the earlier stages of educational expansion, is likely to be partial and misleading at a later stage. Only in so far as we can assume that the rate of economic growth is given from outside can we treat the role of the educational system passively as a supplier of the missing components required to sustain a given target rate of economic development. Even here, the problems of manpower planning, i.e., the problems of preventing bottlenecks of some types of skill and surpluses of other types of skill are pretty formidable. But where the problem is not to supply the "skill-inputs" required for a given rate of development, but to raise that rate of development itself by better education, the "missing component" approach becomes inadequate and misleading. The rate of growth can be raised only by improving the general level of economic competence of the people. Ultimately this can be achieved only by far-reaching social and organizational changes going far beyond expansion of formal education and academic instruction. But in so far as educational policy can help, it is likely to be in the direction of raising the general standard of competence of people, particularly at the secondary school level and at the middle grades of skill. There is a certain analogy between the attempt of the underdeveloped countries to industrialise themselves by erecting steel mills or by concentrating investment exclusively in the manufacturing sector and their attempt to promote economic development by setting up universities and engineering colleges. Both reveal the "fallacy of misplaced concreteness" engendered by the "missing component" view of economic development. In the same way as the underdeveloped countries cannot hope to industrialise themselves successfully except by "industrialising" their agriculture, they cannot hope to accelerate their economic development through better education unless this includes the mass of people, including the people in the rural areas. Wrong investment in material capital, such as an uneconomic steel mill or factory can stay underutilized or can be scrapped. But wrong investment in human capital such as the surplus university graduates or the too highly trained specialists cannot long remain unemployed or underemployed without creating internal political unrest or providing the material for the brain drain.

11 | Trade, Education, and Economic Development

There is a close interconnection between current discussions on trade and development and on education and development: in particular, a certain analogy can be drawn between the currently fashionable view that the "foreign exchange gap" of the underdeveloped countries should be filled in order to enable them to sustain their import-substitution policy of economic development and the equally fashionable view that the underdeveloped countries should carry out "crash" programmes in educational expansion in order to close their "technological gap" with the advanced countries. I shall hope to show that both these views are vitiated by a common fault in reasoning, by the "fallacy of misplaced concreteness."

Let me start with international trade theory. Development economists tend to dismiss the theory of comparative costs as static and inadequate to cope with the problems of the underdeveloped countries. One of the reasons for this dissatisfaction is that the conventional theory of comparative costs is concerned with the "direct" gains from trade and is strictly neutral between the desirability of expanding production for the export market or the domestic market. Starting from a given situation, the question whether more

From *Economic Development and Structural Change,* Edinburgh University Press, 1969, pp. 1–12. Reprinted by permission.

resources should be transferred to the export sector or the domestic sector should be decided strictly according to the given comparative costs. On the other hand, it is rare to find any development economists maintaining this neutral attitude to foreign trade and domestic production. They tend to be either for expanding export production or for expanding domestic manufacturing industry as the mainspring of economic development policy and they tend to speak of the "dynamic" or "indirect" effects beyond the "direct" "static" gains from international trade.

A full-scale discussion of the relative merits of the "export-expansion" versus "domestic-industrialisation" approach to development policy would have to range over a variety of issues, e.g. the economies of scale and the size of the market, technical complementarities and external economies, the long-term prospects of the world market demand for primary exports from the underdeveloped countries and so on. I have discussed some of these issues elsewhere;[1] but for my present purpose, I should like to focus attention on the "educational" element in this controversy. I should like to suggest that, when stripped of its complications, the crux of this controversy consists in a clash between two different views about the type of education which economic policy should seek to promote in the underdeveloped countries in order to accelerate their rate of economic development.

There are various arguments which can be advanced in support of the view that the underdeveloped countries are likely to enjoy rapid economic growth by reducing their existing network of controls over foreign trade and investment and by allowing the world market forces to transform their internal economic structure according to their potential comparative advantage. But when hard-pressed, those who favour this "outward-looking" approach to development policy would probably fall back on their fundamental belief in the powerful "educative effect" of the contact with the outside world on the underdeveloped countries. They would say that "economic develop-

1. Cf. above, Chapter 7.

ment" is a foreign and outside thing for the underdeveloped countries and that if these countries really desire economic development they have somehow or other to open themselves to the stimulus of outside economic forces instead of insulating their economies from them. The advocates of the "outward-looking" approach would then go on to emphasise the enormous educative effect of keeping an underdeveloped country open and receptive to new wants, new activities, new methods of economic organisation from abroad.

The belief in the "educative effect" of an open economy is nothing new and can be traced back to the writings of the classical economists, particularly John Stuart Mill. Similarly, when we examine the arguments for promoting economic development through the protection of domestic industry, they also turn out to be based ultimately on an educational argument. The belief that manufacturing industry is somehow more educative than agriculture was first advanced by Friedrich List, and H. W. Singer sums up the modern interpretation of this belief very well when he writes that manufacturing industries "provide the growing points for increased technical knowledge, urban education and the dynamism and resilience that goes with urban civilisation, as well as the direct Marshallian external economies."[2]

Ultimately, then, we are left with two rival theories of education for economic development. How far can we adjudicate between these rival theories of educational sociology? It seems to me that the economist has a great deal to say towards obtaining a correct perspective on this question before venturing into sociology.

The first thing to be said is that it is misleading and inappropriate to identify "industrialisation" in the sense relevant for economic development with manufacturing industry in the narrow sense. Economic development consists in the growth of national output as a whole and in the expansion of the various sectors which make up this total output. "Industrialisation" in the broader sense relevant for economic development should therefore include not only manufacturing industry but also the creation of social overhead capital such

2. H. W. Singer, *International Development: Growth and Change* (New York, 1964), pp. 164–65.

as transport, and communications, irrigation, power, etc. and, above all, the "industrialisation" of agriculture in the sense of applying modern science and technology to raise agricultural productivity.

The failure to appreciate this broader concept of "industrialisation" and the attempt to identify it with manufacturing industry in the narrow sense is the root cause of the "fallacy of misplaced concreteness" in current theorisings about promoting economic development through "import substitution" of manufactured consumers' goods.

If we define industrialisation solely as the setting up of manufacturing industry, then "capital goods" are automatically identified with durable machinery required by the modern manufacturing sector. Since most underdeveloped countries are too small and too economically backward to be able to set up machine-producing industries successfully, we have the generally accepted doctrine that import-substitution should start from or be confined to manufactured consumers' goods. Since "capital goods" in the sense of durable machinery cannot be produced domestically, the "capital requirements" for economic development are translated into "foreign exchange requirements." The foreign exchange requirements are calculated on the basis of fixed technical coefficients between foreign inputs and domestic output. This type of calculation tends to emphasise the purely technological relations to the exclusion of the economic problem of making the best use of the scarce resources. We are asked to accept the existence of the import-substitution industries as *given* and are asked to confine ourselves to the notion of "import requirements" which would follow purely as the engineering or technological consequence of operating them at full capacity or of maintaining the existing tempo of import substitution. Given the desired target rate of expansion in output and the fixed technical coefficients between foreign inputs and domestic output, the foreign exchange requirements for that rate of growth are projected. Comparing this with the projected foreign exchange receipts from exports (and international aid) we then have the size of the "foreign exchange gap" to be filled up by an increase in international aid.

This type of import-substitution approach emphasising the "foreign exchange gap" of the underdeveloped countries has gained considerable vogue since the first UNCTAD. I believe that it is open to a number of serious objections.

(1) If we accept that "industrialisation" relevant for economic development should be defined broadly in terms of the growth of national output as a whole, then we should be concerned with the capital requirements not only for the manufacturing sector but also for social overhead investment and the agricultural sector. When we consider the nature of investment inputs required in these two latter sectors, it becomes very questionable whether "capital goods" can be narrowly identified with durable machinery and whether it can be presumed that the potential comparative costs of the underdeveloped countries would always lie in the direction of import substitution of consumers' goods and not of the investment goods.

To begin with, at the earlier stages of economic development which characterise the underdeveloped countries, we should expect the capital requirements of social overhead capital and agriculture to be quantitatively more important than the capital requirements in the form of durable machinery by the manufacturing sector. The experiences of the advanced countries tend to support this. Kuznets pointed out that, during the second half of the nineteenth century, the share of producers' equipment in the total capital formation of the major advanced countries was as low as a fifth rising to over a third only during the recent decades. The rest of capital formation was in "construction" both residential and for social overhead capital.[3]

Now social overhead capital, including irrigation and land improvement activities, essentially consists in construction which has to be done on the spot as distinct from machinery which is imported in a prefabricated form. While construction work may require some machinery, it requires to a much larger extent two other forms of input which offer promising scope for import substitution. First, it requires materials such as cement, brick, tiles, etc. which, because of weight and bulk and heavy transport costs, offer a natural protection

3. S. Kuznets, *Modern Economic Growth: Rate, Structure and Spread* (New Haven, 1966), p. 257 and table 5.6.

to domestic production. The domestic manufacture of tubings for irrigation purposes in Pakistan is a notable example of this type of import substitution of investment goods. Second, even more fundamentally, construction work means putting a large number of workers to produce future output as distinct from present output: that is to say, before the work of these people yields consumable goods, they have to be supported by a "subsistence fund" during the waiting period.

We are therefore back in the classical notion of capital as "advances to labour" in the form of the "subsistence fund." It is my argument that in the underdeveloped countries this classical notion of capital as the "subsistence fund" is of greater relevance than the modern concept of capital as durable machinery. If we accept that food is capital, then agriculture becomes a major investment-goods-producing industry! Now a number of underdeveloped countries are having to import food and agricultural materials due to backward agriculture and population pressure. Thus an increase in domestic agricultural production can offer a considerable scope for "import substitution" which would substantially contribute to the "capital requirements" for economic development by enlarging the subsistence fund to maintain workers engaged in the construction of capital goods. Thus, Lockwood, in his well-known study of Japanese economic development, speaks of "the general truth that the real capital assets required in various forms of economic growth must be largely produced at home."[4]

(2) We can go a step further to free ourselves from the "fallacy of misplaced concreteness" which defines "capital goods" and "consumers' goods" according to their intrinsic physical properties and not according to the use they are put to in a given economic situation. If food can be regarded as "capital goods" in the underdeveloped countries, what about the cheap imported consumers' goods which play the vital role of "incentive goods" in many peasant economies of Asia and Africa? It seems to me that where the expansion of

4. W. W. Lockwood, *The Economic Development of Japan* (Princeton, 1965), Ch. 5, p. 243.

peasant agricultural production has been discouraged in spite of the availability of land and other physical inputs, because the highly protected domestic manufacturing industries cannot offer consumers' goods to the peasants on attractive terms, the freer importation of cheap incentive consumers' goods may be more to the purpose in encouraging the expansion of agricultural production than the importation of technical inputs which the peasants may not have the incentive to use. In this case I do not see why incentive consumers' goods should not be treated as "inputs" to agriculture on the same footing as other technical inputs.

(3) Finally, the most serious objection that can be raised against the currently fashionable type of import-substitution approach is that it obscures the fundamental economic problem of choice. This problem is most clearly appreciated when we start from a given and limited amount of scarce resources, including foreign exchange receipts from exports and aid, available to a country and focus attention on the comparative advantage of using these resources among the alternative uses. In our setting, an underdeveloped country may be looked upon as having to face the problem of choice in two stages: first, how to convert the available domestic savings into "capital goods" and second, how to use these "capital goods" to obtain the final consumers' goods. At each stage, there is a choice between the "direct" method of domestic production and the "indirect" method of international trade. Thus, "capital goods" can be either produced at home or imported from abroad; in the latter case, the foreign exchange to pay for them would have to be made available (leaving out aid) either by cutting down other imports or by cutting down domestic expenditure and shifting the resources thus released into export production. Similarly, having obtained the "capital goods," the consumers' goods can be either produced directly at home or acquired indirectly in exchange for exports by using the "capital goods" to produce exports.

Current thinking on import substitution implicitly identifies "capital goods" with complex and sophisticated machinery which the underdeveloped countries have no choice but to import from abroad.

But having obtained the "capital" goods, current thinking implicitly assumes that it will always be preferable for the underdeveloped countries to use the "capital goods" to produce consumers' goods directly at home instead of using the "capital goods" to produce exports and acquire the consumers' goods indirectly through trade. I have been trying to show that, on a broader and more relevant definition of "industrialisation" and "capital goods," neither of these presumptions stand up to scrutiny and that there is a considerable case for taking the opposite view. But my objection at this point is not only that the currently fashionable import-substitution approach makes wrong economic judgments, but also that the habit of thought it engenders tends to push the whole economic problem of choice into the background and with it the necessity of making any explicit economic judgments whatsoever. The habit of assuming the existing import-substitution industries or the current tempo of import substitution to be *given,* and inquiring only into the foreign exchange requirements of their continued operation, means that the problem of deciding which of the import-substitution industries are "economic" and which are "uneconomic" is relegated to the background. Instead of the economic problem of making the most of scarce resources, we are simply left with the technological problem of trying to run the existing industries at full capacity. But the central problem facing these industries is how to improve their efficiency and lower their costs. Their costs are made up of two components: the foreign exchange costs and domestic costs. In so far as they import machinery and other inputs at competitive world market prices, the reason for their high costs cannot be found in the foreign exchange component of their costs but in the domestic component. Yet the constant harping on the foreign exchange requirements of these import-substitution industries distracts attention from the vital domestic component of their costs which can make or mar their future development.

I can now draw the analogy between current thinking on promoting economic development through import substitution and through educational expansion. Both are examples of the "missing-component" approach. Import substitution starts from a given target rate of growth which it is desired to achieve. Then, on the assumption of fixed technical coefficients between foreign inputs and domestic output, the foreign exchange requirements for the target rate of growth is estimated. Similarly, the theoretical model behind current discussions about education and skilled manpower planning starts from an autonomously given target rate of economic growth. It then assumes that there are fixed technical coefficients between various educational inputs and the national output. Thus the number of skilled people of various categories required to sustain a given rate of growth is estimated. The role of the educational system is to perform the passive function of filling the gap in the skilled manpower requirements, to achieve the target rate of growth as distinct from the active function of raising the possible rate of growth.

This notion of education and skills as the "missing component" of economic development is reasonable enough in many underdeveloped countries immediately after their political independence. Then there were obvious gaps in skilled manpower created by the departure of expatriates in the various branches of the administrative and technical services. Sometimes the skills required were fairly specific and whole departments might not be able to function for lack of a few "key" men. The situation then approximated to the assumption of fixed technical coefficients and it was obviously important for the underdeveloped countries to train their nationals quickly to fill these gaps. But since then the situation has changed. In the same way as most underdeveloped countries have passed through the "easy phase" of import substitution, they have also passed through the easy phase of job redistribution from the expatriates to their own nationals. From now on, the rate of expansion in new jobs in skilled occupations must largely depend on the general rate of economic growth itself. In the meantime, as the result of the "crash programmes" in education, the schools and universities in many underdeveloped countries are producing large numbers of fresh graduates at much faster rates than their general rate of economic growth. Thus there is a real danger, already familiar in many Asian countries, of growing unemployment among the educated classes which adds fuel to the fire of "the revolution of rising expectations." Here again there are similarities with import substitution. The process of rapid import substitution in the underdeveloped countries tends to create excess capacity in the newly built factories in spite of the heavy protection given to their products: this surplus of certain durable forms of capital goods tends to co-exist with a shortage of circulating capital in the form of food supply, inventories of all sorts and above all "foreign exchange" which is the most liquid form of circulating capital. Similarly, educational expansion has created excess capacity in certain categories of "human capital" in the form of university graduates, some of them with highly specialist technical qualifications. Yet, in the midst of growing graduate unemployment, there seems to be a genuine shortage of skilled people required for economic development, from competent people at the middle levels of skills to able entrepreneurs and civil servants at the top.

I would suggest that this similar outcome is basically due to the wrong allocation of resources resulting in the creation of wrong pieces of capital equipment, whether material or human, which cannot be economically absorbed into the existing productive structure of the underdeveloped countries. The underdeveloped countries are, for various reasons such as national prestige, easy victims to the lure of gleaming modern factories and imposing university buildings. But this tendency to make a fetish of the tangible outward symbols of economic development has also been encouraged by the "fallacy of misplaced concreteness." The import-substitution approach mistakenly identifies "industrialisation" with the setting up of manufacturing industry in the narrow sense. Similarly, the advocates of "crash programmes" in education mistakenly identify the general improvement in education, skills and training required for economic development with formal education in the narrow sense to be produced by the universities and technical colleges. I shall argue that formal education forms only a part and perhaps not the most important part of education in the broader sense relevant for economic development; and that ultimately the improvement in the economic competence of the mass of people in the underdeveloped contries will largely depend on the "educative" influence of the whole economic environment in which they live.

But even in the sphere of formal education, there are certain biases and distortions in the educational programmes of most underdeveloped countries which can be attributed to the "fallacy of misplaced concreteness." First, there is a bias in favour of producing too many university graduates and too few people at the middle level of skills, reinforced by top-heavy salary structures in favour of the graduates. Thus, many underdeveloped countries are acutely short of people to fill jobs at middle levels of skills while suffering from a relative glut of university graduates. Second, there is a bias in favour of producing graduates with specialist training in some applied branch of technology as against the general arts and science graduates. Now this attempt to produce "technical experts" equipped with highly specific types of "technical know-how" is reasonable so long as there are clearly defined gaps in the skilled manpower requirements of a country into which the "missing components" can be fitted like pieces of a jig-saw puzzle. But after these gaps have been filled, the attempt to produce specialist technicians without any clear notion where they are to be fitted into the existing production structure increases the risk of wasteful creation of wrong pieces of "human capital." This can be seen in the growing number of students from the underdeveloped countries who have pursued highly specialist studies in applied technology in the advanced countries, only to find that their training and skills are too specifically adapted to the economic conditions of these countries to be usable when they return home. This can also be seen in the growing unemployment among the graduates of engineering colleges in some Asian countries, such as India and Burma. Finally, there is the seeming paradox of a genuine shortage of capable entrepreneurs and civil servants side by side with inability to create a sufficient number of new jobs for the army of fresh graduates pouring out of the university. But considering the magnitude of the "explosion" in the number of university students in most underdeveloped countries and their acute shortage of teachers, this is perhaps not altogether surprising. The rapid expansion of universities tends to lower academic standards both among the students and the teachers and, faced with large overcrowded classes, the teachers are in no position to select the more promising students and give them special attention. Thus it seems to me that the really crippling cost of the "crash programmes" in education is to be reckoned in terms of the wastage of human resources: the more gifted students who could have developed into capable entrepreneurs and administrators have been prevented from realising their full potentialities by being crowded out by their less gifted fellows.[5]

Let me now turn to the broader concept of education in the sense of the "educative" influence of the economic environment as a whole on the people of the underdeveloped countries. I cannot enter in any detail into the various ways in which the economic environment including the system of economic "signals" and incentives can affect the economic behaviour of the people of the underdeveloped countries, their ability to make rational economic decisions and their willingness to introduce economic changes. All I can hope to do is to bring out some aspects of this subject sharply by returning to the question I have raised initially: namely, how to assess the rival claims of the "educative effect" of the open economy and the "educative effect" of manufacturing industry.

The answer which suggests itself at this stage is to consider the "opportunity cost" in educational terms of free trade and protectionist policies in the present setting of the underdeveloped countries. To the protectionist, it is unsatisfactory for the underdeveloped countries to adopt free trade on the basis of the given comparative costs as determined by their existing level of skills. To pursue a free trade policy is therefore to miss the opportunity of improving the skills of the people through the process of learning-by-doing afforded by the protection of the "infant industry." To the free trader, the opportunity cost of protection to the underdeveloped countries is the

5. Cf. above, Chapter 9.

insulation of their economies from the stimulus of the outside economic forces transmitting new wants, techniques and new methods of economic organisation. Now, so long as we are concerned with protecting carefully selected individual "infant industries" while permitting free trade in the rest of the economy, it is difficult to say which way the net educational effects would go. The positive educative effect of learning-by-doing would have to be weighed against the possible negative educative effect on the entrepreneurs of a sheltered monopolistic market provided by the protection.

But current thinking on import substitution is concerned not merely with protecting individual "infant industries," one at a time. It insists that the "infant industry" argument for protection should be extended to cover the whole of the "infant" manufacturing sector of the underdeveloped countries or even that the entire "infant economy" of the underdeveloped countries should be insulated and protected from the pressures and disturbances of the external economic forces. Moreover, in a majority of the underdeveloped countries, this insulation is done not merely by tariffs and subsidies, but by a network of economic controls, ranging through quantitative import controls, price controls of agricultural products both for the domestic urban market and for the export market and controls on foreign investment and remittances. In this setting, I am inclined to believe that, leaving aside the wastages through misallocation of resources, the negative educative effects of this general insulation of the economy required to support a wholesale programme of import substitution is likely to outweigh its possible positive educative effects.

First, the typical modern manufacturing industry in the underdeveloped countries tends to adopt high capital-intensive techniques embodying sophisticated technology. It does so, not only for prestige reasons, but also because it has to pay high wages to its workers belonging to the politically powerful urban labour pressure groups and because it is in the privileged position of being permitted to import its capital equipment at official exchange rates in a situation where the domestic currency is highly overvalued through inflation. Thus, from the educational point of view, the modern manufacturing sector in the underdeveloped countries is in danger of growing into an "enclave" employing only a small proportion of its labour force and having to employ a large number of foreign technical experts required by the sophisticated technology. In terms of educational impact there is much to be said in favour of encouraging the more labour-intensive small-scale industries using simpler technology which requires a smaller technological gap to be bridged by the people of the underdeveloped country. Second, the import-substitution policy as currently practised generally entails keeping down the price offered to the agricultural producers. This is done either to keep down the cost of living for the urban workers; or to collect the funds to be invested in the manufacturing sectors as in the case of the state marketing boards in some of the Asian and African peasant export economies. In either case, the lack of incentive to the agricultural producers not merely discourages them from expanding output but what is more important, discourages them from adopting new methods to raise agricultural productivity. Finally, there are the well-known "perverse" educative effects exerted by the foreign exchange controls over the indigenous entrepreneurs of the underdeveloped countries.[6]

To sum up: current thinking on import substitution and educational expansion has been vitiated by the habit of starting from a given target rate of economic growth and by concentrating on the purely technical problem of supplying the "missing components" of durable capital goods and skills required to fulfil that rate of growth on the basis of fixed technical coefficients between these technically necessary inputs and total output. This has obscured the basic economic problem of allocating the available resources efficiently in the formation both of material and human capital so as to raise the rate of economic growth. This confusion between the "technical" and the "economic" problems is closely connected with the "fallacy of misplaced concreteness" which narrowly identifies "industrialisation" and "education" relevant for economic development with

6. Cf. above, Chapter 7, pp. 200–201.

manufacturing industry and the expansion of formal educational facilities. Once we free ourselves from this habit of thinking, it would seem that the underdeveloped countries can facilitate a more efficient import-substitution process according to their potential comparative advantage and can create an economic environment with a more favourable "educative effect" for economic development by relaxing their existing network of controls over international trade and by permitting the outside economic influences to transform their economic structure. This policy of inducing "structural change" for economic development by encouraging the flexibility and adaptability of the internal economic structure to the changing world market forces may be contrasted with the current policy of imposing "structural change" to fulfil target rates of growth on the basis of fixed technical coefficients. I have no doubt that as economic development proceeds, the underdeveloped countries will find themselves with an expanding manufacturing sector and with a large number of highly trained specialists and technicians. But I suspect that the manufacturing industries and the specialists which will have grown up in the process of efficient adaptation to changing world market forces will not be the same as the manufacturing industries and specialist technicians which are now brought into being by the import-substitution programmes and the "crash" programmes for educational expansion.

IV | Internal and External Policies

setting up of heavy capital goods industries requiring the economies of scale. Even Indonesia, which is much larger than the others, is too widely spread out for the building up of a large cohesive internal market.

These two conditions, taken together, suggest that the type of economic development policy appropriate for the Southeast Asian countries will be different from those adopted in India or in China. In these big overpopulated countries, the basic economic problem is the sheer physical problem of combating food shortage and the pressure of population on very limited land. Heroic measures may have to be adopted to control present consumption and raise saving and investment so that in the future, the rate of economic growth may be sufficient to cope with the population explosion. To enforce these measures, it may be necessary to exercise a rigid and detailed control over the use of scarce resources through a system of central planning. In contrast, the basic economic problem in Southeast Asia is how to create a favourable economic environment and economic institutions which will lead to a more effective and fuller use of the relatively abundant and underutilised resources. Given their comfortable surplus production of food above subsistence requirements, the Southeast Asian countries are in a position to experiment with positive economic incentives instead of relying on rigid economic controls, and the rapid economic expansion promised by the underutilised natural resources may be used as a spring board for further economic growth. Again, India or China may attempt an inward-looking autarkic approach to economic development, with an emphasis on heavy capital goods industries and oriented towards their potentially immense domestic markets. But such an autarkic type of development policy is not likely to succeed in the Southeast Asian countries with their relatively small internal markets. The most promising thing for them is to adopt an outward-looking development policy, making a more effective use of their existing opportunities for international trade, and ultimately to seek to widen the size of their markets by some form of regional co-operation.

In spite of these broad *prima facie* considerations, only Malaya,

Thailand and the Philippines have followed such an outward-looking type of economic development policy. Burma and Indonesia, after some vacillations, have tended to follow an increasingly inward-looking path of economic development. The reasons why Burma and Indonesia have chosen this path are deeply rooted in the political and psychological attitudes in these countries and these in their turn are moulded by their experiences, not only during the war and the subsequent transfer of power, but also stretching far back into their colonial days. In particular, the great depression of the thirties seems to have had a profound influence, sometimes subconsciously, on the outlook of the political leaders. In the postwar years these political and psychological attitudes and the economic policies interacted and re-inforced each other and with each round of disappointment and failure, the countries seem to have been driven deeper into their inward-looking path. There is no need to attempt to trace this complex history in detail. Nor should we presume to judge whether these political and psychological attitudes are ultimately right or wrong for the countries concerned. What is useful is to take the various economic reasons which have been put forward to justify these inward-looking policies and consider how far they are appro-priate for the economic development of these countries and how far they have fulfilled their stated economic objectives.

It should be remembered that at the end of the war and on the eve of their independence, all the Southeast Asian countries shared a common reaction against "the colonial economic pattern" and the belief in the need for direct government action to change this pattern and accelerate their rates of economic growth. Thus in the early postwar years Burma's rice marketing board was matched by the Thai government monopoly of the rice export trade, while the Philippines pursued the policy of setting up government-owned factories more vigorously than Burma. Moreover, they all agreed that economic development, apart from increasing national income, should also fulfil two important objectives: (1) to change their status as agricultural countries and reduce their dependence on a few primary exports vulnerable to world market fluctuations and to set up a sizeable domestic manufacturing sector; (2) to transfer a growing share of the incomes, economic activities and economic power from the foreigners to their own people by changing the prewar economic pyramid dominated by big Western enterprises at the top and by the Chinese and Indians in the middle levels.

Starting from this common reaction against the "colonial economic pattern," countries such as the Philippines,[2] Malaya or Thailand seemed to have sensed early that it would be easier and *quicker* to change the economic structure and the pattern of distribution of incomes and economic activities if the total volume of national output were expanding rapidly than in a situation of economic stagnation or slow growth. They also seemed to have realised that, given the basic conditions of their economies, the key to expanding their total national product was to be found in expanding the volume of their exports. Since a large share of these exports was produced by the foreign-owned mines and plantations, the governments of these countries took care to guarantee the security of foreign property and freedom to remit profits, and generally created a favourable economic environment which encouraged the foreign enterprises not only to continue their existing production but also to undertake new investments, to strike out into new lines of exports and to introduce new methods of production and organization. Countries such as the Philippines and Thailand made no secret of their aspiration that a progressively larger share of these enterprises would be taken over by their nationals. But the foreign investors had confidence that such a transfer, when it took place, would be through the ordinary process of buying and selling of shares at the prevailing market prices rather than through arbitrary expropriations.

These countries also came to realise that in order to have a rapid economic expansion, they must use positive economic incentives not only on the foreign enterprises but also on their own nationals. Thus the Thai government, after a few years of experiment with govern-

2. For a fuller account of the Filipino economic nationalism see F. H. Golay, *The Philippines: Public Policy and National Economic Development,* Cornell University Press, 1961, Ch. XIV.

ment monopoly, liberalized the rice trade and, through using economic incentives, encouraged the peasant producers not only to expand rice production but also to adapt to changing world market conditions and produce new export crops, such as maize, all the time making a fuller use of the available supply of land. The Philippines government, disillusioned by the inefficiency and corruption in government-owned factories, sold them back to Filipino entrepreneurs. Thereafter, it switched over to an indirect method of industrialization, providing differential economic incentives and advantages to the Filipino entrepreneurs, through such measures as overvaluation of currency, protection and foreign exchange allocation. In the peasant agricultural sector also the provision of economic incentives led to a rapid expansion in agricultural output mainly through bringing under cultivation new land in the outlying islands.

In contrast, countries such as Burma and Indonesia were obsessed by the fear that once the foreign enterprises were allowed to re-establish themselves in the export industries, they would regain their old "stranglehold" on the economy; they therefore felt that the right policy was to take advantage of the war-time breakdown in production to discourage these enterprises from renewing their activities. These countries were more interested in getting a large share of the cake irrespective almost of what was happening to the size of the total output. Moreover, there was a certain ambivalence in their attitude towards the value of primary export production for economic development. On the one hand, the governments of these countries carried out extensive nationalization of foreign companies on the grounds that the exploitation of natural resources was too valuable and important to be left in the hands of the foreigners. On the other hand, once the governments had obtained control of the mines and plantations and other export enterprises, no great effort was made to expand production. At this point the governments seemed to have switched over to the feeling that it was not important to carry on with this "colonial economic pattern" and diverted their attention and resources to the industrialization programme in the form of building a few more state-owned factories, and, in the case of Burma, to big and costly social overhead projects in transport and electricity. In the earlier period, Burma did explore the possibilities of forming "joint ventures" with Western enterprises, particularly in the field of manufacturing. But apart from the Burma Oil Company (since completely nationalized), nothing much came out of this as the country did not afford adequate security or incentives to the private investors. From then on Burma began to adopt an increasingly negative attitude towards foreign enterprises, both Western and Indian and Chinese. Burma's exports in the mining and forest sectors never recovered their prewar level. The same pattern may be observed in Indonesia with the exception of the new foreign oil companies which were allowed to be set up in the postwar years.

Burma and Indonesia were unwilling to employ positive economic incentives to expand export production, not only for the foreigners, but also for their own nationals. Thus the slow recovery of Burma's rice exports must be attributed, apart from the breakdown of law and order, to the inefficiency of the State Agricultural Marketing Board in almost all its operations, from the collection of crop from the peasants to the sale of rice to foreign buyers and above all, in its pricing policies. These amounted to charging zero transport and storage costs and moreover kept the prices paid to the peasant fixed at the same level over a decade, in the face of the rising prices of everything else. Thus the Burmese peasants, in spite of initial benefits from the expropriation of land from foreign landlords and from having to pay little or no land revenue, became increasingly cut off from the economic incentives of the world market and were not able to expand production or strike out into new export crops as in Thailand.[3]

Under the shelter of import controls, some small-scale domestic

3. By 1954–55, Burma's index of production of all agricultural commodities (on a 1934–38 base equal to 100) was 88 compared to 152 for Thailand, 137 for the Philippines, 131 for Malaya and 122 for Indonesia (ECAFE, *Economic Survey for Asia and the Far East,* 1955, p. 195). But there is general agreement that the value of agricultural output is underestimated in Burmese national accounts.

manufacturing industries sprang up in Burma, in some cases owned and run by Burmese entrepreneurs, who apparently were able to obtain capital from the windfall profits arising out of the allocation of import licenses. But unlike their counterparts in the Philippines, these infant Burmese enterprises never gained strength for a number of reasons. First, there was the misguided policy of wholesale import liberalization in the early fifties which frittered away the foreign exchange reserves accumulated during the Korean boom. Second, re-imposed import controls heavily handicapped the import of machinery and materials by the private entrepreneurs as a larger part of the scarce foreign exchange was diverted to capital intensive projects in the state sector.[4] Third, there was the continual threat and the progressive carrying out of a nationalization policy from large foreign-owned enterprises down to small Burmese-owned enterprises.

The general dimensions of economic development in the Philippines, Thailand and Malaya on the one hand and Burma and Indonesia on the other can be illustrated by the following table showing the percentage growth in their volume of exports and in real national product in the late fifties compared with their respective prewar levels.[5]

These figures comparing the postwar period 1946–60 with the prewar levels give a better picture of the relative economic performance of the two groups of Southeast Asian countries than the usual

---

4. Burma's public investment is estimated to have been about 47 per cent of total fixed investment during the late fifties (compared to 28 per cent in the Philippines and 24 per cent in Thailand) ECAFE, *Economic Survey for Asia and the Far East, 1961,* p. 27 and p. 36. The *Survey* goes on to state: "In the eight-year (1953–60) plan of Burma, for instance, transport, communications and power were to have absorbed 43 per cent of total government expenditure or 77 per cent of public investment. This has been considered excessive in an economy which has barely recovered pre-war levels of production especially in agriculture, and where more attention needs to be given to augmenting direct production."

5. These calculations are reproduced from Douglas S. Paauw's excellent article on "Economic Progress of Southeast Asia," *Journal of Asian Studies,* November 1963. Professor Paauw's calculations strengthen and support the

method comparing the average annual growth rates in aggregate real product starting only from 1950. For instance, taking the period 1950–59, the ECAFE *Economic Survey* gives the following annual growth rates: Burma, 5.1 per cent; Indonesia, 3.6 per cent; Thailand, 5 per cent, and the Philippines, 6 per cent.[6] But these calculations do not bring out the fact that Malaya, Thailand and the Philippines very rapidly recovered their prewar levels of aggregate real national product by 1947 or 1948, whereas Burma did not regain her prewar level of aggregate real product until 1957 and Indonesia, not until 1953. Thus in terms of annual growth rates in aggregate real products, the Philippines is estimated to have grown at 50 per cent during 1946–47, and Thailand at 30 per cent during 1946–47 and at 15.3 per cent during 1947–50.[7] The high rates were possible during the rehabilitation period as these countries were merely making good the war-time interruption or damage to production and were merely retracing their prewar paths of production on the basis of pre-existing land and labour and methods of production. All this took place before the ECAFE figures started. On the other hand, these figures include seven years of Burma's and three years of Indonesia's rehabilitation period when the rate of expansion in national output could have been much higher than the growth rates

---

general view of those acquainted with the postwar economic conditions in Southeast Asia. For my own assessment of the situation see "Problems of Economic Development in South-East Asia," *Royal Central Asian Journal*, July/October 1963.

	1958–60 Export Volumes as % of 1937 level	1960 level of Aggregate Real National Product as % of the prewar level
The Philippines	163	201
Thailand	149	191
Malaya	167	164
Indonesia	121	111
Burma	48	111

6. ECAFE, *ap. cit.*, 1961, p. 11.
7. Cf. Paauw, *loc. cit.*, pp. 70–75 and pp. 82–83.

for the Philippines and Thailand which represented genuinely new economic growth over and above their prewar production.

What then are the causes of slow rates of economic recovery in Burma and Indonesia and the rapid rates of recovery and new economic growth in Malaya, Thailand and the Philippines? There are of course, special circumstances and extra-economic factors which may partly account for these differences. Thus war-time damage to material capital was very severe in Burma but then it was equally severe in the Philippines. The breakdown in law and order and the long-drawn insurgencies in Burma have admittedly been a running sore in Burma's economy. But then Malaya had to cope with her "Emergency" and the Philippines with the Huk rebellion. Even when we have made allowances for the special circumstances, it is difficult to avoid the conclusion that a large part of the explanation for the poor economic performance of Burma and Indonesia must be found in the economic policies they pursued, in particular the inward-looking attitude which failed to appreciate the vital importance of export expansion for economic growth and preferred centralized economic planning and controls based on direct state activity to the use of positive economic incentives to encourage both the foreign and indigenous producers to expand economic activity. The postwar breakdown of production and law and order emphasized the need for using economic incentives to hasten economic recovery. Instead, the governments of these countries preferred cumbrous and complex methods of planning and control which were beyond the decision-making capacity of their politicians and the administrative capacity of their civil servants. Burma in particular was distracted by high expectations from her development plans from pressing forward with the vital tasks of re-establishing law and order and physical reconstruction, particularly in the areas which produced her mineral and timber exports. The hope of some of her politicians that insurgency would automatically die as the fruits of the economic development plans became available showed a complete failure to understand that the fruits of development, even if

they were to be realized, would be much too slow for the urgencies
created by armed rebellion.

Granted that the outward-looking countries of the Philippines,
Thailand and Malaya have been able to expand both their exports
and their national income faster than the inward-looking countries
of Burma and Indonesia, how far do they succeed in attaining the
two further objectives, (1) of expanding domestic manufacturing
industry and reducing their dependence on a few export commodities, and (2) of redistributing incomes and economic activities in
favour of their own people?

In the Southeast Asian economic setting, it is not possible to
sustain the expansion of the domestic manufacturing industry unless
exports are also expanding rapidly at the same time. This is so
because, given their present stage of economic development, the
Southeast Asian countries have to import from abroad much of the
capital equipment, skilled personnel and frequently much of the
semi-processed materials. Thus, while the process of industrialization is likely to be held up by frequent balance of payments crises
in countries such as Burma and Indonesia because of insufficient
foreign exchange earnings, it is likely to proceed further and more
smoothly in the other countries which can command an expanding
supply of foreign exchange through exports or further inflow of
foreign investment. Further, countries such as Burma and Indonesia,
by insisting on state ownership and control for the new industries,
may also be held back by the limited supplies of civil servants who
are competent to run and manage these enterprises. On the other
hand, countries such as the Philippines and Thailand, by encouraging
private enterprise of their own nationals, may be able to create and
draw on an expanding supply of private entrepreneurs who have
gained experience through the assistance of their governments. This
is in line with the statistical evidence provided by Professor Paauw
who has measured changes in the contributions of agriculture, industry in the broad sense (including mining, manufacturing, construction, electricity, gas and water) and manufacturing in the narrower
sense in Burma, Indonesia, Philippines and Thailand during the

1950–60 decade.[8] His results show that the fastest rate of structural change has taken place in the Philippines where the share of agriculture in national output was reduced to 34 per cent by 1958–60, compared to 37 per cent for Thailand, though the rate of decline for Thailand was somewhat greater. The rise in the share of manufacturing was also most rapid in the Philippines, roughly doubling from 9 to 18 per cent. Industry as a whole expanded at the same rate for the Philippines and Thailand, at a rate much faster than for Burma. While Burma showed some expansion in manufacturing, the share of agriculture in her national output remained much higher than in the Philippines and Thailand. There was hardly any change in the relative shares of agriculture and industry in Indonesia during the decade.[9]

What about the objective of reducing dependence on a few export commodities? Here also the outward-looking countries have achieved a little more success, although all the Southeast Asian countries are still highly dependent on a few exports. The rapid expansion of exports from the Philippines, Thailand and Malaya was achieved not only through the expansion of the older exports but also through the addition of new export commodities. For instance, Thailand compensated for the declining Japanese demand for her rice by the expansion of maize exports. Malaya encouraged not only the re-planting of the new high-yielding rubber trees, but also the expansion of new crops such as palm oil. The postwar development of iron-mining in the East coast of Malaya promises not only to contribute to economic diversification but also to longer-run economic development. In contrast, given the drastic reduction in the exports of petroleum, timber and minerals which formed about half of her total in prewar days, Burma is now more dependent than ever on her rice exports. Similarly the quantum index of Indonesian exports covers only her four major exports, petroleum, rubber, tin and copra, and

8. Paauw uses current prices for lack of suitable data at constant prices for Burma and Indonesia and takes three-yearly averages to smooth out short-run fluctuations.
9. Paauw, *loc. cit.*, pp. 83–89 and Figure II.

does not reflect the reduced volumes in a wide variety of minor exports which she has suffered in the postwar period.

The picture is not appreciably different when we look at this matter more broadly in terms of the ratio of exports to total national product in these countries. From the figures given in the table above, we should expect the ratio of export to total national product to be declining in all countries except Malaya, though for somewhat different reasons. In the Philippines and Thailand, the ratio would be declining because the rapid expansion in exports has been accompanied by an even more rapid expansion of total national product. In Burma, it would be declining because of an absolute decline in the volume of exports with very little growth in total national product. This seems to be borne out by the direct estimates of the ratio of exports to national income given by Professor Paauw. According to him, comparing 1938 with the average for 1957–59, the Philippines has reduced the ratio of exports to gross national product from 20 per cent to 9 per cent; Thailand has reduced the ratio of exports to her gross geographical product from 19 per cent to 16 per cent; Burma has reduced the ratio of exports to her gross domestic product from 33 per cent to 19 per cent; and Indonesia from 24 per cent to 5 per cent. These figures have to be interpreted cautiously. First, the concept of the national product used in calculating the ratio varies. Second and more significant, there were varying degrees of overvaluation of currency, particularly in Indonesia and in the Philippines (before the devaluation of the peso in 1962). Taking this into account, Professor Paauw suggests that the ratio of exports to national product in both countries was around 14 per cent in the late fifties.[10] Taking it by and large, we may conclude that the Philippines and Thailand have not increased but have reduced to some extent the ratio of export to national product through a vigorous policy of export expansion and that they cannot be said to be more dependent on exports than Burma and Indonesia.[11]

10. Paauw, *loc. cit.,* p. 80.
11. The ratio of exports to GDP remains high for the Federation of Malaya at about 50 per cent, but she has been able to achieve a considerable degree

Granted that, without increasing their dependence on exports, the Philippines and Thailand have been more successful in increasing the share of industry and in reducing the share of agriculture in their economies than Burma and Indonesia, how far are they successful in achieving the further objective of increasing the share of their nationals in the incomes and economic activities of their countries? Since Burma and Indonesia pursued this goal of economic nationalism through direct takeovers by the state and the Philippines and Thailand pursued this objective indirectly by encouraging the private enterprise of their nationals, it is difficult to make a meaningful comparison. Although statistics are not available, one would guess that through progressive nationalization of foreign enterprises the governments of Burma and Indonesia would by now control a larger share of the total economic activities of their countries than do the governments of the Philippines and Thailand and their private nationals taken together. But as we have seen, while Burma and Indonesia are getting a larger share of a smaller or a less rapidly growing cake, the Philippines and Thailand are increasing the relative shares of their nationals in a setting of rapid economic expansion, progressively acquiring experience and knowledge to better their position further. Most impartial observers in the Philippines and Thailand would agree that the relatively open policy towards foreign enterprise adopted in these countries has not led to foreign economic domination and the re-establishment of the foreign strangle-hold in the way feared by Burma and Indonesia. Moreover, the governments of the Philippines and Thailand have not followed policies of *laissez-faire* which might have handicapped their nationals, but have adopted a judicious system of government support to improve the competitive position of their private entrepreneurs. Here again, the Philippines seem to have achieved the most striking success. As a leading authority on the Philippines economy has said recently:[12]

---

of stability due to export taxes and other factors. Cf. C. H. Harvie, "Export Multiplier and the Stability of the Federation of Malaya's Economy," *Malayan Economic Review,* April 1964, pp. 80–89.

12. F. H. Golay, "Aspects of Filipino Entrepreneurship," paper given April,

Equally remarkable has been the rapid Filipinization of all major economic sectors. Export production, with the major exception of mining in which foreign capital and management is still prominent, has been rapidly transferred to Filipino ownership and management. Commerce, both foreign and domestic, with the exception of the ubiquitous international oil distributing firms, and a few large export-import firms, is now dominated by Filipino ownership and management and heavy nationalist pressures are being maintained on the remaining Chinese and Western interests.

Similarly, public utility services, including transport and communications, are virtually one hundred per cent Filipino owned and managed. Finally, the postwar period has seen the emergence with government encouragement of a sophisticated structure of money and capital market institutions essentially owned and controlled by Filipinos.

What are the implications of these two different patterns of economic development which we have described for the economic future of Southeast Asia? Much will of course depend on the outcome of crises such as presented by the situation in Vietnam. Assuming that these can be settled or contained without widening the area of conflict, we may try to outline the type of economic problems which the Southeast Asian countries may have to face in future.

The Philippines, Thailand and Malaya may be able to carry on for some time with their present pattern of economic development based on the expansion of primary exports and industrialization through progressive import substitution. But, sooner or later, they may encounter difficulties both in export expansion and import substitution. First, the world demand factors, such as the substitution of synthetic for natural rubber, may turn against some of their major export commodities. Second, as their rapid population growth and export expansion press against the limits of their natural resources, they are likely to encounter increasing difficulties on the supply side of export expansion. Third, as they extend their process of import substitution from the simpler types of consumer goods to the more complex types of consumer durables and capital goods,

---

1965 to the San Francisco meeting of the Association for Asian Studies, See also his book *The Philippines, op. cit..* Ch. XIV.

they may increasingly feel the limitations of the smallness of their domestic markets.

Burma and Indonesia have still to solve the primary problem of making a more effective use of their natural resources and their opportunities for international trade. Since their inward-looking economic policies spring ultimately from deep-seated political and psychological attitudes, their problem is essentially a political one which cannot be dealt with purely in terms of economic analysis. Thus it is not the function of a mere economist to urge them to relax some of their prevailing attitudes for the sake of expanding their exports. Ultimately, they must make their own decision about the correct balance between political and economic objectives. What is desirable is to clarify some of the points relevant to this decision. First, the outward-looking policy toward international trade need not affect their "neutralist" position in foreign policy. Indeed, the most advantageous trade policy for them would be a strictly neutralist attempt to trade with whatever country that offers the most favourable trading terms. To shift trading relationships from one country or bloc of countries to another is merely a diversion of trade. To create trade, these countries should increase the number of their trading partners. They must diversify not only their exports but also the direction of exports. Second, it should be pointed out that population is increasing almost as rapidly in Burma and Indonesia as in the other Southeast Asian countries. We have seen that these two countries increased their aggregate national product by a mere 11 per cent above the prewar level by 1960. Allowing for the population growth in the two decades from 1940 to 1960, it is very doubtful whether these countries have so far regained their prewar level of per capita national output. So long as total output cannot be expanded through the expansion of exports, the pressure on standards of living must continue. In Indonesia particularly, population pressure is serious not only because it reduces the standard of living but also because it tends to divert land from cash export crops to subsistence agriculture, thus aggravating the foreign exchange shortage. Finally, even if the governments of Burma and

Indonesia are unwilling or unable to admit direct private foreign investment, they could take more vigorous action to expand exports from the mining and plantation sector, either through state enterprise or joint enterprises with suitable foreign partners. With the resulting increase in foreign exchange earnings, they could expand output of domestic consumer goods thus alleviating the present austerities created by heavy import restrictions. While it might be possible to adopt direct state production methods in the mining and plantation exports, they would still have to make a greater use of the indirect economic incentive methods in stimulating output from the peasant export sector. In Burma particularly, where the peasants have suffered from the fixed prices paid by the State Agricultural Marketing Board, a more vigorous and flexible use of positive economic incentives should not only expand production but also help to diversify peasant exports to meet new trends in the world market demand.

Proposals for regional economic unions and common markets are popular nowadays, and it is therefore natural to ask whether a closer regional co-operation among the Southeast Asian countries might not offer a promising way of widening their markets and perhaps bringing about a more outward-looking frame of mind in Burma and Indonesia. While the long-term advantages of closer regional economic cooperation in Southeast Asia are immense, one cannot help feeling that, at the moment, the more ambitious types of proposal, such as a common market or a regional investment planning authority, are somewhat premature. Without attempting to go systematically into the pros and cons of these proposals, we may draw three implications from the previous analysis which indicate a cautious attitude towards wide-sweeping proposals for regional economic co-operation.

To begin with, there are the hardening patterns of the economic attitudes in Burma and Indonesia on the one hand and Malaysia, Thailand and the Philippines on the other. It is difficult enough to suppress nationalism among the newly independent countries even when they have the same type of approach to economic development. Thus ASA (the Association of Southeast Asia) which is made up of the three outward-looking Southeast Asian countries has so far achieved very little in economic co-operation. The problems are considerably increased when we are trying to combine two groups of countries with very different outlooks on economic development. If the proposed customs union or common market is to be worked on a more or less free enterprise basis, the Burmese and Indonesians would merely dismiss it as a device by which the foreign capitalists, whether Southeast Asian or others, were attempting to obtain the old stranglehold on their economies. If the economic union is to be on the basis of regional planning, co-ordinating investment plans to avoid duplicating productive capacity, insuperable difficulties and jealousies would arise over the geographical allocation of what are considered to be the more desirable types of industry. For instance, which country is to get "the steel mill"? Apart from these subjective obstacles, the different patterns of economic development which have taken place in the last two decades in the two groups of countries are bound to create genuinely serious structural problems for regional integration. To take another obvious example, consider the difficulties of a payments union between the strong and stable currencies of the outward-looking countries with those of the inward-looking countries, particularly Indonesia. Since the weakness of the currencies of the inward-looking countries are deeply rooted in their slow rate of export expansion and their policies which have resulted in a chronic state of suppressed capital flight, it is difficult to see how the rates of exchange of these currencies can be brought into line with the others without radical changes in their economic policies.

We have said that the process of import-substitution in the outward-looking countries may increasingly feel the limitations of the smallness of their domestic markets. Most people jump too readily from this to the conclusion that therefore the only remedy is to have a wider common market. There is also another path which deserves to be explored. It is frequently forgotten that while a small country may have a small domestic market, the size is not necessarily fixed once for all. It can in fact be increased appreciably even within a relatively short period both by the growth of population and by the growth of per capita income. Thus if the out-ward-looking Southeast Asian countries can continue to expand their exports by increasing productivity in their existing lines of primary exports and by creating a favourable economic environ-ment which might enable them to strike into new lines of primary exports, they may be able to expand the size of their domestic mar-kets quickly enough to keep on adding further stages of import substitution, without being held back by a foreign exchange short-age. If they can maintain this process for some time, their domestic industrial base may become strong enough to enable them to supple-ment their primary exports with further exports of manufactured and semi-processed goods. Without this possibility, it is difficult to see how the smaller European countries, such as the Scandinavian countries, have managed to launch themselves into economic de-velopment in the past without the benefits of large regional common markets or colonies. Of course, this escape route may be increas-ingly difficult for the "latecomers" in Southeast Asia who have also to contend with the competition from countries like Hong Kong, India and Pakistan in the export market for the simpler types of manufacture. But perhaps international trade in manufactures may look more promising if we take into account not only finished prod-ucts but also the possibility of trading in semi-processed goods and simpler capital goods affording opportunities for a vertical interna-tional division of labour among Asian countries. When this pos-sibility is supplemented by internal economic measures such as expansion of domestic food production, improvements in internal transport and marketing facilities, a more equal distribution of in-comes between the towns and the countryside, etc., the initial small-ness of the domestic market need not necessarily prove to be a fatal handicap for economic development. It is worth stressing this point, because an underdeveloped country may easily fall into the danger of not pressing forward urgently enough with its own economic reforms because it is distracted by the great expectations held out to it by the proposals for a regional economic union.

Another favourite argument in support of a regional economic association is that it may enable a greater amount of outside economic aid to be funnelled into the region, say, through a regional economic development bank. The Southeast Asian countries can of course use more economic and technical aid of the right type. But as we have seen, the basic reason for the slow economic growth of Burma and Indonesia is to be found, not in the shortage of material resources but in the deep-seated political attitudes which have prevented them from creating a favourable economic environment for making a more effective use of their own existing resources. For these two countries at least the primary problem still remains, namely how to stimulate the expansion of trade, and a mere increase in the amount of aid (even if a country like Burma were willing to accept more aid) may not have much effect unless the fundamental attitudes governing economic policy can be shifted in a more outward-looking direction.

What is the role of Japan in the economic future of Southeast Asia? Given Japan's position as the most industrially developed Asian country, with a high degree of complementarity of resources with Southeast Asia and a high and growing proportion of both her trade and funds for economic co-operation devoted to the region, she is bound to play a crucial role in the economic future of Southeast Asia. If we envisage the immediate possibility of far-reaching forms of regional economic association, Japan must be looked upon, either on her own or jointly with other developed countries, as one of the main pillars on which a regional economic structure may be built. But Japan's importance is even greater if we adopt a more realistic approach, starting from the economic conditions in Southeast Asia as they exist now and assuming a minimum change of attitudes, particularly on the part of Burma and Indonesia.

Given her friendly relations with these two countries, Japan is currently in a more effective position to help them than any other advanced country; and given that the regional economic prosperity of Southeast Asia may be jeopardized by the increasing gap in economic development between these two countries and their neighbours, Japan may find it in her long-run interest to make special efforts to help them. Take for instance the declining Japanese demand for Southeast Asian rice. While Thailand has been able to compensate for it by expansion in exports of maize, the structure of Burma's agriculture has been more rigid and she still depends principally on her rice exports. It would be interesting to explore how far Japan might be able to modify internal agricultural policies to admit more rice from Burma.[13] This however should be looked upon as a "pump-priming" operation to use Japanese capital and technical aid to assist Burma in the expansion of her other non-peasant exports and her import-substituting industries. The Japanese experts are said to have shown a particular flair in analysing the prospects of investment projects in Asian conditions and in suggesting new industries under conditions of limited markets, and their assistance should be particularly valuable in Burma.

Apart from these special efforts directed towards the inward-looking countries, Japan's role is not merely to expand trade along existing lines but also make flexible adjustments to enable the Southeast Asian countries to make their crucial transition from the export of primary products to the export of manufactured goods and to extend the scope of their manufacturing industries from the domestic to the world market. The Southeast Asian countries can learn much from Japan's policies adopted during her own transition period. But they will be further assisted if Japan (together with other advanced countries) were to adopt a policy of progressive withdrawal from the export of simpler manufactures to make room for their export from the underdeveloped countries and to turn progressively towards the export of the more complex and capital and skill-intensive products in which her comparative advantages are increasing.[14]

13. See particularly the suggestive paper by Katsu Yanaihara on "Problems of the Rice Trade between Burma and Japan—A Case Study on Exports of Primary Products in Underdeveloped Countries," *The Developing Economies,* March 1964.

14. Cf. Kiyoshi Kojima, "The Pattern of Triangular Trade among the U.S.A., Japan and Southeast Asia," *The Developing Economies,* March-August 1962, and also Toshiaki Yoshihara, "Japan's Trade with Developing Countries" in the same issue of the journal for further discussion of the adjustments which may be made in the commodity composition of Japan's trade with Southeast Asia.

13 | Market Mechanism and Planning—The Functional Approach

The functional approach to market mechanism and planning which I shall adopt in this paper can be distinguished both from the ideological approach and from the purely formal approach to development planning.

In conventional ideological terms, a preference for using the market mechanism is identified with the laissez-faire policy while a preference for using the administrative machinery to exercise direct controls over the economy is identified with "planning." In the functional approach, value judgments are introduced explicitly at the beginning, in determining the objectives of economic policy. The market mechanism and the administrative machinery are then regarded merely as alternative instruments of economic policy whose relative merits should be judged, not ideologically, but according to their effectiveness in fulfilling the given objectives of economic policy.

The functional approach can also be distinguished from the purely formal approach to market mechanism and planning. The formal models of planning tend to be concerned mainly with the consistency

Presented at the International Conference on the Structure and Development in Asian Economies, Japan Economic Research Center, September 9–14, 1968, Tokyo, Japan.

between the quantifiable magnitudes of the plan, in particular between the target figures of the desired increase in outputs, the estimated sectoral capital-output ratios and the total amount of resources required to achieve the target figures. The economic mechanisms which are to implement the plan are pushed into the background and frequently there is a tendency to assume a perfect planning agency much in the same way as advocates of laissez-faire policy tend to assume perfect competition. But even if all the quantifiable magnitudes of a plan are formally consistent with each other, the plan may still fail if the existing organizational framework of the planning country is unable to cope with the non-quantifiable extra burdens of co-ordination and adjustments imposed on it by the plan. In the functional approach, we start from the market system and the administrative machinery as they exist and operate in the realistic setting of the underdeveloped countries and consider their relative effectiveness in performing the task of co-ordinating the economy under planning. More importantly, we may consider not only their present performance but also their future potentialities of development and the contributions they can make to the improvement of the organizational framework of the underdeveloped countries in the longer run.

The question we are concerned with in this paper may be formulated as follows: assuming that the chief objective of the Asian governments is to promote a rapid economic development of their countries measured in terms of per capita incomes, what is the relative scope and effectiveness at present and in the future of using the market mechanism and the administrative machinery as instruments of economic development policy? This question may be further narrowed down by accepting the proposition that social overhead capital, such as transport and communications, power, and large-scale irrigation works should be provided by public enterprise.

In this paper, I shall begin by showing that the attempt to co-ordinate economic planning by an extensive use of direct administrative controls has proved to be clearly inefficient even where the administrative system is highly developed by Asian standards so that there is a general presumption in favour of using the market mechanism as much as possible as an instrument of economic co-ordination. Next, I shall argue that the development of the market system still offers the most promising method of improving the organizational framework of the Asian economies so that even the most planning-minded Asian government should be concerned with encouraging the development of the market economy. Finally, I shall argue that in some of the highly controlled Asian economies, the development of a more effective market economy has been re-tarded and "economic dualism" aggravated by inappropriate policies of maintaining overvalued currencies, artificially low official rates of interest and unfavourable price policies towards the agricultural sector; and that the correction of these faults can be looked upon as a major step in strengthening the market mechanism.

In economic planning in a "mixed economy," the operational controls which the government can exercise over the rest of the economy fall into two main types: the indirect controls working through the market mechanism and the direct controls worked by the administrative machinery. The instruments of indirect controls in-clude the foreign exchange rate, the rate of interest, pricing policies of state enterprises and public utilities, tariffs, taxes and subsidies and price support programmes. Typically, the indirect controls are operated by correcting the existing prices of selected commodities or factors of production and then allowing the market forces to change the relevant quantities in the desired direction and to the desired extent. Indirect controls are not discretionary in the sense that once the initial market prices have been corrected, any buyer or seller is subsequently free to buy or sell *unlimited* quantities at the ruling prices. In contrast, the direct administrative controls typically attempt to operate on the physical quantities of com-modities and factors of production by various methods, such as quotas, licensing and rationing, although as we shall see, these quantitative controls frequently entail price controls also. The controlling authority also exercises discretion on who should do the buying and selling and in what individually prescribed amounts.

The non-communist Asian countries are "mixed economies" with the larger part of their total economic activity comprised of agriculture, handicraft and small-scale industries and with a large proportion of modern manufacturing industry, trade and commerce in the private sector. The state sector is confined mainly to public utilities and certain categories of large scale industry. But this seemingly uniform facade of "mixed economy" conceals wide differences in the mixture of direct and indirect contols used by different Asian governments in carrying out their economic development plans. When we look more closely at these differences, it is possible to detect a significant relationship between the use of indirect controls and the "open-ness" of the economy on the one hand and the use of direct controls and the "insulation" of the economy on the other. Thus there are the relatively open economies such as Malaya, Thailand and the Philippines where government controls mainly operate through the market mechanism. It should be noted that these countries are by no means laissez-faire economies. They have their official development plans and their governments are as much concerned with promoting rapid economic development as the governments of other Asian countries. On the other hand, there are the highly insulated economies such as India, Burma and Indonesia; Pakistan and Ceylon may also be included in this group with certain reservations.

This broad pattern of relationship between the use of indirect controls and the open-ness of the economy and the use of direct controls and the insulation of the economy is not surprising. In general terms, it is easy to see why the countries which desire to keep their economies open to the influences of the world market forces should resort as little as possible to direct controls. Given the interdependent relationships between their domestic economy and the world economy, the scope for using arbitrary direct controls over the domestic economy is limited. It is also notable that the open economies of Asia have pursued fiscal and monetary policies which control the rate of inflation and keep the external values of their currencies in line with their domestic prices and costs. In contrast, the countries which have tried to insulate their economies from the world market forces may have been initially impelled to impose quantitative import controls to meet a short-run foreign exchange crisis: but subsequently their governments have exalted the reduction of "dependence" on foreign trade and the reduction of "foreign economic domination" as an objective of national economic policy or at least as the necessary condition for the assertion of a genuine national "economic independence." This "independence" is usually interpreted as the freedom of the ruling government to impose any type of control it may choose to exercise over the domestic economy, ignoring its interdependence with the rest of the world economy. Further, one of the freedoms claimed by the government is the freedom from the "orrthodox" fiscal and monetary discipline. Thus, the rate of domestic inflation and the over-valuation of the currencies at the official exchange rates have been greater in the insulated economies than in the open economies.

Historically, however, quantitative controls on imports have been usually imposed in response to a short-run balance of payments crisis. Here it may be noted that while Malaya may have been exceptionally well placed, other open economies like Thailand and the Philippines have not been free from balance of payments difficulties during the post-war reconstruction phase or in the post-Korean boom period. What really distinguishes them from the insulated economies is not that they have been free from balance of payments difficulties, but that they have been able to use import controls as short-run expedients by adopting long-run policies which enable them to liberalise their imports and shift towards indirect controls on foreign trade. In particular, they have adopted an "out-ward-looking" policy towards the expansion of foreign trade and investment combined with the use of market incentives for their peasant producers. In countries like India, Burma and Indonesia, however, the quantitative controls on imports, once introduced tend to perpetuate themselves as an integral part of "planning" and tend to spread to the rest of the economy. This tendency has been aggravated by the adoption of an "inward-looking" policy of domestic industrialization which concentrates only on the expansion of modern manufacturing industry to the neglect both of the export sector and the peasant agricultural sector.

Now, it is not difficult to understand why direct administrative controls tend to perpetuate and proliferate themselves in the "inward-looking" countries. Typically, the government starts by putting on quantitative import controls to meet a short-run balance of payments crisis; but it finds the subsequent rise in the prices of imports "politically unacceptable" either because it would raise the cost of living and strengthen demand for higher wages in towns or because it would raise the cost of capital goods and raw materials for its industrialization programme. Thus it finds itself trying to control both the quantities and prices of the imports at the same time and to suppress the disequilibrium of excess demand at the controlled prices by administrative means such as licensing and rationing. Now so long as there are no fundamental changes in economic policies to improve the balance of payments position, such as the expansion of exports, the expansion of domestic production to absorb the purchasing power which increases the pressure of demand on imports or effective taxation to cut down domestic consumption, the need for the direct controls will continue. As the effects of the disequilibrium spread to the other parts of the economy, there will be a further need to impose more extensive and comprehensive controls over the rest of the economy.

This process is well documented in the case of India by Professor Myrdal in his recent book.[1] In addition to the quantitative controls on imports, the direct controls imposed by the government of India include: the control of new security issues of companies under Capital Issues (Control) Act, 1947; the requirement to have a license for all new major industrial undertakings including any substantial extension of existing plants or change in their location

1. Gunnar Myrdal, *Asian Drama*, 1968, Vol. II, Chs. 19 and 20.

or change in the articles manufactured under Industries (Development and Regulation) Act (1951, amended 1953 and 1956); and the control of production, distribution, transport, trade, consumption or storage of all foodstuffs, all principal raw materials, important industrial components and all iron and steel products and the prescription of their prices under the Essential Commodities Act (1955). Myrdal concludes that "no major and, indeed, few minor business decisions can be taken except with the prior permission of the administrative authorities or at the risk of subsequent government disapproval."[2]

How effective is such an extensive network of direct administrative controls in co-ordinating the various sectors of the economy in a concerted attempt to achieve the target figures of the development plan? One would expect an unfavourable answer both from practical experience elsewhere and from our general knowledge of the effects of such a system of control. Here I shall reiterate some of the basic draw-backs of the direct administrative controls in the setting of the "inward-looking" Asian countries.

In so far as the government's objective is merely to control the total quantity of a given commodity, an indirect method of control working through the market mechanism is a more efficient method. Even taking into account the practical difficulties of fixing the correct price or the correct rate of tax or subsidy, an indirect control tends to minimise the economic cost of bringing about the desired change by permitting the most efficient buyers and sellers to trade in unlimited quantities at the corrected price. For instance, even if a country were unwilling to adopt devaluation, the foreign exchange shortage problem can be alleviated by various methods using the market mechanism, such as a uniform surcharge on all imports or auctioning the foreign exchange permits in the open market. These would be more efficient than the cumbrous system of import licensing, exercising detailed controls over who should receive the import licences, in what individually allotted amounts and for what categories of imports. But the Asian governments which have per-

2. Ibid., p. 921.

sisted in using the method of import licensing do not seem to be very clear whether their prime objective is to conserve the scarce foreign exchange resources or to pursue other economic and political objectives by using their discretionary power.

Thus in many Southeast Asian countries which have suffered from "foreign economic domination," particularly by Indian or Chinese businessmen in the import-export trade, import licensing has been frequently used to discriminate in favour of the less efficient indigenous business men. This has frequently led to the selling of import licenses by the less efficient to the more efficient traders at monopoly profits and has greatly added to the rise in the prices of imported goods. Things are even worse, when the government attempts to counter these abuses by establishing state monopolies to distribute the imported goods. We then have the ultimate inefficiency of scarce foreign exchange being used to pile up stocks of unwanted imported consumers' goods while shortages and black markets flourish for the more popular types of imported goods (which the government shops in their ignorance of market demand fail to stock in adequate quantities).

In the Indian case, where the government uses its discretionary power, not so much to discriminate against persons, but against types of economic activity, the system develops a different kind of defect. A complex system of discretionary controls even when administered honestly and with the best intentions, tends to favour the bigger firms which are already established and which can be relied on to a greater extent to fulfil the government's requirements.[3]

In all the countries which have adopted quantitative controls of

3. "The small business units and newcomers in enterprise are particularly hindered and discouraged by the multiplicity of controls, for their economic power is so weak that they can hardly deal effectively with the control authorities and cope with the delays and red tape involved. On the other hand, existing large enterprises enjoy a semi-monopoly position under the protection of controls and make easy profits through access to scarce factors made available to them cheaply. There is hardly any incentive for them to improve productivity or operating efficiency" (*Economic Bulletin for Asia and the Far East,* Vol. XII, No. 3, December 1961, p. 7).

imports, the notion that these controls are an integral part of development planning has been fostered by a confusion between the type of import controls necessary to deal with the short-run balance of payments problem and the type of import controls necessary to promote long-run domestic industrial development through the protection of the "infant industries." To begin with, the short-run balance of payments difficulties may not even be caused by a genuine increase in developmental expenditure: they are frequently associated with a high level of government consumption expenditure, in social welfare expenditure or defence which can only be indirectly or tenuously associated with economic development. Given the short-run balance of payments difficulties, the typical aim of import controls would be to prevent a sharp rise in the cost of living causing economic distress to the poor and generating an upward pressure of wages and prices. This however calls for a liberal import of "necessities" while prohibiting "luxury" imports. Unfortunately, without effective taxation to cut down urban middle class consumption, this tends to encourage the setting up of domestic luxury goods industries which moreover can usually obtain permission to import machinery and raw materials which are classified as "capital goods" by the import control authorities. Clearly, these luxury goods industries which have sprung up, unplanned, are not likely to be "infant industries" with genuine prospects of lowering their costs in the future. On the other hand, in the typical situation of domestic inflation and indiscriminate rise in the prices of all imports associated with quantitative import controls, the tariffs have lost much of their power to encourage suitably selected "infant industries." Tariff protection works by offering a differential price advantage to the protected industries relative to the non-protected industries. But the differential advantage offered even by a stiff tariff rate is likely to be drowned by successive rounds of rises in the prices of all imports which are induced by purely short-run factors, by speculation and by the vagaries of import licensing.

Behind all these defects is the well known drawback of the method of direct controls: viz. it requires an elaborate bureaucracy to operate the controls. The inefficiency and the delays of red tape are notorious even in the advanced countries. In the underdeveloped countries of Asia with a less developed administrative machinery and a shortage of competent civil servants, the inefficiency of bureaucratic controls is multiplied many fold, frequently resulting in widespread corruption. From the point of view of efficient co-ordination, two difficulties need to be specially pointed out. First, when an extensive system of direct controls is used, there is the extremely difficult problem of co-ordinating the controls to avoid serious contradictions between them which could paralyse all private decision-making processes in the controlled sectors and to avoid loopholes which would lead to black markets. Here, Professor Myrdal has shown that this complex problem of co-ordinating direct controls has been clearly beyond the capacity even of the Indian administrative system which is the most developed one among the Asian underdeveloped countries. Second, efficient implementation of the plans requires the co-ordination of the different sectors of the economy, not just at a given moment of time, but as a continuous process stretching over the whole period of the plan. That is to say, each sector must not merely fulfil its allotted target but must do so according to a strict time-table. The delay in the fulfilment of the plan in one sector will cause delays in the fulfilment of the plans in the related sectors. Thus the delays associated with direct administrative controls are not only costly in themselves but can also throw the whole process of implementing the plan out of step. This danger is greater, the greater the degree of "integration" between the different parts of the plan and the different sectors of the economy.

Enough has been said, I think, to show that Asian experience tends to confirm the general proposition that extensive and detailed controls by the administrative machinery are extremely inefficient and cannot offer a workable method of co-ordinating the economy. This leaves us with the general presumption against using the administrative machinery and for using the market mechanism as much as possible as an instrument of economic planning. While this may be accepted in general terms in current writings on development planning within the framework of "mixed economies," I do not think that its full implications have been appreciated.

If we accept the general presumption in favour of using the market mechanism, then the government in a mixed economy can no longer take a laissez-faire attitude towards the growth of the market economy. On the contrary, the more planning-minded a government is, the more it should pursue deliberate policies to encourage the growth of the market economy; for it is only through the growth of a well articulated market economy and a wider basis for taxation that the government can expect to exercise a more effective control over the economy to promote economic development. I have emphasised this point because current discussions, particularly on the "mobilization" of resources for economic development, are vitiated by the facile assumption that the market economy would grow automatically, irrespective of whatever actions are taken by the government. Thus governments have been urged to take more vigorous action to increase taxation, but there is no discussion of the disincentive effects of taxation nor of the longer term policies to broaden the tax base through the enlargement of the market economy. Governments have been urged to mobilise domestic savings, but the role of an appropriate level of the official rate of interest as an instrument of developing the domestic capital market is neglected. Finally, governments have been frequently condoned, if not encouraged, for resorting to deficit financing on the ground that it creates "forced savings" for economic development, but there is no serious concern for the possible effects of inflation in discouraging savings at low official rates of interest or in discouraging the spread of the money economy by undermining the confidence in money among the subsistence producers who are in the process of entering the money economy.

However, before we can discuss policies to strengthen and develop the market economy in the underdeveloped countries, it is necessary to face up to the fact that, in spite of repeated failures to plan the economy by direct administrative controls, there is still a considerable resistance to the use of the market mechanism as an instrument of development policy. The critics start by pointing out the various deficiencies in the existing market systems of the underdeveloped countries. From this, they not only draw the conclusion that the market mechanism works imperfectly in the underdeveloped countries but also the more questionable conclusion that we should not adopt policies to develop and strengthen the market mechanism and turn it into a more effective instrument of development policy. One can readily concede that the market mechanism works very imperfectly in the underdeveloped countries, but the drift of our previous analysis has been to suggest that, *relatively* speaking, the market mechanism still offers a more workable instrument of economic co-ordination than the administrative machinery. But the more important question to my mind relates to the *future* potentialities of developing the market systems of the underdeveloped countries and transforming them into a more effective organizational framework for their economic development. To answer this, let us look a little more closely at the various deficiencies which prevail in the market systems of the underdeveloped countries.

These deficiencies are of two main types: viz. "market imperfections" common to both the advanced and the underdeveloped countries and the incomplete development and spread of the market economy which is a special feature of the latter. In the Asian setting, the incompleteness of the market economy can be seen in two different ways. First, there still remains a considerable amount of "subsistence" production in agriculture and handicraft industries and there is only a rudimentary development of markets for the factors of production, particularly for capital funds, in the rural sector of the economy. Second, the different parts of the economy are only imperfectly connected with each other and there is a broad "dualistic" division of the economy into the traditional unorganized sector and the modern organized sector. This incomplete development of the market system can be only partly explained in terms of the time-lags and frictions in the transition process to the money economy. In most underdeveloped countries, there would also be various "imperfections" of the market which tend to aggravate incompleteness and fragmentation of the economy. Now these market imperfections can be classified into three types. First, there are those caused by the imperfect mobility and divisibility of the factors of production and imperfect knowledge which may be considered as arising naturally from the existing economic conditions. Second, there are those artificial distortions and rigidities introduced into the economy by private monopoly power or by government policy or by both. Third, there are the "divergences between social and private costs."

I would accept that all these possible defects of the market system are present in varying degrees in all the Asian economies. But let me go quickly down the list to show that none of these defects constitutes a serious objection against trying to make a more effective use of the market mechanism as an instrument of economic development policy. First, the incomplete development of the market economy may be interpreted as *prima facie* evidence for further possibilities of extending and strengthening the market mechanism through appropriate policies to encourage the growth of the money economy. Second, the accepted method of overcoming or reducing the immobility and indivisibility of factors of production is for the government to provide better social overhead facilities, particularly in transport and communications and power. This in no way conflicts with, and is in fact complementary to, the policy of promoting the growth of the market economy.

Third, we have the artificial distortions and rigidities created by private monopoly power or by government policy. Here, we may repeat that the use of the market mechanism as an instrument of economic policy does not imply a laissez-faire policy towards monopolistic enterprises. But it does imply that the monopoly power should be regulated through the market mechanism: that is to say, by encouraging potential competitors or, if that is not possible, by taxing away the monopoly profits, instead of the government taking over the monopolistic firms and running them as state enterprises. However, under the fear of "foreign economic domination,"

Burma and Indonesia have pursued a policy of nationalizing the foreign-owned mines and plantations in the export sector. Whatever the ideological justifications for such a policy, from a functional viewpoint of promoting economic development it seems fairly clear that this policy has greatly slowed down the growth of their exports and their general rate of economic development.[4] Even when we turn to India where nationalization has been used only moderately, it seems clear that the more important source of the artificial distortions and rigidities in the economy is not the old fashioned private monopoly power but government policy promoting and sheltering monopolistic firms under a network of direct controls necessitated by inappropriate pricing policies in the key sectors of the economy. I shall argue that in all the highly controlled "inward-looking" countries of Asia, the development of a more effective market economy has been retarded and "economic dualism" aggravated by inappropriate policies of maintaining overvalued currencies, artificially low rates of interest in the modern organized sector of the economy and unfavourable price policies for the agricultural sector. I shall argue that the removal of these government-created rigidities by itself can be looked upon as a major step in strengthening the market mechanism.

Before I do this, let me touch briefly on the last item on our list of market imperfections, viz. "the divergences between social and private costs" in the underdeveloped countries. I am myself inclined to consider that, from the viewpoint of promoting economic development in the present-day context of Asia, the static problem of correcting these divergences within the *given* market framework is likely to be of less immediate importance than the problem of expanding and developing the framework of the market economy. First, in so far as these divergences between social and private costs arise from the technological external economies and diseconomies in a setting of physical proximity and interrelationships, there is no reason to suppose these divergences are more important for the underdeveloped countries than for the advanced countries. In fact,

4. See above, Chapter 12.

the familiar problems of air and water pollution, noise, the problem of urban sprawl into the countryside are likely to be more important for the advanced countries than for the underdeveloped countries. The type of divergence which is likely to be more important for the underdeveloped countries is the wasteful utilization of natural resources, e.g. soil erosion through over-grazing or "shifting cultivation," despoliation of forest cover to land through fire, wood-cutting, over-fishing or over-hunting, etc. But as F. H. Knight has pointed out long ago, this type of divergence arises through a lack of a proper private or state ownership of these resources which can regulate their use by charging economic rent.[5] Thus they may be regarded as symptoms of an underdeveloped market for land and natural resources rather than external economies and diseconomies in the strict sense of the term. Further, the corrections of the divergences between social and private costs have to be made by taxes and subsidies and I am doubtful whether the fiscal machinery as it exists in most Asian countries is developed enough to make the finer corrections and adjustments called for by theoretical welfare economics. For instance, the most interesting application of the optimum analysis for the underdeveloped countries is in the field of international trade. Here it has been frequently argued that tariff protection should be given to domestic manufacturing industry in the underdeveloped countries either because the wage level in the industrial sector is above the true social cost of labour measured in terms of its marginal product in agriculture or because the "educative effect" of manufacturing industry yields social returns in excess of private returns. Recent analysis has however shown that, in so far as these domestic distortions exist, they should be cured by *subsidies* applied to the source of the distortion within the domestic economy. To try to cure domestic distortions by imposing tariffs operating on international trade is inefficient as it introduces a new distortion to cure the existing one.[6] But I feel that until

5. F. H. Knight, "Some Fallacies in the Interpretation of Social Cost," *Quarterly Journal of Economics,* 1924.
6. See H. G. Johnson, "Optimal Trade Intervention in the Presence of

the Asian countries are able to broaden their tax base through the expansion of their market economies, this recommendation to use subsidies instead of tariffs is likely to remain a counsel of perfection for many of them.

This leads me back to my main theme of expanding the framework of the market economy. The general process in which the money economy has developed in Asia through the expansion of export production induced by the growth of new wants for the imported consumers' goods has been extensively analysed elsewhere.[7] Here I need merely to recapitulate its salient features which are: the expansion of peasant exports bringing in the underutilised land and labour from the subsistence sector into the money economy; the expansion of mining and plantation exports bringing in the underutilised labour from the subsistence economy into the wage economy; the extension of money economy through improvements in transport and communications bringing in a wider circle of peasants producing cash crops on a part-time basis and "migrant labour" which is only partially in the wage economy; the intensification of the market economy through specialisation which turns these "part-time" cash earners into whole-time cash earners; and the spread of the money economy from the foreign trade sector to the domestic sector and the development of the modern urban manufacturing sector side by side with the traditional rural sector.

Now, this process has rarely been permitted to happen in a "neutral" way. Both during the colonial period and after independence, government policy has always played an important part in encouraging or discouraging it. Thus, the so-called "laissez-faire" policy of the colonial governments was in fact a policy of promoting the growth of foreign trade. This was motivated, not only by a desire to provide the raw materials and the markets for the metropolitan countries, but also by a desire of the local colonial govern-

---

Domestic Distortions" in R. E. Baldwin *et al., Trade, Growth and Balance of Payments,* 1965.

7. See my book *The Economics of the Developing Countries,* London, 1964, Chapters 2–5.

ments to expand the source of their revenues required to finance the setting up of a modern government and the provision of social overhead capital, particularly improved transport and communications which served to open up the colonial territories to foreign trade. Now there are various objections one can raise against the practical execution of this policy in a colonial setting; but from the strictly functional standpoint of promoting economic development in terms of per capita national income, I believe that this was and still is the appropriate type of policy for the smaller and less densely populated countries of Southeast Asia. Thus, in functional terms, the export expansion policy pursued by the "outward-looking" countries of Malaya, Thailand and the Philippines may be regarded as a continuation of the "colonial policy," adapted to serve the national interests of the independent governments. Through such a policy these "outward-looking" countries have been able to enjoy a rapid rate of economic development in the post-war decades and their governments have been able to influence the pattern of distribution of incomes and economic activities in favour of their own nationals and against the foreigners. In contrast, Burma and Indonesia which are no less abundantly endowed with natural resources relative to population and which also produce the same type of export commodities, have very clearly fallen behind the other Southeast Asian countries in export expansion and economic development. I believe that this must be mainly accounted for in terms of their violent reaction against the "colonial pattern" of economic development.[8] Given their fears about "foreign economic domination," they have nationalized or otherwise discouraged foreign enterprises in mining and plantation. Given their ideological distrust of the market mechanism, they have relied extensively on direct administrative controls and state enterprises; and these together with heavy taxation and shortage of imported consumers' goods have robbed their peasant producers of any economic incentive to increase export production. In pursuing their "inward-looking" policies they have in effect cut off their relatively abundant

8. I have developed this argument at greater length above, Chapter 12.

endowment of natural resources from the world market demand for the exports which these resources can readily produce. They have thereby denied themselves a fairly easy method of economic development through export expansion which could have been achieved without any great improvements in techniques of production or any heavy outlay of capital investment except in the traditional sphere of improving transport and communications.

Granted the importance of the market mechanism in promoting export expansion in the smaller and less densely populated countries of Southeast Asia, what is its role in the larger and more densely populated countries like India or Pakistan? Here, given the larger size of the countries, one would expect the development of the export sector to be relatively less important than the development of the domestic sector. Again, given their less abundant natural resources relative to their populations, one would expect that there is much less scope for the expansion of agricultural exports without considerable changes in techniques and increase in productivity. I have drawn the contrast somewhat more sharply than the facts justify[9] so that we may accept the proposition that for India and Pakistan the development of manufacturing industry is likely to be more important than the expansion of primary exports and consider its implications for the role of the market mechanism in the economic development of these countries.

The way I now see this question may be stated as follows. I

9. For one thing, in spite of their denser population, the type of agriculture prevalent in India and Pakistan may be described as the inefficient *extensive* method of cultivation in contrast to the truly intensive form of agriculture, say in Japan. For another, neither country has exhausted its opportunities for expanding primary exports, particularly the "minor" primary exports where their share of the world market is small and they face a relatively price-elastic world demand. This feeling is strengthened when we observe India taking countervailing action against her devaluation by abolishing subsidies and imposing duties on a wide range of her exports. Cf. G. Myrdal, *Asian Drama,* Vol. I, Ch. 10, and Vol. II, Part V on the extensive agriculture of India and Pakistan. Cf. A. B. De Vries, *The Export Experience of Developing Countries,* International Bank for Reconstruction and Development, Washington, 1967 on the importance of the "minor exports" for the underdeveloped countries.

think that countries like Burma and Indonesia would readily gain much more by making use of the market mechanism for export expansion. But compared with this simpler process of export expansion based on underutilised natural resources, the expansion of the industrial sector in India and Pakistan would require the development of a more articulated market economy, including a better developed internal capital market and the development of the agricultural sector. Thus India and Pakistan would need to develop the framework of their internal market economy more than Burma and Indonesia. In discussing the "inward-looking" policies of these two latter countries, it has been sufficient to concentrate on the effects of import controls and overvalued foreign exchange rate on their foreign trade sector. In the case of India and Pakistan however it is necessary to supplement this analysis by considering the effects of inappropriate levels of the official interest rate and inappropriate policies towards the agricultural sector in aggravating the "dualism" inside the domestic economy.

Before the second world war, the Asian colonial countries could borrow at lower rates of interest than, say, a country like Japan could obtain in the metropolitan capital markets; but the rates of interest in the modern sectors of their economies were closely linked with the metropolitan rates of interest. After the second world war, the underdeveloped countries of Asia could still borrow cheaply from international organizations such as the World Bank or obtain "soft loans" from the aid-giving countries. But, with the establishment of their own central banks and the attainment of monetary independence, their internal capital markets have grown increasingly insulated from the international capital markets. Thus we have the paradoxical situation in which the central banks in the capital-scarce countries like India and Pakistan have maintained a consistently lower level of interest rates than the prevailing level in the capital-abundant advanced countries in the post-war period. The "cheap-money policy" was first advocated in the context of the advanced countries trying to get out of a short-run economic depression. The rationale of this policy for the underdeveloped countries trying to promote long-run development has never been seriously discussed, but seems to have been adopted implicitly in the general reaction against the orthodox classical economics.

The artificially low rates of interest which do not reflect the economic reality of capital scarcity have very deleterious effects on the underdeveloped countries, both by perpetuating the need for extensive direct government controls over the organized modern sector of the economy and by aggravating the financial dualism between the organized sector and the unorganized rural sector. In India and Pakistan, the combined effect of overvalued currencies, domestic inflation and low rates of interest have the effect of raising the profits of the bigger firms which can run the gauntlet of the controls to abnormally high levels. This creates a demand for investible funds which cannot be supplied in unlimited quantities at the ruling rates of interest thus perpetuating a system of controls under which "most officials have to devote much of their time and energy to limiting and stopping enterprise." Professor Myrdal has likened this state of affairs to "driving a car with the accelerator pushed to the floor but the brakes on" and has forcefully argued for correcting the overvaluation of currency and raising the official rate of interest as a necessary step in removing the wasteful and ineffective network of discretionary controls.[10]

There are some obvious advantages to be obtained from raising the official rate of interest to a more realistic level. First, one would expect an increase in the supply of savings, both new savings and the attraction of the funds which are now hoarded or used for speculation. Second, a higher rate of interest (combined with a higher price of foreign exchange for imports of capital goods) would prevent the adoption of excessively capital-intensive techniques of production in both the public and the private sectors. Above all, from the longer-term point of view, it would encourage the development of a more integrated domestic capital market, reducing the dualism between the organized and unorganized sectors of the market. Here again one may quote Professor Myrdal:

10. G. Myrdal, *Asian Drama*, Vol. II, Ch. 19, p. 925.

The way to gradually break down the dualism in the credit market would seem to be, first, to increase interest rates substantially in the organized market and second, to decrease or eliminate the subsidies involved in public lending to the traditional sectors; requests for aid should be treated as a separate issue. . . . If credits in the traditional sector were placed on a business basis, so that the volume of credit could be expanded without cost to society, the state could more seriously compete with the usurious moneylenders, and the average interest rate would eventually be lowered. In any case, consideration for the traditional sectors cannot be invoked in defense of the low interest rates in the organized sector. It is worth noting that in Japan, where the rural and small-scale industrial sectors are much more integrated in the organized credit market (more than half of all agricultural credit is provided by financial institutions), interest differentials are much smaller: on the average, interest rates are lower in the traditional sector, but considerably higher in the full organized sector than in India and Pakistan [G. Myrdal, *op. cit.*, p. 2095 and Appendix 8].

Finally, we come to the role of the market mechanism in the development of the agricultural sector. This is a vast subject and I shall confine myself to two main points.

The first is the possibility of using the market mechanism to a greater extent to encourage the agricultural sector to use improved inputs by means of subsidies. This can be illustrated both in relation to irrigation and to the dissemination of better methods of farming, improved seeds and fertilizers. No one would deny that only governments can undertake large-scale capital-intensive irrigation works. But the real question has always been whether these capital-intensive methods of irrigation, particularly those large-scale multi-purpose river valley projects, are the most economical method of providing irrigation. Recently, the rapid growth in the spread of tube wells and pump sets in Pakistan and to some extent in India also has provided fairly strong evidence of the advantage of small-scale over large-scale irrigation methods. There would seem to be a good case for subsidising the small-scale private enterprise spreading this more economical and popular method of irrigation. Again, no one would question that it is the function of the government to undertake research and experiments on improved methods of farming. What is questionable is whether these technically improved methods can be spread to the farmers simply by relying on an army of undertrained agricultural extension officers to preach at the farmers instead of providing economic incentives for the adoption of the improved methods. Moreover, the task of distributing the fertilisers and improved seeds in the right place, and in right amounts at the right time in rural areas has generally been beyond the cumbrous machinery of agricultural departments. I think that there is much to be said for the policy (which I believe has been adopted in Pakistan) of subsidising the distribution of seeds and fertilisers through the normal trade channels of the village shop.

The second point relates to the maintenance of a favourable price level for agricultural products to induce the expansion of output in the agricultural sector in some sort of "balanced growth" relationship with the manufacturing industry and to bring the rural sectors into an articulated framework of the national economy. Here most countries encouraging domestic industrialization tend to turn the terms of trade between the manufacturing and agricultural sector against the latter in a variety of ways, such as controlling the rise of agricultural prices to keep down the cost of living of the workers in the urban manufacturing sector. In the case of India, the situation has been complicated by the receipt of large quantities of PL 480 wheat to meet short-run food shortages which may have unfavourable longer-run effects on the expansion of food production. This brings me to the point which I am concerned with here: viz. the *maintenance* of a favourable price level for the agricultural sector. One of the reasons why the money economy has spread so easily in the less densely populated Southeast Asian countries was that the farmer could grow cash crops by bringing waste land into cultivation without having to reduce the production of his food crop. This is the strategic role which the "part-time" cash farmers played in the widening of the market economy. This mechanism is not available in India or Pakistan although it would be misleading to think of all Indian and Pakistan farmers as struggling at subsistence level on over-crowded small holdings with no economic reserves to meet the risks of entering the money economy. In fact, there is a considerable class of medium and large-scale farmers in India and Pakistan and they seem to have played a leading role in increasing the marketable agricultural output. But even so, it is generally recognized that the reduction of risks by some form of price support programme would have a powerful effect in encouraging the expansion of output from all classes of farmers. Now, as we have seen, India, in spite of her elaborate planning machinery and sophisticated methods of planning, has been extremely vulnerable to fluctuations in harvest caused by weather conditions. Thus there would seem to be a strong case for solving the two problems together by means of an internal buffer stock scheme for food, maintaining the price level during bumper harvest years by adding to the stocks and preventing high prices and speculation during years of bad harvest by drawing on stocks. This is by no means a new idea and I believe that this has been recommended to India by the World Bank. But it is an excellent illustration of the type of planning using the market mechanism which I have been advocating in this paper.

To sum up: the general approach I have been advocating in this paper is to make a deliberate use of the theoretically unsophisticated but practically more dependable working of the market mechanism as an instrument of economic development policy. The underlying assumption of my argument is that, even in the underdeveloped market setting of Asia, the basic market laws operate in the sense that the government can control either the price or the quantity of a commodity and that the attempt to control both and to suppress the resulting disequilibrium by administrative methods has generally turned out to be ineffective and has led to extensive growth of further controls which further stifle longer run economic development. This may be contrasted with the case for more comprehensive planning which is derived from more sophisticated theoretical models of planning. These in general tend to concentrate on elaborate exercises to test the formal consistency of the quantifiable magnitudes of the plan. However, as I have suggested earlier, even if all the quantifiable magnitudes of a plan were consistent, the plan would still impose unquantifiable extra burdens of co-ordination and adjustments on the existing organizational framework of the economy and would fail if the organizational framework proved unequal to perform the complicated tasks imposed on it. As I have pointed out, the co-ordination of planning over time requires that each sector not merely fulfil its allotted target but fulfil it according to a strict time-table covering the whole period of the plan and the delays associated with bureaucracy exercising direct controls are not only costly in themselves but tend to throw the whole process of implementing the plan out of gear. Thus in any realistic setting of the underdeveloped countries, I believe that the external diseconomies transmitted from one sector to another in a closely integrated plan are likely to outweigh the theoretical advantages claimed for it. Theoretically, it can be shown that a perfect planning agency co-ordinating investment plans over time can reap the benefits arising out of external economies and complementarities in a way not possible in any realistic market situation, particularly with imperfect capital markets. But theoretically, it can also be shown that provided we assume perfect compeition, including perfect competition in the capital market, the free play of market forces will automatically bring about an optimum allocation of resources over time.[11] The former is no more an argument for comprehensive development planning than the latter is an argument for a laissez-faire policy.

11. For a well-known exposition of the theoretical advantages of integrated planning see T. Scitovsky, "Two Concepts of External Economies," *The Journal of Political Economy,* April 1954. For an equally well-known exposition of the theoretical advantages of perfect competition in relation to the problem of efficient programmes of capital accumulation, see Robert Dorfman, Paul A. Samuelson and Robert M. Solow, *Linear Programming and Economic Analysis,* McGraw-Hill, New York, 1958, Ch. 12.

14 | Dualism and the Internal Integration of the Underdeveloped Economies

In this paper, we shall re-examine the nature and causes of economic dualism in the underdeveloped countries and consider some of its implications for development policy.

Dualism may be defined as the continuing co-existence of a "modern" sector and a "traditional" sector within the domestic economic framework of an underdeveloped country. One version of dualism identifies the modern sector with the exchange economy and the traditional sector with the subsistence economy. The other version, with which we shall be mainly concerned, defines the modern sector as consisting of large-scale economic units employing capital-intensive methods of production and the traditional sector as consisting of small-scale economic units employing labour-intensive methods of production.

Existing theories of dualism attempt to explain the differences between the two sectors in terms of sociological and technological factors. In contrast, we shall argue that the most significant aspect of economic dualism as it exists in the present-day underdeveloped countries is that scarce inputs such as capital funds, foreign exchange and public economic facilities, notably transport and communica-

From the *Banca Nazionale del Lavoro Quarterly Review*, No. 93, June 1970. Reprinted by permission.

tions and power, are being made available on excessively favourable terms to the larger units in the modern sector including the public sector, and on excessively unfavourable terms to the small economic units in the traditional sector. Our interpretation of dualism emphasises the importance of domestic economic policies to promote internal economic integration between the modern and the traditional sectors of the underdeveloped countries by removing as far as possible the causes of unequal access to the scarce economic resources by the two sectors.

This conclusion is in sharp conflict with the policies of domestic industrialization and import substitution currently adopted in the underdeveloped countries. Here, in order to encourage the expansion of domestic manufacturing industry, the whole apparatus of government controls has been used to discriminate in favour of the modern sector and to discriminate against the traditional sector thus aggravating the unequal access to economic resources which already exists because of the underdevelopment of the domestic economic organisation. The advocates of domestic industrialization moreover invoke the concept of dualism to support their argument and to attack the application of the "orthodox" theory of optimum allocation of resources to the underdeveloped countries. They maintain that the neo-classical model of an economic system making smooth and flexible adjustments cannot be applied to the underdeveloped countries because of their dualistic economic structure created by the various sociological and technological rigidities and by the existence of "disguised unemployment" and factor disproportionalities. They further maintain that the static norm of efficient allocation of resources has limited relevance for the purpose of promoting rapid economic development by introducing "dynamic" economic changes into the underdeveloped countries.

The drift of these arguments is to emphasise, not the importance of domestic economic policies to reduce dualism, but rather the impotence and limitations of the purely domestic economic policies which the underdeveloped countries can pursue on their own because of the "structural" difficulties created by dualism. The final effect is to emphasise the importance of external economic aid to the underdeveloped countries. Thus we have the familiar UNCTAD thesis[1] that the slow rate of economic growth in the underdeveloped countries is mainly due to the external economic factors beyond their control, notably the unfavourable trend in the world market demand for primary products. On the other hand, it is maintained that the current tempo of domestic industrialization must be maintained to provide acceptable target rates of economic growth, to absorb the "disguised unemployment" and above all to introduce "dynamic" economic changes. Thus the burden of promoting economic development is shifted from domestic economic policies to external economic assistance to finance the strategic imports required in fixed proportions as technical inputs for the expansion of the output of the domestic manufacturing sector. Given the implicit belief in the economic superiority and the "dynamic" effects of the large-scale modern manufacturing industry much attention is devoted to the formation of regional economic unions and multi-national economic integration while the more fundamental problem of promoting internal economic integration within each individual underdeveloped country is neglected.

In re-examining the concepts of dualism, we are inevitably involved in a critical review of these arguments for domestic industrialization. In Section I we shall argue that in order to understand the economic significance of dualism we have to go beyond the sociological and the technological explanations and take our bearings from the theory of the optimum allocation of resources. Thus dualism may be interpreted as a species of distortion in the allocation of resources arising out of the unequal terms on which economic resources such as capital, foreign exchange and public economic services are made available to the two sectors. In Section II we shall argue that the "financial dualism" which is aggravated by domestic industrialization policies, not only leads to a distortion in the allocation of capital funds but also tends to impede the longer-

1. Cf. *Towards a New Trade Policy for Development,* United Nations, New York, 1964.

term growth of a more integrated domestic market for capital. In Section III we shall examine dualism in relation to labour supply and "disguised unemployment." We shall argue that current views on domestic industrialization seriously underrate the possibilities of introducing labour-intensive methods both in agriculture and in manufacture and that in particular, the development of complementary relations between the large- and the small-scale industries offer a more promising prospect for absorbing abundant labour than the current policy of trying to expand large-scale manufacturing industry on its own. This will also lead us to re-examine the role of the modern sector in introducing "dynamic" changes into the traditional sector. In Section IV, we conclude with a broad review of the implications of our analysis of dualism on the external aspects of development policy: on international trade policy; on the "absorptive capacity" for international aid and "economic enclaves"; and on the formation of regional or multi-national economic integration.

I

Let us begin with the concept of dualism based on the dichotomy between the exchange economy and the subsistence sector. Dualism in this sense may be said to exist as soon as a hitherto self-sufficient traditional society is opened up to international trade. We then have the familiar process of the expansion in export production bringing the labour from the subsistence economy into the mines and plantations and inducing the peasants to devote their surplus land and labour to the production of export crops. At first, the exchange economy is mainly confined to the foreign trade sector, but gradually as the export producers spend a part of their cash earnings on home produced goods, a growing part of the domestic economic activities will be drawn into the exchange economy. There is also the well-known complementary relationship between the growth of the exchange economy and the fiscal system. The foreign trade sector initially provides the government with the revenues and the borrowing power to set up a modern system of administration and the basic framework of social overhead capital. Improvements in transport and communications widen the area of the exchange economy which in turn widens the scope of government revenue and expenditure. Thus as the boundary line of exchange economy moves further outward, it draws a larger part of the national economic life into the organized domestic economic framework. In general, one would expect the position of the boundary line between the exchange economy and the subsistence sector to be influenced by a number of economic factors, such as the state of development of the tastes and preferences of the people in the subsistence sector for the goods and services available in the exchange economy, the state of export and domestic demand for the goods and services which can be produced by the resources still remaining in the subsistence sector and above all, the state of development in transport and communications.

What economic significance can we attach to the concept of dualism based on a boundary line between the exchange economy and the subsistence sector existing in an underdeveloped country at a given moment of time? Those who favour the "sociological" interpretation of dualism seem to look upon the mere co-existence of the exchange economy and the subsistence sector as evidence of sociological rigidities creating special obstacles to economic development.[2] They tend to assume that there are two completely different groups of people, one in the exchange economy and one in the subsistence sector, each living in separate worlds of their own. Thus the people in the subsistence sector are not supposed to respond to economic incentives in the normal way, either because they have limited wants for the commodities available in the exchange economy or because of their conservatism and ignorance. Now, in so far as it is true that the subsistence sector persists because people there do not want the goods and services in the exchange economy, there is no question of economic irrationality: they do not have "economic development" measured in terms of money income because they do

2. Cf. J. H. Boeke, *Economics and Economic Policy in Dual Societies*, 1953, for a well-known exposition of these views.

not want it. However, this type of pure subsistence society insulated from outside influences must nowadays be regarded as a very small and shrinking part of the underdeveloped world. In the rest of the underdeveloped world, with growing contacts with the outside world, the tastes and preferences for the new commodities and the new ways of life have been developed only too rapidly. Once this happens there is no lack of evidence to show that people in the underdeveloped countries follow the normal economic behaviour of maximising their utility according to their given tastes and preferences.[3] What is even more important for our present analysis, in the general run of the underdeveloped countries, the majority of the people are neither in the pure isolated type of subsistence society nor are they completely absorbed into an organized wage economy. Rather they are in the vast intermediate zone of economic activity with a very low degree of economic specialization, devoting varying parts of their time and resources to subsistence activities and cash-earning activities.

Now assuming normal economic behaviour, this means that these people will make appropriate switches in the allocation of resources between subsistence and cash-earning activities until the balance of net advantages from these two types of activity are equal. Thus, although we may draw a statistical line to indicate the proportion of resources devoted to the exchange economy and the subsistence sector, there is no sharp discontinuity in the actual decision-making processes which have resulted in this boundary line. Thus if we wish to attach a special significance to the concept of dualism based on the dichotomy between the exchange economy and the subsistence sector, we must not merely show that a boundary line can be drawn between the two, but also that the boundary line actually existing is in the wrong position because, say, the exchange economy has not expanded to the extent consistent with the economic factors governing the situation. In other words, there has been a genuine distortion in the allocation of resources between the exchange economy and the subsistence sector.

3. Cf. P. T. Bauer and B. S. Yamey, *Markets, Market Control and Marketing Reform*, 1968, Parts 1 and 2.

As a matter of fact, in many underdeveloped countries the expansion of the exchange economy is likely to be retarded, not because people in the subsistence sector behave irrationally, but because of economic policies which have distorted the relative attractiveness of subsistence and cash-earning activities. For instance, there may be no incentive to switch from subsistence to cash crops because of transport difficulties in bringing the produce to the market, although the expansion in production would have been profitable enough to pay for the cost of extending or improving the transport system. This is particularly likely to happen when there is a "dualism" in the provision of public services favouring the larger type of social overhead projects serving the modern sector located in the bigger towns to the neglect of the traditional sector located in the remoter parts of the country. Again, the incentive to switch from subsistence to cash crops may be reduced because domestic industrialization policies have turned the "terms of trade" against the agricultural products which can be produced by the subsistence sector. In each case, the expansion of the exchange economy has been retarded in a significant sense because there has been some distortion in the allocation of resources.

A similar reasoning can be applied to the "technological" concept of dualism based on the dichotomy between the modern sector consisting of the larger-scale economic units employing capital-intensive techniques of production and the traditional sector consisting of small-scale economic units employing labour-intensive techniques. The mere fact that the modern sector uses capital-intensive techniques while the traditional sector uses labour-intensive techniques is not significant in itself: the two sectors may be producing two entirely different non-substitutable types of product. Technological dualism becomes significant only when it is observed that the two sectors are producing similar or potentially substitutable products but using different techniques involving different scales of production and different proportions of the same type of factors of production and inputs. The significance arises because there is a *prima facie* case for suspecting a distortion in the allocation of resources.

Now it is true to say that technological dualism in this significant sense seems to be more pronounced in the underdeveloped countries than in the developed countries. It can sometimes be found even in some export industries, notably rubber in Malaya and Indonesia, where small producers co-exist with larger plantations. But the most interesting case of economic dualism for our analysis is that which occurs in the manufacturing sector in the underdeveloped countries. Here the new import-substituting factories set up in the modern manufacturing sector are mainly confined to consumers' goods industries, notably food, drink, tobacco, textiles, etc. which are also produced by the traditional sector.[4] There are of course considerable differences in quality, design and standardization of the product between the goods produced by the small-scale industries and those produced by modern style factories. But the case for regarding the traditional sector as producing the same type of "commodity" as the modern sector is stronger than it appears at first sight. It is true that the small industries produce inferior quality products compared with the modern factories in the underdeveloped countries; but there is a similar quality gap between the products of the latter and the imported goods they seek to replace. Further, while the small industries produce inferior quality goods, their prices are also lower. In contrast, the modern factories, set up under heavy protection in the underdeveloped countries, frequently produce goods which are not only inferior in quality but also higher in price compared with the imported goods. Thus, if we are prepared to accept the possibility of import substitution, we should also accept the possibility of substitution between the products of the modern style factories and the products of the small-scale industries.

If the modern and the traditional sectors produce a similar range of consumers' goods which are in some degree substitutes for each other, why do the economic units in these two sectors use such markedly different methods of production? Writers on dualism tend

4. Cf. Masanori Koga, "Traditional and Modern Industries in India," *The Developing Economies*, September 1968, for a useful summary of the empirical data on this point.

to explain this in terms of the sociological or technological rigidities. Thus the small industries are supposed to employ the traditional labour-intensive methods because of conservatism and technological backwardness. On the other hand, it is said that the capital-intensive methods in the modern sector are the inevitable result of the under-developed countries' need to adopt the ready-made advanced tech-nology from abroad. But these explanations are unsatisfactory because they ignore the glaring differences in the prices of the factors of production in the two sectors. Thus, given the underdevelopment of the domestic markets for capital funds and labour, the level of interest rates is markedly higher while the level of wages is markedly lower in the traditional sector compared with the modern sector. In commonsense terms, this striking pattern of high interest rates and low wages in the traditional sector and low interest rates and high wages in the modern sector would be sufficient to account for a large part of the differences in the factor proportions used in the two sectors without introducing special assumptions about socio-logical and technological rigidities. What is however more significant is that in many underdeveloped countries trying to promote domestic industrialization, the gaps in the factor prices arising out of the underdevelopment of the factor markets tend to be widened arti-ficially. In some countries where labour is strongly organized in the urban manufacturing sector or the mining sector, there are restric-tions to free entry of labour from the traditional sector. In almost all countries, the apparatus of government controls tends to be used to divert the lion's share of capital funds and foreign exchange to the larger-scale economic units in the modern sector, including the public sector, while the small economic units in the traditional sector are starved of these vital resources. In particular, this has resulted in the maintenance of artificial factor prices in the modern sector which go against the pattern of factor endowments of the country taken as a whole. Thus interest rates are kept artificially low in flagrant contradiction to the general scarcity of savings and wages are main-tained artificially high in spite of the abundant supply of labour. In terms of the optimum theory, this implies a distortion in the allocation of resources between the two sectors and the use of excessively capital-intensive methods in the modern sector. Thus the economic significance of technological dualism may be found, not so much in the differences in techniques of production by themselves, but in the fact that the two sectors are producing similar or potentially substitutable products but with markedly different factor proportions because of the artificially accentuated unequal access to economic resources.

II

Let us now consider "financial dualism" in the domestic market for capital funds in the underdeveloped countries. Given the well-known facts about the much higher risks and costs involved in lending money on a retail basis to a large number of small borrowers than in lending to a small number of large well-established borrowers, one would normally expect the rate of interest in the "unorganized" credit market in the traditional sector to be higher than the rate in the "organized" credit market in the modern sector. Further, one would expect this normal gap in the interest rates to be larger the more underdeveloped the domestic credit market and the financial institutions in a given country. Financial dualism in this sense has of course existed in the underdeveloped countries long before they embarked on their present policies of domestic industrialization. But there are two differences between the old financial dualism which existed in the "open economy" of the colonial period and the new financial dualism which now exists in the "closed economy" of the underdeveloped countries pursuing domestic industrialization policies.

First, under the colonial financial system, the disadvantage which the small economic units suffered compared with the big economic units was in obtaining credit in terms of local currency. Once that was obtained, the small economic units were at least on equal terms with big economic units in their access to foreign exchange. The automatic currency system ensured free convertibility at fixed rates of exchange; there was no balance of payments problem and no foreign exchange shortage. In contrast, domestic inflation and balance of payments difficulties have now become endemic in the underdeveloped countries. This means that the small economic units in the traditional sector not only have to face their previous handicaps in raising loans in local currency; they now have to face a new handicap in their access to foreign exchange and imports.

Second, under the colonial system, the organized credit market of the underdeveloped countries, made up of the branches of foreign banks, was closely linked with the international financial market. That is to say, the low rate of interest which prevailed in the organized credit market was not an arbitrary rate. It represented the market rate at which the modern sector of the economy, mainly consisting of the mines, plantations and the export-import firms, could borrow from the international capital market. In the organized credit market at least the demand and supply of loans was equated at the equilibrium market rate. In contrast, since attaining financial independence, the organized credit market in many underdeveloped countries has become increasingly insulated from the international capital market. Given the increasing use of foreign exchange controls which restrict profit remittances and transfers of banking funds, the foreign branch banks no longer function as significant links channelling outside capital funds into the underdeveloped countries. This has been aggravated by the attempt of many underdeveloped countries to stimulate their economic development with the "cheap money" policy. Thus during the last two decades, there has frequently been the anomalous situation in which the official rates of interest in the organized credit markets of the capital-poor underdeveloped countries have been kept well below the prevailing level of interest rates in the capital-rich advanced countries.[5]

Given the pressure of domestic inflation with fixed exchange rates, there is a chronic excess demand for foreign exchange at the overvalued exchange rates. Given the "cheap money" policy of maintain-

5. For an elaboration of this anomalous situation, see above, Chapter 13, pp. 309–11.

ing artificially low interest rates in the organized credit market, there is a chronic excess demand for loans above the volume of domestic savings forthcoming at these rates of interest. The government in most underdeveloped countries atempts to cope with this disequilibrium situation by setting up a network of direct controls to ration the scarce capital and foreign exchange resources between rival claimants: and it is this rationing process through the apparatus of government controls which has aggravated the unequal access to scarce resources suffered by the small economic units in the traditional sector. Even if the government's policy towards the different sectors were neutral, there would be a considerable amount of unintended or unofficial discrimination against the small economic units. Compared with the larger economic units in the modern sector, they are notoriously at a disadvantage in coping with the complexities and delays of the bureaucracy which administers the various economic controls.[6] But government policy far from being neutral has the avowed aim of encouraging the larger economic units in the modern sector, including the public sector. With given resources, this implies discriminating against the small economic units in the traditional sector. This discrimination applies not only to access to capital funds and foreign exchange but also to public economic services supplied by the government. In particular, social overhead facilities such as transport and communications and power are more readily available and frequently on cheaper terms to the larger economic units in the modern sector than to the small economic units in the traditional sector. In this setting of rationing through direct quantitative controls, the extent of unequal access to economic resources can no longer be adequately depicted in terms of the gap in the rates of interest in the modern and the traditional sector. For instance, the use of the excessively capital-intensive methods by the large-scale economic units in the modern sector is encouraged, not only by the low rates of interest, but also by the easier availability of foreign exchange which enables them to import capital goods on very

6. Cf. *Economic Bulletin for Asia and the Far East,* Vol. XII, No. 3, December 1961, p. 7.

favourable terms at the over-valued official exchange rates. This is re-inforced by easier and cheaper access to public economic services.

All this has the effect not only of distorting the allocation of resources between the modern and the traditional sectors but also of impeding the longer-term growth of an integrated domestic capital market in the underdeveloped countries. The development of an integrated domestic capital market requires two conditions: (a) the growth of a financial centre which can effectively collect the savings from both the modern and traditional sectors as well as from the international capital market and channel these funds into different parts of the domestic economy according to the highest obtainable returns on investment; and (b) the growth of a financial network which links the financial centre with the lenders and borrowers in all parts of the country, including the public sector. The financial links may be branches and subsidiaries which are vertically integrated with the headquarters of financial institutions located in the centre, such as the district branches of the commercial banks and co-operative societies. Or the links may be independent financial intermediaries such as a professional class of moneylenders who have access to the funds collected at the centre to be re-lent to the rest of the country. In any case it is clear that in order to reduce the financial dualism between the organized and the unorganized markets for credit, there would have to be more effective links facilitating the mobility of funds between the two.

We have already seen that the policies followed by many underdeveloped countries since attaining financial independence have insulated their organized credit markets from the international capital market. But these policies also have the effect of insulating the organized credit market from the free market for credit within the country. Indeed, given the multiplicity of government controls, much of the unofficial or free market for credit is reduced to the status of the "black market." To begin with, given the pressure of domestic inflation with overvalued exchange rates, there is a chronic tendency for speculative flights of capital abroad. Where the government has succeeded in blocking these leakages, the funds, instead of remaining in the official organized credit market, are diverted into the purchase of gold, jewelry, real estate and into speculative activities. This is not surprising when, thanks to the "cheap money" policy, the official rates of interest offered to the lenders are so markedly below the returns on investment in any of these alternatives. Indeed, in many countries the rates of interest offered to the lenders by the organized credit market yield negative real returns because the rate of depreciation in the value of money exceeds the rate of interest. The growth of an unofficial market for credit may serve to relieve the shortage of savings in the traditional sector by diverting some of the capital funds into money-lending and trading. But the fact remains that the "cheap money" policy imposes the very heavy long-term cost of retarding the growth of an effective financial centre.

The growth of the financial intermediaries is also retarded by the way in which the governments of the underdeveloped countries usually exercise their controls to ration the scarce capital supply. These controls discriminate not only against the small borrowers but also against the moneylenders and others who are the chief source of credit to the small borrowers. There are two underlying beliefs behind these controls which are inimical not only to the growth of the capital market but also to the development of a domestic market economy in general.

The first is the belief that the only "productive" way of using capital funds is to invest them in durable capital goods and machinery embodying modern technology. The vital role of capital as the "subsistence fund" in agriculture is not understood and the financing of trading activities is regarded as "unproductive." Credit discrimination against trading not only serves to widen the wholesale and retail prices because of the high costs of holding stocks but has a general consequence in undermining the development of the market economy in the underdeveloped countries which is not clearly appreciated. The truth of the matter is that most underdeveloped countries tend to hold a much lower level of stocks of commodities and circulating capital than is required to run their economies smoothly given the underdevelopment of their transport and communications and market organization. Consequently, their internal economic organization is extremely "brittle," liable to frequent breakdowns and speculative instability of prices in the face of unforeseen changes, such as an unfavourable harvest threatening famine conditions in a particular locality. Now although much has been said about the vulnerability of the underdeveloped countries to the instability in the world market demand for their exports and their need for adequate foreign exchange reserves, little has been said about their vulnerability to internal instability and their need to hold adequate stocks of circulating capital. It may well be that international trade and the opportunity to draw on an elastic world market supply of goods is a greater stabilising force on the underdeveloped countries than is generally realised.

The second belief underlying government economic controls is the traditional belief in the wickedness of moneylenders and the need to suppress or curtail their activities by regulating the rates of interest at which they are permitted to lend. Few such regulations have succeeded because the moneylenders perform a genuine economic service in the unorganized credit market which the government cannot provide. There are two contradictory strands in the popular arguments against the moneylenders. The first is that the moneylenders, landlords and the village shopkeepers make use of their entrenched position in the local community to extract monopolistically high rates of interest from the peasant borrowers. If this is true, the logical remedy would be to increase the competition among the moneylenders, and this can be done by facilitating their access to the central funds of the organized credit market. The second argument states, not that there are too few moneylenders, but that there are too many middlemen intervening between the financial centre and the final borrowers in the traditional sector who are obliged to pay excessive rates to cover the middlemen's commission. This argument really amounts to saying that it is always cheaper to cater for the small borrowers through the branches of the lending agencies which are vertically integrated with their headquarters located in the

financial centre rather than through independent financial intermediaries who form the market links between the financial centre
and the final borrowers. This is however not supported by the
experience of the commercial banks which have generally found
that the cost of opening sub-branches in the remoter districts of the
underdeveloped countries is too high to compete with the lower
overheads of the moneylenders. Yet the popular belief that the
excessive profits of the middlemen and moneylenders can be cut by
"direct" links with the official lending agencies persists. It seems to
arise from ignoring or underestimating the costs of vertical integration between the central lending agencies and the numerous branches
and sub-branches which are necessary to cater for the credit needs
of the small borrowers: these costs include not only the overhead
costs and salaries of the officials but also the relative inefficiency of
the official employees dealing with small borrowers according to
rigid rules of creditworthiness and inefficient co-ordination between
the headquarters and branches by bureaucratic methods.

So far, apart from the abortive attempts to control the activities
of the moneylenders, most underdeveloped countries have done little
to improve the working of the unorganized credit market beyond
ad hoc attempts to supply limited amounts of subsidized loans
through co-operative societies to some favoured parts of the rural
sector. The model villages enjoying the subsidised loans from the
government may be "showpieces" like the steel mills, but they have
very little general effect in lowering the prevailing high levels of
interest rates in the rural sector. Indeed, frequently they benefit
the moneylenders, who have managed to get themselves elected as
members of the co-operatives. Moreover, the bona fide members of
the co-operatives wishing to borrow more than the officially permitted amounts of cheap loans can now afford to pay a higher
rate of interest on their extra borrowings from the moneylenders.
This is not to deny that the co-operative societies may be able to
compete with the moneylenders either because they are more
efficient in collecting information about the creditworthiness of their
members or because they can reduce risks better by mutual guar-

antees undertaken by their members. But the correct way of testing this is, not by giving limited amounts of low-interest loans to the co-operative societies, but by giving unlimited access on equal terms at the ruling market rate of interest both to the co-operatives and the moneylenders so that they can compete to lower the rates of interest for the small borrowers.

The conclusion of this analysis is clear. In order to reduce financial dualism and build up a more integrated domestic market for capital, the underdeveloped countries should raise the official rates of interest in their organized credit market high enough to reflect their existing shortage of capital funds. This would encourage the growth of a financial centre which can effectively attract savings both from within the country and from abroad. It would also equate the available supply of savings to the demand for loans including the demand for funds by the moneylenders to be re-lent to the unorganized credit market. The granting of an equal access to capital funds by the traditional and the modern sectors would serve to reduce the distortion in the allocation of resources between the two sectors. The familiar argument that the raising of the official rate of interest would raise the cost of government borrowing has limited significance for the underdeveloped countries. Given the unattractively low rates of interest offered on government securities, there has been little public demand for them. The bulk of the government securities are in fact held by various government agencies and their affiliates so that the raising of the interest rate would mainly have the effect of changing the accounting relationships within the public sector. Indeed, the case for raising the rate of interest is strengthened, not weakened, by taking into account the longer-term effects on the government's ability to borrow from the public.

III

We have noted that the level of wages is generally higher in the modern sector than in the traditional sector of the underdeveloped country. How far does this imply the existence of a dualism in the labour market, discouraging the expansion of the modern sector and distorting the allocation of resources in the opposite direction from that caused by financial dualism? Without entering into a detailed enumeration of the possible causes of the wage differentials between the two sectors, we may consider them under three heads.

First, there are the wage differences which reflect genuine economic differences in skills, in costs of living, etc. which clearly do not distort the allocation of labour between the two sectors.

Next, there is the less well-recognized fact that in the underdeveloped countries the wage rate in the modern sector reflects the payment to the head of the family to induce him to move with his dependents on a permanent basis to the place of his work, whereas the wage rate in the traditional sector reflects the payment to a single worker on a casual or temporary basis. Now even in the absence of government regulations and trade union pressure, the larger-scale concerns in the modern sector may prefer to pay higher wages to obtain a regular labour force, for at least two reasons. First, the gains in productivity from a stable labour force and a low rate of turnover may more than pay for the higher wage bill. Second, if the concerns are run by foreign entrepreneurs or managers, they do not have the necessary local knowledge and skills in labour relations to cope with the casual type of labour. Indeed, from their point of view the cost of re-adapting their whole system of production and organization to make use of the cheaper casual labour would be much too high and they would be prepared to pay considerably higher wages to obtain a labour force approximately similar to the type of regular labour force they are used to in their own countries. Historically, this can be illustrated by the contrasting labour policies adopted in the development of the textile industry by foreign entrepreneurs in India and by indigenous entrepreneurs in Japan. The former recruited their labour force from adult males, paying them a wage rate sufficient to maintain their dependents; the latter took advantage of the cheaper, but equally efficient, labour of young farm girls available for a few years before they got married.[7] The present-day expansion of the modern manufacturing sector in the underdeveloped countries relies heavily on foreign managers and technical experts, not to speak of the branch factories of international corporations set up to jump the tariff and import controls. Thus we have a pattern of wage policy and labour organization based on a high differential between the ruling wage rate in the regular labour market and that in the unorganized market for casual labour. How are we to interpret this type of wage differential between the modern and the traditional sector? In so far as the large-scale modern concerns are willing to pay a higher wage rate, voluntarily and without any external pressure, there can be no distortion of resource allocation originating from the labour market. Yet the wage differential is associated with a distinct dualism in industrial organization and may be a sign of managerial rigidity on the part of the modern sector failing to make a more effective use of the abundant supply of casual labour. In so far as this creates a distortion, it is not due to a high wage rate discouraging the expansion of the larger-scale economic units in the modern sector, but due to an insufficient development of the small-scale indigenous economic units which are more likely to be able to take advantage of the abundant supply of casual labour.

Lastly, we have the factors which arbitrarily widen the wage differential between the modern and the traditional sectors and clearly distort the allocation of labour between the two. However, these need to be disentangled from the concept of "disguised unemployment." A familiar argument for the protection of domestic manufacturing industry based on this concept may be summarised as follows. Because of heavy population pressure on existing land,

7. For a comparative analysis of the labour policies adopted in the development of the textile industry in India and Japan see S. J. Koh, *Stages of Industrial Development in Asia,* University of Pennsylvania Press, 1966, Chs. II and III; see also W. W. Lockwood, *The Economic Development of Japan,* Princeton, 1954, pp. 213–14; for a theoretical analysis of this point, see D. Mazumdar, "Underemployment in Agriculture and the Industrial Wage Rate," *Economica,* November 1959.

the marginal product of labour in agriculture is reduced to zero. But the income level in the traditional sector is equal not to the marginal product but to the average product of labour on land because of the prevalence of the extended family system sharing the total output among its members. In recruiting labour from the traditional sector the modern sector must pay a wage rate equal to the income level in the traditional sector plus an incentive margin. Thus the modern sector is being penalised by having to pay a wage rate high above the social opportunity cost of labour as measured by its marginal product in agriculture, and in order to correct this distortion the modern manufacturing industry should be given tariff protection.

In order to argue that a person in the traditional sector can enjoy an income equal to the average product of labour even when his marginal product is zero we need, first of all, to assume that his family owns the land and that he is being supported in a state of "disguised unemployment" out of what is, properly speaking, rent from the land. Once we introduce the landlords into the picture, then the income left to the family after paying economic rent must be wage income: i.e. the marginal product of family labour on land must be positive. Even if the family owns the land, the marginal product of labour on the farm will not be zero if there are alternative opportunities of using some part of the family labour elsewhere. Once we introduce some form of market for agricultural labour, the marginal product of labour on the family farm will approximately reflect the wage rate in the neighbourhood. Finally, even in the absence of landlords and a labour market, the marginal product of labour on the family farm will not be zero unless we are prepared to make the highly unrealistic assumption that the marginal disutility of work on the farm is zero. But the notion of the zero marginal product is not needed for the purpose of showing the existence of a distortion in the labour market. All that we need for the purpose is to show that there are certain factors arbitrarily or artificially widening the wage differential between the modern and the traditional sector beyond the extent required to reflect the genuine economic differences in the two sectors.

It is possible to find three such factors. The first consists of the various government regulations on labour and minimum wage rates. These exert a differential effect in that while they can be strictly enforced in the bigger economic units in the modern sectors they are unenforceable for the small economic units in the traditional sector. The second arises from the greater ease with which the urban labour force in the manufacturing sector can organize itself into strong trade unions restricting free entry of labour. The third factor is important in countries which have a prosperous foreign-owned export industry such as petroleum or copper. Here the high wage rates which the trade unions are usually able to extract out of the export sector tend to spread, by a series of sympathetic wage rises, into the rest of the modern sector, imposing a heavy burden both on the domestic manufacturing industry and on the public sector. While all these three factors can cause a serious distortion in the allocation of resources, none of them constitutes an argument for special protection of domestic industry. The distortions have to be cured by reforms within the labour market. In particular the third source of distortion is similar to the point we have discussed in connection with "disguised unemployment" in agriculture. Here also the distortion arises from the fact that the rent income which the government should have extracted from the foreign companies in the extractive industries and kept for its own use has been unjustifiably permitted to inflate the wage level in the modern sector above the marginal productivity of labour.

Finally, we may turn to the main argument for domestic industrialization which underlies much of the current writings on economic dualism in the underdeveloped countries. This argument combines the concept of "disguised unemployment" with that of technological dualism and attempts to make out the case for the expansion of domestic manufacturing industry, not in terms of deviations from the static optimum but in terms of "dynamic" considerations. Thus it is argued that, given the heavy pressure of population on land, it is no longer possible for the underdeveloped countries to absorb any more labour in agriculture: the only way of absorbing the surplus labour is through the expansion of the manufacturing sector. But the underdeveloped countries are obliged to import modern technology in a ready-made form from the advanced countries: this means that the expansion of the manufacturing sector has to be based on methods of production which are not only capital-intensive but also require capital and labour in fixed proportions.[8] In terms of the static optimum theory, this pattern of economic development goes against the grain of the factor endowments in the underdeveloped countries, but it is argued that it can be justified on two grounds. First, given the factor disproportionalities and technological rigidities which characterise the dualistic economic structure of the underdeveloped countries, there is really very little scope for smooth and flexible substitutions and adjustments assumed in a neo-classical model of the economic system. Second, the "dynamic" gains from the expansion of the modern manufacturing industry will tend to outweigh the static losses from the distortion in the allocation of resources.

We shall now show that these arguments do not stand up to a critical scrutiny and that they seriously underestimate the scope for the introduction of labour-intensive methods of production both in agriculture and in the manufacturing sector by appropriate domestic economic policies. Even the exponents of the population pressure argument recognise that the underdeveloped countries in Africa and Latin America are not so thickly populated as some of the Asian countries. Thus they tend to use countries such as India or Pakistan as prime examples of agricultural overpopulation. But a broad survey of the Asian agricultural scene is sufficient to cast doubts on the assumption that the agricultural sector in these countries is so saturated with labour that there is no further scope for the introduction of labour-intensive methods along any known lines. As

8. Cf. R. S. Eckaus, "The Factor-Proportions Problem in Underdeveloped Areas," *American Economic Review,* September 1955.

a matter of fact, the highest population densities on land and the smallest-size peasant holdings are to be found in countries such as Japan, Taiwan and Korea. On the other hand, these countries are also outstanding illustrations of how agricultural output can be rapidly increased by intensive methods of farming based on small peasant holdings provided that appropriate economic policies. are followed. These include (a) the adequate provision by the government of agricultural inputs, notably the irrigation facilities which enable multiple cropping on the same piece of land, reduce seasonal unemployment and encourage the use of fertilisers and improved seeds; and (b) improvements in agricultural credit and marketing. Compared with the genuinely intensive agriculture of Northeast Asia, the agriculture in the so-called overpopulated countries of India and Pakistan may not unfairly be described as an inefficient *extensive* type of farming offering great potentialities for the introduction of labour-intensive methods.[9] In terms of our analysis, the agricultural backwardness of these countries may be attributed to two types of dualism: (a) unequal provision of government economic services to the modern manufacturing sector and to the agricultural sector with some degree of dualism within the agricultural sector itself, created by unequal access to public economic facilities between the larger and the small farmers; and (b) financial dualism, which is a serious obstacle to the adoption of improved methods by small farmers. Thus it is no accident that

in Japan, where the rural and small-scale industrial sectors are more integrated in the organized credit market (more than half of all agricultural credit is provided by financial institutions), interest differentials are much smaller: on the average, interest rates are lower in the traditional sectors, but considerably higher in the fully organized sector, than in India and Pakistan.[10]

9. For two very important recent contributions to this subject, see Shigeru Ishikawa, *Economic Development in Asian Perspective,* Kinokuniya, Tokyo, 1967, Ch. 2 and also charts 2–4; and G. Myrdal, *Asian Drama,* 1968, Vol. I, Ch. 10 and Vol. II, Part V.
10. G. Myrdal, *op. cit.,* Vol. III, Appendix 8, p. 2095.

Let us now turn to the argument that the scope for substitution of labour for capital is severely limited by the need to adopt modern technology in the manufacturing sector and that, given this technical rigidity, the only method of absorbing surplus labour is to expand the size of the manufacturing sector on a capital-intensive basis. This implicitly identifies the manufacturing sector with the larger-scale modern style factories. But in many underdeveloped countries small-scale industries of various types employ by far the largest proportion of the labour and contribute a substantial proportion of the output of the manufacturing sector.[11] If we define the manu-facturing sector to include both its modern segment of the larger-scale economic units and its traditional segment of the small-scale economic units, then one thing becomes clear: even if all the large-scale modern factories operated rigidly on the basis of fixed tech-nical coefficients, there would still be considerable scope for in-creasing the proportion of labour to capital in the manufacturing sector as a whole by substituting the output of the small-scale economic units for that of the larger-scale units. As we have seen, the possibilities in this direction are greater than generally allowed, for two reasons: first, the modern factories set up for the purpose of import substitution in many underdeveloped countries are pre-dominantly in the field of light consumers' goods which are also produced by the traditional sector; and second, the lower quality of the products of the small-scale industries is compensated for by their cheaper prices. But, as we have shown, this overlap in the range of goods produced by the larger and the smaller manufactur-ing units is associated with and attributable to the glaringly unequal terms on which capital funds, foreign exchange and the economic services provided by the government are made available to the two types of manufacturing industry by the prevailing policy of

---

11. For quantitative evidence for the importance of small-scale industries in the underdeveloped countries, see S. Kuznets, *Modern Economic Growth: Rate, Structure and Spread,* 1966, table 8.1 and pp. 417–20; also E. Staley and R. Morse, *Modern Small Industries for Developing Countries,* 1965, Ch. 1.

domestic industrialization. These policies may be said to protect the larger-scale modern factories not only from foreign competition but also from the domestic competition of the small-scale economic units. Thus it would seem reasonable to expect that a reduction in the unequal access to scarce economic inputs between the larger-scale and small economic units would make the latter more competitive and increase their share of the manufacturing output, thereby raising the proportion of labour to capital employed in the manufacturing sector as a whole. A reduction of economic dualism in this sense would have the effect of encouraging a greater degree of economic specialization between the larger and smaller economic units and thus introduce a new pattern of complementary economic relationships between the two types of manufacturing industry.

Complementary relationships based on vertical linkages between different industries are a familiar theme in development economics. But so far the analysis has been handicapped by confining the concept of complementarity only to the modern segment of the manufacturing sector. Further, given the popularity of the input-output models, complementarity tends to be interpreted in purely technical terms: in terms of fixed technical co-efficients linking up insufficiently disaggregated sectors. When, however, we broaden the concept of complementarity to the possible economic linkages between the larger and smaller industries and apply the older Adam Smithian notions of division of labour and specialization[12] to the situation, we begin to have a richer understanding of the possible complementary relationships within the manufacturing sector which would have the effect of introducing a greater degree of economic flexibility into the domestic economic organization of the underdeveloped countries. With a reduction in dualism, the small economic units may be typically expected to take over a larger share of the output in the light consumers' goods industries while the larger economic units shift into the production of inputs for the small industries. As a matter of fact, the small industries in the under-

12. See G. J. Stigler, "The Division of Labour is Limited by the Extent of the Market," *Journal of Political Economy,* June 1951.

developed countries have shown considerable enterprise in changing over from their traditional materials to new imported materials in such inputs as dyes, yarns, plastics, etc. and this is the reason why they are so handicapped by foreign exchange controls which restrict their access to imports. But the division of labour between the larger-scale and the small economic units may take various other patterns: the larger economic units may sub-contract any part of their productive processes to the small economic units; the small economic units may set up repair shops and other servicing activities for the bigger economic units; and so on. In general, given easier access to capital and foreign exchange, the small economic units may be expected to increase their share of economic activities in the manufacturing sector whenever their lower overhead costs and their access to cheap family and casual labour give them a comparative advantage over the larger economic units. These various possibilities are well illustrated by the history of the economic development of Japan, where the small industries have played a very important role. Significantly, the growth of the small industries was greatly facilitated by access to cheap electric power—a reduction of the dualism in the supply of public economic services. W. W. Lockwood describes the development of complementary economic relations between the larger-scale economic units and the small economic units as "a skilful utilization of Japan's limited capital resources and technical experience to employ a large and expanding population in productive pursuits."[13]

But what about the "dynamic" effects of the modern manufacturing industry? We may examine this argument under two main heads.

First, there is the dynamic "educative" effect of the modern manufacturing industry in imparting new technical knowledge and skills and in building up a permanent pool of trained labour adjusted to the rhythm and discipline of factory production. This is clearly important. But we should also remember that successful economic

13. W. W. Lockwood, *The Economic Development of Japan,* 1954, p. 211. See also the rest of his Ch. 4.

development requires the adaptation of modern technology to the local economic conditions of the underdevelped countries: detailed and intimate knowledge of local resource availabilities and local market conditions are as important as the imported "technical know-how" for this purpose. It is in the acquisition and the spreading of the relevant knowledge about the local economic conditions that the small-scale units are better placed than the large-scale modern factories. Thus if we accept the view that the underdeveloped countries suffer from a lack of indigenous entrepreneurs, the "educative" effect of the small-scale industries in providing the training ground for a large number of potential entrepreneurs must be rated at least as high as the "educative" effect of the modern manufacturing sector in training a regular labour force. Moreover, by insisting on the latest technology, many underdeveloped countries are in real danger of adopting techniques of production which are too advanced and specialised to be sustained and transmitted to the traditional sector. As Stigler points out the vast network of auxiliary industries and educational facilities taken for granted in the advanced countries will not be available in the underdeveloped countries.

At best, the small economies that imitate us can follow our methods of doing things this year, but not our methods of changing things next year; therefore, they will be very rigid.[14]

Conversely, the role of small-scale industries in spreading innovations is emphasised by Lockwood.

If Japan's experience teaches any single lesson regarding the process of economic development in Asia, it is the cumulative importance of myriads of relatively simple improvements in technology which do not radically depart from tradition or require large units of new investment. The big, modern establishment with its concentration of capital in advanced forms of technology was essential in many fields, of course. . . . Much of the real substance of Japanese growth, however, is found in the more modest types of improvements which are more easily and pervasively adopted, more economical in cost, and often more productive of immediate returns in income. For any poor country beginning to indus-

14. G. J. Stigler, *loc. cit., Journal of Political Economy,* June 1951, p. 193.

trialize, one of the crucial problems is to introduce and spread such innovations as widely as possible.[15]

Second, there is the argument that the use of durable capital equipment embodying modern technology would *ipso facto* raise the productivity of labour in the modern manufacturing industry and that since the wage rate would be kept constant by the availability of "unlimited" supplies of labour from the subsistence sector, this would raise the share of profits. The re-investment of these profits, it is argued, would generate a continuous process of dynamic economic expansion, absorbing the surplus labour from the subsistence sector. This is the familiar theme of various growth models, notably the "Lewis model."[16] When we try to apply this type of growth model to the actual process of domestic industrialization which has been brought about by import substitution policies in the underdeveloped countries, a number of difficulties become apparent. To begin with, the employment-creating capacity of the modern manufacturing sector has not been impressive even during the so-called "easy" phase of import substitution; now that import substitution has entered into the "difficult" phase characterised by foreign exchange shortage, its capacity to absorb the abundant supply of labour is clearly very limited. On this ground alone, one would be justified in trying to promote a complementary development of the large- and the small-scale industries instead of trying to expand the modern segment of the manufacturing sector on its own. However, in the typical "closed economy" conditions of the present-day underdeveloped countries the larger economic units in the modern manufacturing sector frequently enjoy high profits. The question is how far are these profits due to a genuine increase in productivity arising out of the adoption of modern technology? The drift of our preceding analysis has been to cast doubt on this and to suggest that the profits of the larger-scale economic units in the modern

15. W. W. Lockwood, *The Economic Development of Japan,* pp. 198–99.
16. W. Arthur Lewis, "Economic Development with Unlimited Supplies of Labour," *The Manchester School,* May 1954.

manufacturing sector have been artificially inflated by government policies. On the one hand, the shortages created by import controls and domestic inflation provide the modern manufacturing sector with an easy and lucrative market. On the other hand, the modern manufacturing sector has a differential access to capital funds, foreign exchange and the public economic services on specially favourable terms. This suggests that the real economic resources which have gone into the expansion of the modern manufacturing sector in the underdeveloped countries have been obtained, not so much from a self-generating process of increase in productivity resulting in an expanding stream of re-investible resources, but from the transfer of resources from other sectors, notably from the export and domestic agricultural sectors. As we have seen, these transfers have been carried out mainly by deficit financing and cheap money policy combined with the apparatus of direct quantitative controls to channel resources into the modern manufacturing sector. So long as these policies continue, one may expect the larger economic units in the modern manufacturing sector to continue to make high profits—in terms of local currency. But their failure to use resources productively on the basis of capital-intensive modern technology will be increasingly reflected in terms of a foreign exchange shortage. Given the buoyant expansion of international trade, both during the 1950–60 decade and the immediate post UNCTAD period of 1960–65, the familiar argument that the foreign exchange shortage of the underdeveloped countries is caused by stagnant world market demand for their exports is not convincing.[17] A more satisfactory explanation of the foreign exchange shortage has to be sought in the failure of their domestic economic policies both in export expansion and in import substitution.

17. See Bela Balassa, "The First Half of the Development Decade: Growth, Trade and the Balance of Payments of the Developing Countries, 1960–65," *Banca Nazionale del Lavoro Quarterly Review,* December 1968; also W. Arthur Lewis's "Closing Remarks" in W. Baer and I. Kerstenetsky, eds., *Inflation and Economic Growth in Latin America,* 1964, pp. 27–28.

IV

We may round off this paper by reviewing the implications of our analysis of dualism on the external aspects of development policy. In current discussions, domestic industrialization policies are frequently described as "inward-looking," while free trade and export expansion policies are described as "outward-looking." Our analysis suggests that this terminology is unsatisfactory because it obscures the intimate relationship which exists between the internal and the external aspects of development policy. As we have seen, the advocates of domestic industrialization policies tend to underrate the potentialities of internal economic policies and seek to relieve the effects of domestic distortions in the allocation of resources by means of external aid. Thus it is paradoxical to describe such policies as "inward-looking" when their main underlying emphasis is on economic aid (and trade concessions) to be administered from outside. Conversely, the policy of internal economic integration reducing the dualism outlined in this paper is based on the building up of more integrated domestic markets for capital funds and labour realistically reflecting the factor endowments of the underdeveloped countries in terms of high interest rates and low wages both in the organized and unorganized sectors of the economy. This is nothing but the inverse application of the Heckscher-Ohlin theory of comparative costs: that is to say, the policy of internal economic integration is the other side of the coin to the policy of expanding international trade according to comparative costs. Again, it is paradoxical to describe export expansion policies as "outward-looking" when their success vitally depends on domestic economic policies designed to reflect the comparative costs and factor endowments of the underdeveloped countries.

While the main drift of our policy of internal economic integration is towards freer trade, it is still of considerable importance even if the underdeveloped countries wish to pursue a protectionist policy. We have seen that the domestic industrialization policies as currently practised in the underdeveloped countries have the effect of protecting the modern segment of the manufacturing industry against the competition not only of imports but also of the domestic small-scale industries. It is therefore possible that in some line of simpler labour-intensive consumers' goods, the small industries may prove more competitive with the imports, at a given tariff rate, than the larger modern industries: provided that there is a more equal access to capital and foreign exchange. Thus the underdeveloped countries, in trying to encourage domestic industrialization by discriminating in favour of the modern segment of the manufacturing industry, may well be missing genuine opportunities of import substitution by the products of the small-scale industry which they have neglected. Our analysis is merely concerned with the reduction of the artificially created unequal access to economic resources between the larger and the smaller economic units. But it is possible to make out a stronger case for the positive encouragement of small industries if we take seriously the avowed aim of the governments of many underdeveloped countries to cut out "luxury" consumption both on grounds of economic equity and to increase savings. At present this has merely resulted in the restriction of imports of "luxury" consumers' goods while freely permitting the imports of the "capital goods" and inputs which are used for the domestic production of these luxury goods. A more effective way of restricting luxury consumption would be to impose a revenue tariff both on imports and on the higher priced factory products mainly catering for the wealthier urban population on those lines of consumers' goods in which the small-scale economic units can produce lower priced substitutes for them. Given the readiness of the small industries to change over to new materials and inputs and to imitate the factory products, the quality gap will tend to get narrower.

Let us now turn to the implications of our analysis for external aid. The policy of raising the rate of interest high enough to reflect the capital scarcity in the underdeveloped countries would have the effect of setting up pressures on their domestic economic organization to make readjustments in the allocation of resources so as to raise the returns on investment. These adjustments are bound to be painful but, if successfully carried out, they would have the effect of raising the underdeveloped countries' "absorptive capacity" for aid. But the essential condition for success is the willingness and ability of these countries to make appropriate and flexible changes in their domestic economic organization. This conclusion differs sharply from the UNCTAD type of argument for aid which rules out beforehand any possibility of making flexible domestic readjustments. Aid is treated by UNCTAD as a means of providing the underdeveloped countries with strategic imports which they are supposed to require in fixed proportions as technical inputs for the expansion of their domestic manufacturing sector. In the earlier writings on the underdeveloped countries, it was frequently argued that foreign investment in the mines and plantations in the underdeveloped countries created "economic enclaves" because they relied heavily on imported capital equipment and foreign personnel and only required the natural resources and unskilled labour from the underdeveloped countries. The present-day expansion of the modern manufacturing industries in the underdeveloped countries on the basis of imported capital equipment, imported materials and frequently foreign technicians has obvious similarities with this notion of "economic enclaves." The mere fact that the foreign inputs are to be financed out of aid does not alter the basic fact that the modern manufacturing sector has limited "dynamic" impact in creating secondary rounds of economic activities precisely because its expansion requires the foreign inputs in so rigid a manner. From the point of view of our analysis the UNCTAD concept of aid as a method of financing import-substitution industries on a capital-intensive basis would have the effect of perpetuating the existing technological rigidities and the dualistic economic structure—the very problems which external aid is supposed to alleviate.

We now come to the final point on which our analysis differs from prevailing views on economic development. The UNCTAD notion of strategic imports is based on the proposition that the only "productive" way of investing resources is in the form of durable capital equipment embodying modern technology. This implicit identification of capital with durable capital goods and complex machinery requires to be seriously qualified when applied to the underdeveloped countries. In the economic setting of these countries the older classical notion of capital as a "subsistence fund" to support labour engaged in producing future output still retains great importance. This applies with particular relevance to labour engaged in various construction work in agriculture and in social overhead capital projects. Further, if, as we have suggested, the reduction of economic dualism leads to an increasing share of economic activities by the small-scale economic units, this would expand the demand for simpler types of tools and equipment which the underdeveloped countries can more easily produce at home. However, given the idea that capital goods can be produced only by a complex of large-scale capital goods industries, current discussions on economic development tend to place a great emphasis on the formation of regional economic unions to overcome the limitations of scale imposed by the smallness of the domestic market in individual underdeveloped countries. But the trouble is that the "domestic market" of an underdeveloped country is not a single integrated market: and without a prior attempt to increase the internal economic integration within each member country, the economic union will be merely a collection of the advanced sectors of these countries, each with only a tenuous connection with its own traditional sector, not to speak of the traditional sector of another country. This is where the analogy between the European Common Market and the proposed Regional Common Markets for the underdeveloped countries breaks down. Given the economic dualism in the underdeveloped countries, internal economic integration is a prior condition for the success of external economic integration on a regional basis.

Index